The
BOOK
COLLECTOR'S
Fact Book

The
BOOK
COLLECTOR'S
Fact Book

Margaret Haller

ARCO PUBLISHING COMPANY, INC.
219 Park Avenue South, New York, N.Y. 10003

Z
118
H34

Published by Arco Publishing Company, Inc.
219 Park Avenue South, New York, N.Y. 10003

Copyright © 1976 by Margaret Haller

Library of Congress Catalog Card Number 74-27436
ISBN 0-668-03756-3

Printed in the United States of America

To
EDWIN HALBMEIER,
for whom reference books fall open,
by themselves, at the right page

Preface

It is hoped that this book will prove useful to the person who is still new to book collecting as a hobby, although no doubt an old friend to books. It presents, in one compact volume, many essential facts about collecting today, including information on books as physical objects, their construction, the artistry of fine bookmaking, illustrated and press books, and the history of modern books. There is information on the current status of the market in old books, and there are hints on how to check on prices. Present-day trends in book collecting are covered. The reader who takes some time to browse through this book, as well as using it to check facts, will, it is hoped, find helpful suggestions on making the most effective use of these facts in building an interesting and possibly even significant collection.

The interests of the modern collector extend over a very wide area indeed. To begin, there is a vast amount of kinds of materials which not so long ago would have been politely if condescendingly called "ephemera" and which are presently newly dignified by the term "paper collectibles." These include posters, broadsides, advertising brochures, pamphlets, and many magazines.

Perhaps there are, as possibly there have always been, more collectors of first editions, in all sorts of categories, than collectors of any other single kind of book. Collectors of first editions in the traditional mode have, however, been fairly recently joined by those who want the first publications printed in a town, territory, or state, even though these

1

"firsts" may be only a page or two and flimsy scraps of paper sadly worn by time.

The collectors of "firsts" today include not only the man or woman who wants such exotics as the first editions of the first-printed books by winners of the Pulitzer Prize, first editions of the Caldecott or Newbery Award winners, or other highly regarded firsts for which he must struggle in a highly competitive market, but also collectors of American comics, the Sunday "funnies," and material from the Walt Disney Studios.

Among traditional collectors there is still, of course, your "uncut" man, who admires the deckle edge of a limited edition which was set by hand and printed on handmade paper, and possibly even bound by hand. Another traditional type of collector is the one who particularly enjoys the heft and the luxurious feel of a leather-bound classic and likes the gleam of its shining gilt edge.

There are collectors for almost any subject you can imagine: music, botany, scientific discoveries, aeronautics, photography, Mesmerism, battle armor, orchid-growing, the ballet, Indian captivities, typography, wrecks at sea, mushrooms. There are collectors who want the works of only certain authors, or certain authors on certain lists, such as one of the Grolier lists, or of certain authors because of their associations with certain other authors. Some collectors look for books containing the work of their favorite illustrators, possibly Dulac, or Rackham, or Rockwell Kent, or Darley, or Phiz. Some are interested in the work of book designers famous for their striking innovations and handsome typographic layouts, such as Bruce Rogers. And there are people who collect books in miniature, three inches or less (their storage problem is certainly minimal), and persons who collect only books published in odd and mostly very large sizes (and their storage problem, on the other hand, can certainly be considerable).

Yet all of these collectors, whatever they collect, do have similar problems. They all need practical and, if possible, up-to-the-minute information on how the old-book business operates, how to buy books from catalogues and at book auctions, and which are the standard bibliographic and other reference works to be consulted. Certainly all have the same need to check on the prices of books offered for sale and to determine the fair or "going" price of items in various stages of condition.

C. E. Frazer, a bibliographer and a collector of the works of Hawthorne, has said that in his opinion a collector needs not only "convictions born out of experience" but also a "dependable hip-pocket experience." But if study, as well as experience, can build conviction, perhaps this handbook will prove helpful. Limiting oneself to first-hand experience has a way, unfortunately, of proving expensive—as well as instructive.

This handbook has been designed for the collector of moderate means, whose passionate longings for books and hankering after some of the most expensive editions must be tempered by a knowledge of the limitations of his own wallet. But there can be, after all, an undeniable satisfaction in building a collection which not only reflects one's own personal interests and bent, but which also constitutes the most exciting collection possible within the limitations of time and money imposed by a workaday world.

In this sense, then, we can let the big collectors have their *Tamerlane* by the youthful Poe (a book which brought $123,000 at auction in New York in December, 1974). We'll skip over the notion that we ourselves might bid for Dickens in the original parts, or the first-published edition of one of his works, or that first-edition *Leaves of Grass*. Yet even so, since we are always looking at old books, it might be wise to be in the position to recognize an original *Tamerlane*, know how to check up on an 1842 *Barnaby Rudge* published at

Philadelphia (a first) . . . and it can be a wonderful feeling to be clever enough to know that the Walt Whitman with the 1860 title page is the pirated edition.

There are, of course, a number of other excellent books on book collecting. They include the *Bookman's Glossary* by Mary C. Turner written, however, more for dealers than for collectors; and those two classics, *A B C for Book Collectors* by John Carter, and *A Primer of Book Collecting*, by John T. Winterich and David Randall, each containing a wealth of useful information. This present volume's justification is that it updates some standard information, and adds a great deal about market conditions and modern practices.

There are many other books on the pleasures of book collecting. One cannot be around old books and old-book stores long without discovering that books about books are one of the staples of the old-book trade. At least a few examples are almost invariably to be found on a dealer's shelves. In them the bookhunters of the past have written of their adventures in tracking down the elusive volume. (Usually they had money of their own or someone else's money to spend, it appears.) The great story-tellers assume the privileges of an old friend. You wander with them back down the winding paths of discovery, to locate a long-lost incunable on a dusty shelf or that rare example of Americana locked away in an attic trunk.

This handbook does not offer competition. The tempting anecdote has been let slip by, in order to present a useful array of facts, but perhaps these facts will help in the further enjoyment of the books by A. Edward Newton, A. S. W. Rosenbach, and others.

The information here has been arranged in glossary form for the convenience of the collector who wishes to check on the meaning of words customarily in use in the old-book trade, including those which are unique to rare-book collecting. Many of these words have been in general use but have come to acquire a specialized meaning. This vocabulary necessarily covers many of the terms used in printing and publishing, book illustration, the history of the book, bibliography, book-cataloguing, and the buying and selling of books.

In addition, a number of general subject headings have been included. These headings accommodate the kind of information which does not easily fit under the definition of a single word or phrase but which nonetheless seemed to be essential for the understanding of book collecting as practiced today.

Some attention has been given to bibliographies, but the subject is too large to be dealt with in depth. Where it seemed appropriate, we have included the names of some of the standard general subject bibliographies, such as Wright Howes' *U.S.iana*, a work of paramount importance for collectors of Americana.

For books currently in print, the publishers' prices have been given, even though these prices may be subject to some change. Similarly, some books described as in print may be going out of print or already be difficult to obtain. It seemed important, however, to be able to give the reader some idea whether we were discussing a book which cost $10 or less, or one which might set him back close to $100 if he decided to purchase it. Of course, a few of the books described here as out of print may yet come back, in reprint. Many are to be readily found in any fairly busy old-book store.

Included in this glossary are a number of foreign words and expressions. Collecting books definitely takes one across language barriers. The collector interested in almost any broad subject area soon discovers that he needs some elementary knowledge of one or more other languages, if only to decipher the title page of a book written in a language other than his own. Also, book collectors travelling abroad can rarely resist the impulse to search out a few volumes in a bookstore, even though the language may be different. Some French terms have been included here, and, since German is the language which seems to afford the most difficulty to the English-speaking, a good many words in German.

Interest in book collecting seems to have been expanding of late, possibly because many people have begun to realize that book prices hold fairly steady and that old books may therefore constitute a good investment. Whatever the reason, there appear to be a growing number of publications in this field. The list is, of course, headed by *AB (Bookman's Weekly)*, which was established in 1948. In addition, each year sees the addition of new periodicals and journals. Some are published by special-interest clubs such as that dedicated to the collection of the *Wizard of Oz* books by L. Frank Baum. By consulting with a specialist dealer who is equipped to handle the type of books in which you are interested, you should be able to locate other collectors with interests similar to yours. Possibly this book will inspire you to find the collectors with whom you can most profitably exchange information.

This book is specifically designed for collectors, not for the bibliographer, the librarian, or the dealer in old books. They have their own interests, point of view, and resources.

We salute our fellow inkhorn mates (bookish fellows), as we close this proem (introduction). Good bookhunting!

The
BOOK
COLLECTOR'S
Fact Book

A

AB Foremost American publication in the old-book field. (See *Bookman's Weekly.*)

Abbildung German for illustration.

Abbreviations Book dealers' catalogues are usually filled with numerous abbreviations, and most catalogues assume a knowledge of the meaning of these abbreviations without offering an explanation: "Evans 315. U.S.iana Z-20. First edition, first issue. 12mo, ½ cont sheep, lea label, a e g. Bumped, some light chipping. O/w vg, but lacks blank. Ex-lib. Np, nd." Obviously, book dealers and the book collectors who buy from them have a vocabulary all their own and a system of abbreviations which assumes knowledge of this vocabulary. Since a great deal of the old-book business is conducted through the mails by the use of these catalogues, any collector should become familiar with the abbreviations and their meanings. The following are those found to occur most regularly in book dealers' catalogues:

A B	*Bookman's Weekly*
A B A A	Antiquarian Booksellers Association of America
A B A C	Antiquarian Booksellers Association of Canada
A B P C	*American Book Prices Current*
abr	abridged
ACs	autograph card, signed
adds	additions
ADs	autograph document, signed
ads	advertisements *within* a book

7

a e g	all edges gilt
A I G A	American Institute of Graphic Arts
ALs	autograph letter, signed
A M N H	American Museum of Natural History
A Ms s	autograph manuscript, signed
A N	absque nota: without information
ANs	autograph note, signed
a p	author's proof
b	born; or back of page (verso)
B A E	Bureau of American Ethnology
B A L	*Bibliography of American Literature*
B A R	*Book Auction Records*
bdg	binding
bds	boards
bev	bevelled
b f	bold face (type)
bib	bibliography
bkrm	buckram
bkstrp	backstrip
b l	black letter
Blanck	B A L, usually
B I P	*Books in Print*
B S	Bibliographical Society (English)
B S A	Bibliographical Society of America
b/w	black and white
bxd	boxed, as it came from the publisher
c	copyright; or circa
c & p	collated and perfect
ca	circa (about)
capt	caption
cat	catalogue
C B E L	*Cambridge Bibliography of English Literature*
cf	calf
chpd	chipped
cl	cloth
cm	centimeter (approx. 2/5 inch)

c o a	cash on arrival
c o d	cash on delivery
col	color or colored; column; colophon
c o r	cash on receipt
comp	compiler
cond	condition
cont	contemporary (*not* continued)
cor	corrected
cov	cover(s)
cpl	complete
cr	crown (a book size)
cvr	cover(s)
C W	Civil War
c w o	cash with order
D°	duodecimo (12mo) (a book size)
d	died
D A B	*Dictionary of American Biography*
D N B	*Dictionary of National Biography*
doc	document
Ds	document, signed
dup	duplicate
d w	dust wrapper (also d/w)
E B	*Encyclopaedia Britannica*
ed	edited or edition
ed d l	de luxe edition
ee	edges
e g	edges gilt
. . .	ellipsis (omission)
eng	engraved or engraving
est	established
e p	endpaper(s)
Evans	*American Bibliography*
ex	exchange allowed
ex lib	library copy
ex ill	extra-illustrated
F	folio (a book size)

f	in fine condition (*not* fair)
fac	facsimile(s)
fcp	foolscap (a British book size)
f d c	first-day cover
f e	fore-edge
ff	folios (leaves); or following
fg	fine-grain (leather)
fig	figure(s)
first	first edition
f/l	flyleaf
fl	lived (flourished)
fldg	folding
fly	flyleaf
fo	folio
fp	frontispiece
fs	facsimile
fx	foxed or foxing
g	gilt; or in good condition
g b	gilt back
g b e	gilt bevelled edge
g e	gilt edges
g l	Gothic letter
glo	glossary
G P O	Government Printing Office
gr	grain
h c	hard cover
hf bd	half bound in leather
hf cf	half bound in calf
h m	handmade
id	idem (the same)
I F T	indexed, folio'd, and titled
i h m	imitation handmade (paper)
I L A B	International League of Antiquarian Book-sellers
ill	illustrated or illustration(s)
imit	imitation

Imp	Imperial (a British book size)
impf	imperfect (a book condition)
impr	imprint
insc	inscribed or inscription
intro	introduction
I P T	indexed, paged, and titled
ital	italics
J C B	John Carter Brown Library
J P	Japanese vellum
l	leaf; or lower
ll	leaves
L C	Library of Congress
l e	limited edition
L E C	Limited Editions Club
lev	levant
lg	large (as in large-paper copy)
loc	located
l p	large paper
Ls	letter, signed
m	marbled
mco	morocco
m e	marbled edge
m p s	marbled paper sides
M O M A	Museum of Modern Art
mor	morocco
ms	manuscript
mtd	mounted
n b	nota bene (mark well)
n d	no date given
n e p	new edition in preparation; also N E/nd.
n p	no place, publisher, or printer given, as the case may be
n u	name unknown
n v	new version
n y	no year indicated
N Y P L	New York Public Library

O°	octavo (8vo) (a book size)
ob	oblong
O E D	*Oxford English Dictionary*
o p	out of print
o p p	out of print, at present
orig	original
o s	out of stock
o/w	otherwise
p (or pp)	page (or pages)
p	paper; or post (after); or a poor copy
p d e	paste-down endpaper(s)
pict	pictorial
pl	plate
pol	polished (leather)
port	portrait(s)
pp	printed pages
p p	privately printed; or private press; also postpaid
pref	preface
prelims	preliminary leaves
pres	presentation copy
prtg	printing or printed
pseud	pseudonym
pt	part or in parts
ptd	printed
pub	published, publisher, or publication
Q	quarto (4to) (a book size)
qto	quarto
rb	rubbed; or rebound or rebinding
ref	reference
revis	revision or revised
rpt	reprint or reprinted
s	signed; or sprinkled
s a	sine anno (no date)
Sabin	*A Dictionary of Books Relating to America*
S A S E	self-addressed stamped envelope (to be included for reply)

ser	series
sg	signed or signature
s n	sine nomine (no publisher indicated)
sq	square book
S O E D	*Shorter Oxford English Dictionary*
sm	small
spr	sprinkled
spec bdg	special binding
S T C	*Short Title Catalogue*
stns	stains
stp	stamped
swd	sewed
t	title page; or translated
t e g	top edge gilt
thk	thick (volume)
TLs	typed letter, signed
T L S	*Times Literary Supplement*
t p	title page
tpd	tipped in
ts	typescript
unbd	unbound
u c	upper cover (top, in British use); or upper case
u p	university press
v d	various dates
v g	a very good copy
vol	volume
v p	various places
w/	with
w a f	with all faults; as is
wrps	wrappers
Wing	*Short Title Catalogue*
X	Christian
Xc	excellent condition
X-lib	library copy
Xr	no returns permitted

Abbreviations: book size

American

F	Folio
4to	quarto
8vo	octavo
12mo	duodecimo
16mo	sextodecimo
24mo	vigesimoquarto
32mo	trigesimosecundo
48mo	fortyeightmo
64mo	sixtyfourmo

(See **Size categories, American** and individual headings for definitions.)

British

Im Fol	Imperial Folio
Ry Fol	Royal Folio
Cr Fol	Crown Folio
Fo Fol	Foolscap Folio
Imp 4to	Imperial Quarto
Ry 4to	Royal Quarto
Med 4to	Medium Quarto
Dy 4to	Demy Quarto
Cr 4to	Crown Quarto
F 4to	Foolscap Quarto
Imp 8vo	Imperial Octavo
Ry 8vo	Royal Octavo
M 8vo	Medium Octavo
Dy 8vo	Demy Octavo
L Cr 8vo	Large Crown Octavo
Cr 8vo	Crown Octavo
F 8vo	Foolscap Octavo

(See **Size categories, British** and individual headings for definitions.)

Abbreviations, bibliographic   For the novice, one of the mysteries of reading a book dealer's catalogue is that within the description of a book there often appears a reference simply to a single name, often all in capital letters, followed by a number which is sometimes placed in parentheses. Thus: HOWES 23, or WRIGHT (110). The name is that of a bibliographic authority, and the number is part of the reference system used within the work of this particular bibliographer. Some bibliographies number each item; others which are arranged alphabetically throughout do not need a numbering system aside from the page numbers. You are being called upon to observe that this particular book is cited in Howes or in Wright. There you may find full bibliographic details, a description of the first edition, often an analysis of the points which identify a first issue, and frequently some comment on the importance of the book, its scarcity and occasionally its price range. A collector soon comes to know the authorities most often cited for the special kind of book he is interested in collecting. Some collectors enjoy limiting their efforts to books mentioned in some bibliography, such as the books on westward migration across the Rocky Mountains cited in Wagner-Camp, or the children's books noted in Jacob Blanck's *Peter Parley to Penrod.* Collectors of the first editions of one author, because of the intensity of their concentration, have been known to culminate their effort by writing the definitive bibliography themselves. A warning should be issued against slavish adherence to bibliographical references: that a book is *not* listed does not necessarily mean that it is unimportant or some sort of forgery—it could be excessively rare and therefore extremely valuable!

Abdruck des Künstlers   German for artist's proof.

Abhandlung   German for treatise or dissertation. *Abhandlungen* may mean transactions or proceedings.

Abkürzung   German for abbreviation.

Abonnement   French for by subscription.

Abrégé   French for abridged.

Abriss   German for abridgement, or summary.

Abschnitt   German for Chapter.

Absque nota   Latin for absence of information regarding the publication of a book. Abbreviated A.N.

Acarus   A kind of insect that lives on the paste used in bookbinding. Not, of course, the same as Icarus.

Accession number   A serial number used to denote the place of an individual book within a collection, such as the books in a library.

Accordion fold   A multiple fold whereby a printed sheet may be opened out to several times the size of a book.

Accroc   French for a tear.

Achevé d'imprimer   French for imprint.

Acidity   In books, a characteristic of both paper and leather which is one of the chief causes of deterioration. The stains observed in some old books may have been caused by acid migration from the binder's boards to the end papers, from endpaper to flyleaf, or from the turn-in of a leather cover, etc. Barrier sheets may be placed in the book to prevent further migration, but little else can be done. Some kinds of paper and some leathers are more acid than others. Even sophisticated modern methods of book manufacture apparently cannot avoid some acidity. Authorities on book preservation have pointed out that today's air pollution also threatens books with exposure to acid fumes.

Sometimes the protective tissue which was inserted in a book to separate an illustration from the opposite page will itself prove acid, turn an unsightly brown, and transfer its own stain both to the illustration and the page. By the time this happens the ink of the illustration has probably dried sufficiently so that it constitutes no threat—the only sensible thing to do may be to tear out the offending tissue guard.

Crystal-clear sheets, as well as folders and envelopes, made of acetate which is itself free of acid, are now available in suitable sizes for the protection of not only books but also documents, maps, broadsides, etc. One supply house, among several, which specializes in acid-free protective materials is Cohasco, Inc., 321 Broadway, New York, N. Y. 10007.

Ackermann von Böhmen Title of the first illustrated book printed from movable type, circa 1460.

Added copy A book added to a library collection which already had included one or more copies of the same book.

Added edition An edition of a book differing in some manner from a previous edition.

Addenda Items which have been added (singular: addendum). Addenda are material added to a book to supply omissions or to correct errors in the body of the text. These omissions or mistakes have been discovered after the book was printed but before it could be bound. Addenda are frequently found in compilations such as genealogies, since new information relating to the text may still be coming in as the book is being made up at the publishers'. (See also **Errata**.)

Advance copy A copy of a new book sent to a potential reviewer or some other person before the official publication date. Sometimes known as a review copy. When such books come into the old-book market they are often in close-to-mint condition.

Advance copy sometimes consists only of a few of the first sheets of a book, furnished in the hope of securing orders while the rest of the book is still being printed.

Advance sheets The unbound pages of a book or part of a book, issued in advance of publication date.

Advertisements In a book, advertisements are almost invariably extra pages furnished by the publisher to be bound in either at the front or back of a book to advertise his other current offerings. These advertisements are frequently found in nineteenth-century books and sometimes furnish a clue as to the particular issue. But advertisements can prove misleading. The presence of the publisher's advertisements for the same year as that of the book's publication could indicate either that they were contemporary or that the publisher, assembling a later edition or issue, simply took up some of the earlier ads he still had on hand. However, many issue points are made over which books are listed in the advertisements, and specifically how the book itself is announced: "almost ready," "just out," etc. Since the wording of any advertisement can be misleading it is wise to consult the appropriate bibliography: There is, for example, no other way of knowing that the first edition of *The Scarlet Letter* by Nathaniel Hawthorne contained ads dated 1850, the book's date of publication. The second edition, for some strange reason, carried ads dated 1849.

Another example of how advertisements may provide issue points is furnished by John Habberton's *Helen's Babies*, published in 1876 by Loring of Boston. The ads in the first issue include a listing of three titles inside the front wrapper headed by "How I Managed my Home on £200 a Year," and, inside the back cover, more ads, headed by "Zerub Throop's Experiment," with the back cover itself carrying an ad for the book of title. In the later issue the ads were different.

Ajouté   French for added.

Album   A book consisting of blank leaves to receive photographs, clippings, etc.

Album de découpures   French for scrapbook.

Alchemic gold   A kind of gold ink in imitation of gold leaf used for decorating the covers or edges of a book.

Aldine Classics   The innovative small pocket editions of the Greek and Roman classics produced by Aldus Manutius, circa 1500.

Aldus   Aldus Manutius (circa 1450–1515) was one of the great men of the Renaissance, both a scholar and an innovator in the area of printing. Combining these two interests, he became the first major printer to publish many of the Greek and Latin classics. The press which he established in 1495 in Venice also produced the first small books for popular reading. Published in what amounted to sizable editions for that day, the Aldine books, with their familiar insignia of the anchor and dolphin, were the forerunners of such later popular publications as the American Modern Library series. Aldus was also the first to employ *italic* type, by means of which he managed to squeeze more words onto the page.

Alignment   The arrangement of type all level at the base . . . a necessary procedure for good printing. This type is not aligned.

All by   Some collectors are ambitious to own *all* the works *by* one particular author. Thus, collectors and dealers will sometimes advertise that they will be willing to buy all by some certain writer. This statement may be misleading. What they probably mean is "many by" rather than all. If you should send a quote to such an advertiser, do not be surprised to learn that the items you have to sell are not actually needed, or that they may duplicate some already on hand.

All edges gilt   The top, side and bottom edges of the body of a book (the pages), having been cut smooth, have been burnished, usually with an imitation gold leaf called gilt.

All firsts   The books listed are all firsts: first editions, though not necessarily first issues.

Allibone   *A Critical Dictionary of English Literature*, by Samuel A. Allibone, a work published in five volumes at Philadelphia between 1859 and 1891.

Allongé   French for tall (format).

Allonym   The name of some person, other than the real author, whose name appears on the title page, used to hide the identity of the author; or, any work which carries such a disguised authorship.

All published   This term indicates all the books actually published out of a great number which were at some time announced for publication. Many items on a longer, original list perhaps never reached the publisher from the author. For example, Volume I may be all that was published of a series of volumes which, although announced, never advanced beyond the first volume. (See also **All by.**)

All rag   Paper which is all rag is of a high quality, containing all rag fibers; it is also frequently made by hand as well.

All rights reserved   Fully protected by copyright.

Allusion book   A work describing or illustrating the allusive designs of heraldry.

Allusive typography   Also called period typography, more or less in the sense that any furniture not clearly modern in style may be termed "period." Allusive is, however, the more accurate term, since allusive typography attempts to be in the style of the historical period of the text of a book. The period may, however, be either that which the book describes (such as the ancient tales of the Knights of the Roundtable), or in the mode of the period when the book itself was published (1920's). Although Bruce Rogers was not the inventor of this particular style of typography, he produced some of the most magnificent examples of the style. The great care which this style of printing requires has made it the special province of some of the private presses.

Almagest   Any treatise on alchemy or astrology; derived from Ptolemy's work on geometry and astronomy, c. 140 A.D.

Almanac   Also spelled almanack: a popular annual issued in wrappers both in England and Europe and in America since the earliest colonial days. When few households owned any book other than the Bible, and when newspapers were scarce, the almanac served both as entertainment and as an important source of general information. It might contain its "judgment" of the weather for a whole year, advice on when to plant crops, and it suggested home remedies for any of the illnesses which customarily beset man and beast; it furnished astronomical charts, tables of coins and interest, and thoughtfully provided reminders of the multiplication table and other matters taught in school. The almanacs also sometimes provided the schedules for travel by coach and maps showing the distances between principal towns. There were also articles of practical information for the farmer and his wife, stories, inspirational essays, and just plain hair-raising yarns of the supernatural.

Some collectors limit themselves entirely to almanacs, paying about $50 for those American almanacs dated about 1750, and considerably more for many of the earlier ones.

It is useful to know that the last page of an almanac is so frequently missing that many dealers routinely omit to mention the absence. This last page usually contained a chart of the distances between cities. Travellers liked to tear it off and tuck it into their pocket for ready reference.

A basic work on this subject is *Almanacs of the United States*, by Milton Drake, in two volumes, published by Scarecrow Press at $35.

Alternative title A title which appears beneath the major title of a book, and adds to it. The alternative title is frequently introduced by the word "or"—as in *Ashenden, or the British Agent*, by W. Somerset Maugham.

Alum-tawed Alum-tawed leather is that which has been treated with both alum and some other agents to render it hard-surfaced and thus extremely durable. Pigskin is often treated in this manner. It then becomes an extremely rugged material for the cover of a book.

Americana Publications either originating in the United States or concerned with the history of the United States or some part of that country—or both. A great deal of Americana pertains to the settlement and development of the eastern seaboard from Colonial days on, no doubt in good part because of the extraordinary wealth of material available. However, today some of the greatest activity around

Americana is taking place in the area of western exploration and the settlement and establishment of the various western states.

The suggestion that "all-Americana" be used as the term to indicate both North and South American material together has never caught on, nor the word "U.S.iana" coined by Wright Howes to refer just to the United States.

Americana (some firsts)   The first American press was one brought over from England in 1638, and the first work to be printed on this press was *The Freeman's Oath*, published two years later. Although the press was owned by a man named Glover, and then by his widow, the first printer was actually a man by the name of Stephen Daye.

American Antiquarian Society   Located in Worcester, Massachusetts, this Society, founded in 1812, maintains one of the outstanding collections in America of early American documents, pamphlets, and newspapers. The Society is also an important publisher of bibliographical works on such subjects as early children's books, books on American penmanship, American books on cookery, and American poetry in Colonial newspapers.

American Bibliography   For the work by this title, see **Evans.**

American Biography, Dictionary of (See *Dictionary of American Biography*.)

American Book Collector, The   A bi-monthly magazine issued for the collectors of scarce and rare books, available at $7.50 per year from the publisher at 1434 So. Yale Avenue, Arlington, Illinois 61312. Single copies are available at $1.25, and special numbers at $2. This magazine periodically publishes a directory of private book collectors, along with information on the kind of books they collect. Subscribers who are book collectors are invited to have their names and interests listed.

American Book Prices Current   A report in book form issued annually of the prices realized at auction not only for old books but also for autographs and manuscripts, maps, charts, pamphlets, and broadsides and other items of closely related nature. There is some time lag in reporting; the 1972 report, for example, came onto the market in 1974. *American Book Prices Current* is now annually covering about 30,000 sales made at about 150 auctions. Only lots bringing $20 or more are included. *A.B.P.C.* used to be published by Columbia University; the present publisher's address is 121 East 78 Street, New York City 10021. The cost of each annual report is about $50, and in recent years issues have been sold out before the succeeding one appears. For this reason, the price for previous issues of *A.B.P.C.* stands up well in the old-book market. *A.B.P.C.* is not cumulative; however, a five-year cumulative index is published separately, with abbreviated entries referring to the annual volume in which the sale was originally recorded. This index is priced at $100. When a book auction house catalogue states that no copy of a certain book has been offered for sale in a certain number of years, this probably means that *A.B.P.C.* has carried no record of it.

Most old-book dealers find it essential to have their own copies of *A.B.P.C.* on file. Some collectors buy each issue as it comes out, but unless you are in the market fairly consistently for books worth $50 or more, you may not need it. Public libraries of any size usually have a full run of *American Book Prices Current*, which you may consult as needed.

Of course, even though prices are accurately reported, they may be, nonetheless, misleading. Auction prices can be affected by temporary market conditions as well as reflect the long-term value of a book. The competitiveness of the bidding on any one day may skew the price, driving it up if two or more bidders are unusually determined to acquire the same book, or resulting in an unusually poor showing if it should happen that the market for this particular book has already been recently satisfied.

Still, as a price reference, *American Book Prices Current* is invaluable—if only for the reason that collectors can assume that any astute dealer will be constantly checking with it.

American Booksellers Association A trade association of the dealers in new books—not old ones. Abbreviated to A.B.A., it should not be confused with the A.B.A.A.—Antiquarian Booksellers Association of America.

American Book Specialists The title of a directory of the antiquarian book dealers in the United States and Canada, setting forth the specialties of each. A 1974 edition is available from the publisher, Continental, 1261 Broadway, New York, N.Y. 10001, at $12.

American cloth Also called "American leather," a cheap fabric sometimes used for bookbinding, referred to as American in countries other than America.

American edition The American edition is usually so designated in a dealer's catalogue only if there also happens to be an earlier foreign edition. If the very first publication of a book, for example, took place abroad, the first edition to be published in the United States might possibly, then, not be the most valuable. This might even be true where the author is an American and the publication of his book creates the widest stir of interest in the United States, passing almost unnoticed abroad at the time of its publication. (See also **Following the flag.**)

American First Editions An important book of this title, considered by many dealers and collectors of first editions to be practically indispensable. *American First Editions*, by Merle Johnson, is more generally known as "Merle Johnson." Now out of print, copies at auction have been known to bring as much as $75. A limit is placed upon its usefulness, however, because of the fact that it does not cover the first editions of books published since 1940. Also, through personal prejudice or some lapse, the works of F. Scott Fitzgerald are not included at all.

American Institute of Graphic Arts   A membership organization formed in 1914, devoted to the promotion of the best in the graphic arts, and with headquarters at 1059 Third Avenue, New York City 10021. An annual exhibit honors A.I.G.A.'s choice of the Fifty Books of the Year. The catalogues issued for these exhibits, which have been held during the past twenty years, are still mostly available from the Institute at a moderate fee. They form an important and fascinating record of excellence in the art of bookmaking, and especially the illustration of books.

-ana   A suffix added to the names of persons or places to denote material pertaining to, or a collection of, some subject. This device is particularly favored as a kind of shorthand among book collectors, who have helped popularize such unpronounceables as Lincolniana and New-Englandiana.

Analyse   German for abstract, or summary.

Anastatic   Referring to the printing process by which facsimiles are produced from a zinc plate.

Anastrophe   An inversion of words, such as "Bright was the sun," rather than "The sun was bright," a device sometimes employed for book titles.

Anhang   German for appendix.

Anmerkungen, versehen mit   German for annotated.

Annals   A narrative of events, arranged by year.

Année   French for year of publication.

Annexe   French for supplement.

Annual   A book issued once a year; in the old-book trade, the term specifically means the type of gift book which was popular in the mid-nineteenth century, usually issued in handsome binding and fancifully illustrated, often colored by hand. These were the "coffee-table books" of an earlier day. The text of these annuals is characteristically made up of previously published poems, articles, essays, and stories, but among the annuals considered most valuable are those containing the first-published works of authors who later became famous. Therefore, it is always worthwhile to check the table of contents of an annual of this type.

Anonyma   A collection of anonymous literature. Although the monumental work on anonyma is the *Dictionary of Anonymous and Pseudonymous English Literature*, by Samuel Halkett and John Laing (See **Halkett**), a more recent and supplemental work is *Political Works of Concealed Authorship in the United States, 1789–1810.* Compiled by Pierce Welch Gaines, a revised edition published in 1965 is available from the Shoe String Press at $6.50. There is also *Anonyms*, by William Cushing—a "Dictionary of Revealed Authorship"—originally published at Cambridge in 1889 and now made available by Mark Press, 16 Park Place, Waltham, Mass. 02154, at $17.50. Also available from the same press is Cushing's *Initials and Pseudonyms*—a "Dictionary of Literary Disguises"—in two volumes, originally published in 1885–88, at $27.50.

Anonymous literature   Works which do not provide the name of the author. There are collectors who specialize in anonymous literature; part of the fun is in tracking down the identities of hitherto unknown authors. However, there is a major work on the identities of early unspecified authors. (See **Halkett**.)

Anopisthographic   Descriptive of a book which has the leaves printed on one side only—a handy word, but not often used.

Anthology   Any literary collection, for example, a single volume containing the works of a number of authors. Originally an anthology was a collection of "flowers of verse"—small and choice poems.

Antiquar   German for an antiquarian book dealer.

Antiquarian Book Fair   An exhibition of old, scarce, and rare books, most of which are being offered for sale. At a book fair, dealers exhibit their wares, exchange the gossip of the trade, and join to publicize their business as well as to sell to each other and to the members of the public who attend. A fair is usually held in a large city and may last for as long as three days. Most of the book sales are apparently made to other dealers, although the general public seems to account progressively for a larger proportion of the sales each year. Prices for books at a fair range from a low of $20 to about $1,000, with a few exceptions upward. Fairs have recently been held in Japan, Great Britain, Germany, and Canada, as well as the United States. Forthcoming fairs are always well publicized in *AB (Bookman's Weekly)*.

Antiquarian Bookman (See *Bookman's Weekly (AB)*.)

Antiquarian Bookman's Yearbook An annual publication issued by *AB (Bookman's Weekly)* for members of the antiquarian book trade, but also made available to the general public. The first issue appeared in 1949. Since then the *Yearbook* has become a major reference work for the trade, providing not only an annual up-to-date directory of dealers and other useful current information, but also furnishing important editorial comment. The *Yearbook* is published in two parts (actually, three sections). Part Two, entitled "The O.P. Market," contains a handy reference directory to specialist and antiquarian book dealers. The advertisements also provide a valuable range of information, since the advertisers include many publishers, both large and small and including many of the university presses, as well as search services, firms specializing in the repair of bindings, and other types of businesses serving both old-book dealers and collectors in a wide variety of ways. The two parts of the *Yearbook* are available separately at $5 each, or together for $7.50, from *Bookman's Weekly* (q.v.). An annual subscription to *AB* includes the *Yearbook*.

Antiquarian Book Monthly Review A magazine for book collectors, librarians, and dealers in the antiquarian book field, published in England at £4 per annum, and available from 3 Brayfield House, Cold Brayfield, nr. Olney, Bucks.

Antiquarian Booksellers Association The international organization, with headquarters at 154 Buckingham Palace Road, London, S.W.1.

Antiquarian Booksellers Association of America   A membership organization consisting of persons admitted after having been in the old and rare book business for at least three years, and for whom this is their principal business. Headquarters are at Shop Two, Concourse, 630 Fifth Avenue, New York 10020. The Association's objectives are to further a friendly and cooperative spirit among its members and to "uphold the status of the antiquarian booktrade and maintain its high professional standards." Approximately 300 firms belong to this Association, and there are about 100 associate members.

Antiquarian Booksellers Association of Canada   A membership organization with headquarters in Toronto. Communications may be addressed to Box 148, Station M, Toronto, Canada.

Antiquarian Booksellers Association of Great Britain   The oldest antiquarian book dealers' association in the world, founded in 1906, with a present membership of about 400 dealers and with headquarters at 29 Revell Road, Kingston-upon-Thames, Surrey, England.

Antiquarian dealer   A dealer in scarce and rare books, as distinguished from the book dealer who handles a wide variety of books which are old, used, and out-of-print.

Antiquariatskatalog   German for a catalogue of second-hand books.

Antique   A kind of finish in paper. In the book trade, antique paper does not mean that the paper is old, but paper which has been manufactured to appear old and thus, usually, handmade. Such paper has a rough uneven surface and is of a yellowish to brown tone rather than white.

Antique binding   "Binding in the antique manner" would be more accurate. A modern binding in imitation of a binding which is truly old. If a book does indeed have an old binding which is properly described as antique, the binding is of leather, usually calf, and although it may be stamped or embossed, no gilt or other color has been added.

Antique finish   In paper, a rough and uneven paper which is in imitation of a genuinely old handmade paper.

Antique stores   Antique stores, as well as stores which handle less valuable secondhand articles, rarely carry books as anything more than a sideline. They may, however, be excellent sources for old and sometimes rare books—which may sometimes be priced unusually low. Books which are offered as precious objects along with antique furniture tend, on the other hand, to be priced high for those people who can afford to buy antiques.

Apocryphal   Of unknown authorship, or of doubtful authenticity.

Appendix   Any addition to the main body of a work or document, having some contributing value but not essential to the completeness of the main body of the work. The appendix is usually placed at the end of the main body and contains information which either illustrates or enlarges upon the textual information. (See also **Addenda, Errata,** and **Supplement.**)

Appraisals   Although some dealers do not mind giving an off-the-cuff opinion of the value of one single book, dealers everywhere expect to be paid a fee for the appraisal of a collection of any size or value. The appraiser generally expects to be paid for his time and expertise at a rate commensurate with that paid to the appraisers of other types of antiques or valuable property, such as works of art. This fee usually amounts to 10% or more of the value of any collection. The appraiser will wish to know the purpose of this appraisal: to determine the value of the property, to determine how much it might be worth if sold, or to replace or duplicate the collection—should it become necessary, for example, in case of a fire. According to the American Society of Appraisers, "there are several kinds of value and several

kinds of cost estimates, each of which has a legitimate place
as the end point of some class of appraisal engagement . . ."
A set of authoritative principles and a code of professional
ethics has been established by this Association, which has
headquarters at 1101 17th Street N.W., Washington, D. C.
20006.

Appraisers   The best thing to do in seeking an appraisal
for a collection of valuable books is to locate the nearest
member of the Antiquarian Booksellers Association of
America or the American Society of Appraisers, then entrust
the matter to him. The worst thing to do is to pack your
books into a box and take them down to the nearest dealer in
old and used books. Unless this dealer knows you well and
has some idea of the value of your books, he will probably
only give a quick look and offer you a few dollars. In any
event, the most businesslike procedure is to make an accurate
list of the books you wish to sell—title, author, date and
place, and condition if other than good—and submit this list
in advance when discussing the terms of an appraisal. You
will have a more accurate idea of what you are offering for
sale, and the appraiser can judge the time he will have to
spend and the approximate value of your collection. If you
are planning to give your collection away, to a library for
example, the responsibility to seek an appraisal rests with
you rather than with the recipient of the gift. The American
Library Association (Rare Book Division) has a set of
recommended procedures about which you might care to
enquire.

Aquarelliert   German for colored by hand.

Armed Services Edition   One of the series of paperbacks
issued during World War II by the (American) Council of
Books in Wartime. Some of these by authors who are most
popularly collected in first editions have already become
collectors' items.

Arming   The impressing of a heraldic device into the
cover of a book.

Armorial binding A leather binding which has been stamped with a coat of arms, possibly that of an owner who had the book bound to his specifications.

Armorial bookplate A bookplate displaying the coat of arms of the owner of the book. Such bookplates are especially valued by many people whose special hobby is collecting bookplates.

Ars Typographica A publication created by Frederic W. Goudy, issued in New York between 1918 and 1934 in three volumes (all published). Illustrating the history of type and of printing in general, *Ars Typographica* included articles on the work of individual printers.

Art canvas A kind of buckram used sometimes for bookbinding.

Artist's proof The impression of an etching or other work, at its most satisfactory stage for the artist. This will probably constitute its best "state."

Ashendene Press A famous private press founded in Hertfordshire in 1894 by C. H. St. John Hornby.

As issued In the condition in which the printed pages emerged from the bindery: the text has been printed but the book is as yet unbound. It is, therefore, unstitched, unbound, and uncut. The expression "as issued" is also used, however, to indicate that a binding is as it came from the publisher. This is most often applied to a work in wrappers, and the publication might, for example, be described as "in wrappers, stapled as issued," to indicate that this was its original condition.

As new Exactly the same as on the day it was published. Not, therefore, the same as "as issued" (q.v.).

Association copy Any book which, whether or not it separately has value for itself, derives value from being linked in some manner with an important person or event. This link is indicated in some manner within the book itself, through an inscription by the author, or by someone else, by the signature of the book's owner, or possibly through a bookplate. Books which were once part of the library of a famous person might, for example, qualify as association copies; a 48-volume set of Scott's Waverley Novels recently achieved a high price of $200 because this set had belonged to T. S. Eliot, with his elephant-head bookplate to prove it, and, furthermore, his signature in four of the volumes. An association copy may be the personal copy of a book owned by the man to whom the book was dedicated. Sometimes a book becomes an association copy when a famous person scribbles his comments in the margin: John Adams in Mary Wollstonecraft's book on the French Revolution: "more wit and point than sense in this." Collectors and dealers can sometimes stretch the concept of association fairly thin. For example, collectors of the works of Sir Arthur Conan Doyle may extend their collecting interests to the works which were mentioned as residing on Sherlock Holmes' bookshelves: fairly recently an 1892 limited edition translation from Catullus commanded a high $250 because it was thought to have been "probably the rarest book in Holmes' library."

* (Asterisk) The asterisk is frequently used in dealers' catalogues to indicate different items within one lot. Thus four, five, or even more may form a series offered as one lot. Books may be thus grouped to be sold because they form a logical entity or because no one of them is worthy of standing alone. In auction catalogues one moderately attractive book may be "lotted" this way to attract bids for the entire lot.

The asterisk is also used to indicate the first footnote in what may be a series; to indicate an omission in the text; or, in biographies, guide books, etc., to indicate birth.

Atlas A collection of maps in a single volume, often annotated. The word atlas is derived from the name of the Titan in mythology who supported the world on his shoulders. Although nineteenth-century school atlases are not particularly esteemed, early American atlases may command a high price if they contain maps of the frontier lands in good condition. The 1776 large folio *American Atlas* with 49 copperplate engravings by Thomas Jefferys, for example, may be worth about $4,000.

Atlas German for a volume of plates; or a geographical atlas, as in English.

Auction Buying books at auction is increasingly popular: one of the largest and most successful of the auction houses recently reported a 30% increase in its sales of old and rare books over the previous year.

Book auction houses issue catalogues advertising the items (lots) which will be offered for sale at any auction. Bids are accepted by mail, phone, and in person on the day of the auction. In most cases, bids for the absentee bidders are executed without fee. The successful bidder, when notified of his purchases, is expected to remove his books from the auction premises.

The auction house receives the books which are subsequently placed for auction from its consignors; one sale may consist of the books of a single consignor or of dozens. Most houses now follow the practice of providing an estimate of the worth of each lot, as a general guideline for bidders. Although these estimates are closely based on what has been paid before, bidding, of course, does not always stay within the confines of the estimate. Every auction has its own surprises.

Among the advantages of bidding at auction are the opportunity to study the description of a book in advance, do one's own research, and, if convenient, the opportunity to examine the books in advance; also, at any auction, the bidders competitively set the price—or, to put it another way, the buyer himself sets the price he is willing to pay.

Book auctions are quite different from the more familiar auctions of household goods. Some country book auctions are still conducted by auctioneers using the familiar stylized patter, but the regularly established book auctions are conducted at a fast clip, without displaying the books before the audience. It is customary to auction between three and four hundred books in this way at a session of no more than two hours.

Auction catalogues   An auction house issues a catalogue for each of its sales. These catalogues are available singly or by subscription, at varying fees. For a single charge, the subscriber may also receive the list of prices realized at each auction after it has been held. Auction houses are at great pains to describe the books they offer with great accuracy and in considerable detail, since many of their customers will not be able to inspect the books. The catalogues of certain sales held by some of the great auction houses have become important bibliographic works and may now command considerable money at auction themselves.

Although the first book auction in history is thought to have been conducted on the Continent, apparently the first auction catalogue was issued in England. This was for the sale of the library of a certain Dr. Seaman in 1676. A Mr. Cooper, the book dealer who handled this historic auction, stated in his first catalogue that he hoped his new method for conducting the sale "will not be unacceptable to Schollars."

Auction houses   At the auctions conducted by the well-established auction houses, most of the bidders are usually dealers, and a great deal of the bidding is conducted through the mails or by phone. The auction itself is conducted swiftly and efficiently, with the same degree of cool displayed whether the bidding is under $20, around $50 to $100 as it frequently is, or up to $28,000 for a work printed before 1460 and ascribed to Gutenberg. Because of the amount of business conducted at these sales, and because they serve as bellwether for prices, bookmen's publications, including *AB (Bookman's Weekly)* devote considerable space to reporting the auctions. The types of materials sold at auction include not only books but also maps, autographs, posters, photographs, and a variety of other graphics—recently even tape recordings.

One general auction house which holds occasional sales of books is Sotheby Parke Bernet, at 980 Madison Avenue, New York City 10021, and, on the west coast, at 7660 Beverly Boulevard, Los Angeles, Cal. 90036. There are additional offices at 232 Clarendon Street, Boston, Mass. 02116 and at Galleria Post Oak, 5015 Westheimer Road, Houston, Tex. 77027. Although book auctions are held infrequently, this house handles some of the most rare and thus expensive items.

The largest American auction house dealing exclusively in books, with weekly sales ten months of the year, is the Swann Galleries at 104 East 25th Street, New York City 10010. Each sale features a different category of literature, including sporting books, first editions, Americana, early and rare books, books on medical history, and the works of individual authors, including many moderns. The house policy is to alternate good general antiquarian material with special sales. "Super sales" may feature both a morning and afternoon session or even run for two successive days.

Other well-known American auction houses include the California Book Auction Galleries (224 McAllister Street, San Francisco, Cal. 94102) which especially seeks to encourage absentee bidding, and Samuel T. Freeman and Co. (1808–10 Chestnut Street, Philadelphia, Pa. 19103), which claims to be "the oldest auction firm in America" and handles not only rare books and manuscripts but also a variety of other antique property. One small but active house is Plandome Book Auctions on Long Island (113 Glen Head Road, Glen Head, N. Y. 11545).

There are still other American houses, some specializing in books only. Any recent issue of *AB (Bookman's Weekly)* might be able to furnish their names. The Harris Auction Galleries (874 North Howard Street, Baltimore, Md. 21201) holds a fine library sale six or more times a year, often including autographs. The Maxwell Scientific International, a division of Microforms International (Fairview Park,

Elmford, N. Y. 10523) specializes in mail auctions for back issues of collected learned publications, books, and microforms.

In Canada, there is Montreal Book Auctions Ltd. (L'Encan des Livres de Montreal) at 1529 Sherbrooke Street W., Montreal 109, P.Q., Canada.

The most familiar British auction house dealing in books is undoubtedly Sotheby & Co. of 34–35 New Bond Street, London, W1A 2AA, with a second division in Hodgson's Rooms, 115 Chancery Lane, London, W.C.2. Other auction houses include Jolly of Bath at the Auction Rooms, Old King Street, in Bath; Morrison, McChlery & Co., 98 Sauchiehall Street, Glasgow, C.2, Scotland; Henry Spencer & Sons, 15 Exchange Street, Retford, Notts; Northern Book Auctions, 33 Merrion Street, Leeds 1; and P. F. Windibank, The Dorking Halls, 18–20 Reigate Road, Dorking, Surrey.

Auction prices Prices paid for books at auction can sometimes be deceptive. First, the condition of the book may be highly important; some auction houses, such as Swann's, usually deal only in books in very good or better condition, and any unusually high prices paid may be a reflection of this fact. Second, an auction house usually has been able to advertise a sale internationally, attracting the best possible competition for each lot offered. And third, prices sometimes escalate wildly if two equally determined bidders collide over one purchase. This is not to say, of course, that all auction prices are unusually high. As anyone who has ever attended a book auction knows, an auction always presents some fine opportunities for bargains. (See also *Book Auction Prices.*)

Aufgeklebt German for mounted, or pasted.

Auflage German for issue. *Auflagenhöhe* means run, or number of copies printed.

Aungerville Or, Aungervyle, Richard (1287–1345), Bishop of Durham, better known by the name of De Bury. Considered by many authorities the father of bibliography, he is the author of *Philobiblon* (q.v.), in which he relates his experiences as a book collector—before printing was invented.

Ausgabe   German for edition. *Originalausgabe* is first edition.

Ausgebessert   German for repaired, or restored.

Authenticity   In 1973 Sotheby Parke Bernet announced that all property sold through its New York auction house would henceforth be "guaranteed authentic," not counterfeit. This action was in response to a growing demand that old-book dealers and dealers in other antiquities, and auction houses in particular, stand behind the statements they make about items offered. Specifically, this house led the way in promising to guarantee the authenticity of authorship of any book for five years from date of purchase. Authorship is defined as identity of the creator, the period, culture, source, or origin of any property. Other auction houses have informally been offering such a guarantee.

Fortunately, the forgery of old books appears to be a fairly rare occurrence, scarcely comparing with the difficulties offered by forgeries in the art world, for example. A book forgery requires not only the duplication of text and type, but also of paper, ink, glue, binding materials, etc. Forgeries are more likely to turn up in single issues of newspapers, broadsides, or maps.

Authorized edition   Any edition which is not the result of piracy; not necessarily, therefore, the same as a first edition. It is usually easier to identify an *un*authorized edition than one which is authorized. It is helpful to remember that up until well into the nineteenth century it was not unusual for books to be pirated—printed and sold—without their authors' consent.

Authorized version   The 1611 English translation of the Bible, authorized by King James and considered one of the most beautiful examples of the use of the English language.

Authors   There are excellent bibliographies in print for a great many of the authors who are currently being collected: among others, Steinbeck, Conrad, Lorca, and Dickens. The list is long. It includes bibliographies for such contemporary authors as Philip Roth, Norman Mailer, and Elie Wiesel. To discover the bibliography or bibliographies for any particular author, one can check *Books in Print*, the very useful *Bibliography of Bibliographies* edited by Charles H. Nilon, or the description of an author's work and career in a standard work such as the *Encyclopaedia Britannica*, which frequently concludes with this information.

A series of bibliographies called *Authors-at-Auction* is scheduled to come from Gale Research, each volume presenting a facsimile of the auction catalogues for an author, with prices noted. The first volume issued was on Hawthorne, and successive volumes are planned for Hemingway, Whitman, Thoreau, and Melville.

Author's binding A book in author's binding is one bound to the author's specifications. Often this book is to serve as a gift from the author to relatives and friends. Although such a binding may be fancy, it is often simply of a different color of cloth.

Author's copy A complimentary copy of the author's book, furnished to the author by his publisher. There may be as few as six. In the old-book trade, however, the meaning of the term is extended to include any copy owned by the author and, possibly, bearing his signature or his bookplate.

Authors in magazines Collectors interested in the works of one author should not neglect magazine appearances. There may even be a very special fascination in being able to trace the germination of an idea through a first appearance in print to its final flowering in a best seller. For any one particular work, the "first published edition" in hard cover may actually follow the first appearance in a magazine. The complete first appearance may be scarce, because of problems in assembling six to eight issues of a magazine. There are fortunately an increasing number of magazine bibliographies available for the most popularly collected authors. Many first appearances have been in truly obscure publications. This is one of the reasons for the great popularity of collecting the "little magazines."

Authors, living Buying the first-edition copies of the works of living authors as they are published is considered a tedious, not to say chancey, way of trying to build a valuable collection. In the first place, the true first edition may not be the trade edition made available to the general public . . . and it may be a very long wait before you can know whether your author is going to stand the test of time.

Author's proof The proof which is returned to the publisher by the author after he has inserted his corrections.

Author's rights Those rights assured to an author under the copyright law.

Autogramm German for autograph.

Autograph Signature, and, in the book business, the signature of the author of the particular book. If the signature is that of any other person, this is explained.

Autograph copy A copy of a book signed by its author. Less commonly, any book which bears a signature. "To form a collection of books, chosen for the sole reason that they contain the autographs of the eminent, would be a poor thing to do; but the collector may not ungraciously cherish an especial tenderness for books which—while otherwise conforming to the general scheme of his library—yet have the added charm of bearing the mark of some sympathetic previous owner. When that owner was the author himself, or was a friend to whom the author presented a copy, the pleasure of now owning his book is many times increased; and, naturally, in the second of these cases, it is the donor's, rather than the recipient's, handwriting that we hope to find."—Iolo Williams, *The Elements of Book Collecting*.

Autograph document, signed A document which is entirely in the handwriting of the signer. Abbreviated to A.D.s.

Since the invention of the typewriter, such documents are produced less frequently.

Autonym   A literary work published under an author's true name. As distinguished from pseudonym.

Autorenexemplar   German for the author's own personal copy of a book.

Avant–propos   French for foreword.

Avis   *The Bookman's Concise Dictionary*, compiled by F. C. Avis, published by the Philosophical Library, New York, 1956.

Azured   In a leather binding, ornately tooled in closely parallel lines, frequently in gilt.

B

Back The part of a book which is sewn or stitched and therefore holds the book together; the spine. *Not* the back cover, which is one of the book's two "sides."

Backbone The spine of a bound book, connecting front and back covers (sides). The backbone is the part of the book which shows when the book is shelved in the conventional manner.

Back cover A book has both a front and back cover; these are called sides, to distinguish them from the one back (spine) every book has.

Backed A book is termed backed (1) when its spine is covered with a material different from that used on the covers (sides), or (2) when the book's spine has been newly recovered ("newly backed in calf"). "Rebacked" is the more precise term for "recovered" in this instance.

Backing pages The verso and recto, comprising one leaf.

Back lining A book manufacturer's term for the paper or fabric which adheres to the spine of a hardcover book for reinforcement.

Back page The page which appears on the left-hand side of an open book; or the last page in a book.

Backstrip The covering of a book's spine, usually of cloth or leather, and frequently lettered with the title of the book and other information, and decorated as well. The backstrip will often show signs of wear before the rest of the book, fading, fraying, becoming chipped or discolored.

Backstrip label A label printed with the title of the book, sometimes also the name of the author, which is affixed to the backstrip. The label may be leather or paper. In either case, this type of label, which adds to the cost of manufacturing the book, is rarely used on modern books except as a special finishing touch on fine and limited editions.

Band German for wrapper. In French, *bande*. The German *band* also means volume.

Bands The cords to which the signatures of a book are sewed, and thus part of the back of the book. When these bands project across the back of the book in a prominent position, they are called raised bands. If heavy cording is used, the bands appear raised. The appearance is that of ridges (although the term "ridges" is never used).

Bank note engraving Fine steel engraving in the style used for bank notes in the nineteenth century, when machines were employed to render the finest possible small detail.

Banned books Although old-book dealers may be presumed to have less trouble with the laws on pornography than dealers in new and as yet untested books, still the subject of pornography has seemed important enough to merit special attention in the *AB* 1973–74 *Bookman's Yearbook*, where the leading article was the text of a lecture delivered before the Copyright Society in New York by Robert B. McKay, Dean of the New York University Law School. Until 1870, he pointed out, America seemed able to contain both "drawing-room prudish" and "frontier coarse" without great strain. In 1896 the Supreme Court expressed its confidence in the public knowledge of what "is meant by decency, purity, and chastity in social life, and what must be deemed obscene, lewd, and lascivious." Since then, both the Court's confidence and ours, not to mention that of the dealers in books challenged as obscene, has steadily drifted off, until today, in a highly permissive society, what should be banned, or whether any printed works should be banned, is hotly debated. Dean McKay's article makes good reading.

For those interested in this subject, there is also a book by Anne Lyon Haight, now in its third edition, entitled *Banned Books*, published by R. R. Bowker at $9.50. In the old book trade, there is a steady business in curiosa, exotica, and erotica, a great deal of it in books of greater historical than prurient interest.

Bariolé   French for multicolored.

Barrier sheet   A piece of paper, acetone, or other material used in a book to prevent the migration of oil or acid from one page onto another or from one material to another, as from leather to vellum or to paper.

Base line   An imaginary line upon which type characters stand.

Baskerville   John Baskerville (1706–1775), designer of a popular type face. Baskerville was already a successful businessman and in his mid-forties when he gave up his business to experiment with printing and typography. In 1750 he established a paper mill, a print shop, and a foundry at Birmingham, England, and began to experiment with different combinations of paper, ink, and type, eventually producing his first book in 1757. He also was fascinated with designing type, and since he had started life as a writing master, the Roman letter which he designed, although derived from Caslon, was both rounder and more sharply incised, showing clearly the graceful influence of calligraphy.

Bastard title   The bastard title precedes the title page. Because it usually states only the main part of the title, it is sometimes called the half-title. In common use the three terms bastard title, half-title, and short title are used somewhat interchangeably. It may be helpful to remember that the bastard title serves little or no purpose to the reader, being primarily inserted for the convenience of the printer and often bearing his imprint.

Battledore   A modified form of the horn book, which was used for the instruction and entertainment of children up until the middle of the nineteenth century. The battledore provides lessons based on the alphabet, arranged on a series of folding cards. Examples of the battledore still in good condition have become scarce.

Bay Psalm Book The first book printed in the British American colonies. The date was 1640; the press was operated by Stephen Daye.

Bearbeitet German for adapted, or arranged. *Bearbeitung* means an adaptation.

Beaumont Beaumont Press, a private printing press founded by Cyril William Beaumont in London in 1917.

Beilage German for an annex or supplement.

Belles lettres Light literature; or the aesthetics of literary study.

Belletristik German for a work of fiction.

Bennett (See **First editions, American.**)

Bericht German for bulletin. *Berichtigungen*, on the other hand, means corrigenda.

Berieben German for rubbed (as a binding may be rubbed).

Beschädigt German for damaged. *Beschmutzt* means dirtied or smudged.

Beschränkt German for limited.

Besprechungsexemplar German for a review copy.

Bestiary A medieval work containing allegorical stories about animals. Such books are often profusely and charmingly illustrated. Some modern children's books are still produced in imitation of this style, which otherwise has lapsed.

Best seller Today's best seller, as we all know, is not necessarily going to be tomorrow's most valued book. Collecting first editions of the best sellers as they come out is a tedious way to build a fine collection—as well as highly uncertain. A best seller sometimes proves "the gilded tomb of a mediocre talent"—Logan Pearsall Smith.

Bevelled boards The covers of a book which have been angle-cut (champfered) to create a sloped edge.

Bewick, Thomas   The English wood-engraver (1753–1828) who restored end-grain engraving and introduced—and became master of—the white-line technique. His work appeared in many books, influenced other artists, and helped create the illustrated book as we know it today.

Bibelot   A term sometimes applied to a miniature book which is both interesting because of its small size and its beauty, charm, and, sometimes, rarity as well.

Bible   Most old Bibles, even treasured family heirlooms, have little value on the old-book market. Bibles dating as far back as the sixteenth century are not particularly scarce. This is not surprising when one considers that the Bible, over all the years, has been consistently the best seller, and that when many households could afford to own no other book, they at least had their copy of the Bible. If there should be a demand for a particular edition of the Bible, most dealers say they would have little difficulty locating it. However, since in general the demand for old Bibles is exceedingly small, most dealers do not handle them unless there is something special to recommend a particular copy.

Only two categories of Bibles interest the dealers: the firsts, and the oddities. Leading all other firsts is, of course, the first example of a printed book, the Gutenberg Bible, issued in 1455. Other first Bibles which may be valuable are the first to be printed in any language, such as the first translation into an American Indian dialect, or the first for a particular country or immigrant population, or the first polyglot Bible. The oddities include a number containing typographical mistakes. There is the 1560 edition which has "making themselves breeches out of fig-leaves" rather than aprons. The so-called bug-Bible substituted "afraid of bugs by night" for "terror by night," and a 1562 edition managed to print "Blessed are the place-makers" rather than peace-makers. A Bible printed in 1568 had treacle instead of balm in "Is there no balm in Gilead?" Then there is the odd parable called "Parable of the Vinegar" rather than vineyard, which appeared in another Bible. The 1652 "wicked" Bible omitted the Seventh Commandment entirely.

Bible paper   A thin but strong paper which is opaque and often used for books with many hundreds of pages, such as the Bible. India paper.

Bibles, American   The first Bible in English was issued in America in 1782. This is one of the few early American Bibles which have value. Many of the old Bibles found in America are those issued by the American Bible Society, which gave away huge numbers of copies. There are a number of firsts, however, which have value, including the first Bibles for the Indians. Association copies can be of great interest: any Bible, for example, which had belonged to the family of a man who became President of the United States would be of interest.

Biblia-a-biblia   Non-books, or books not considered worthy of the name.

Biblio-   A prefix meaning of or pertaining to books, as in bibliokleptomaniac (book thief) or bibliolatry (excessive admiration for books).

Bibliognost   A book collector's magazine issued quarterly, published by Denis Carbonneau, bookseller, and available by subscription at $8 per year from Box 50, Cooper Station, New York City 10003. A bibliognost is one who knows books well.

Bibliographer's Manual of English Literature   An important reference work on books which were issued before 1864, by William T. Lowndes, published in London between 1858 and 1864, in four volumes.

Bibliographical Society   A British organization founded in 1892 to further bibliographical research and publishing.

Bibliographical Society of America   An organization which welcomes into membership all those interested in bibliographical problems and projects of all sorts. One or two meetings are held in the course of a year, with the annual meeting customarily convened each January in New York

City. The Society publishes *Quarterly Papers.* It also has sponsored publication of a number of important bibliographical works, most notably Sabin's *Dictionary of Books Relating to America* and Blanck's *Bibliography of American Literature.* A subscription to the *Papers* of the Bibliographical Society costs $10 per year. Persons interested in becoming members of this society are invited to send a brief statement of their special bibliographical or book collecting interests to the Society at Post Box 397, Grand Central Station, New York City 10017. There are currently about 1550 members.

Bibliographies There are individual bibliographies for practically every major author. Almost all are of a high standard of scholarship and invaluable to the collector of old books, especially first editions. For example, for Dickens, a standard work is the *Catalogue of the Exhibition of the Works of Charles Dickens,* with an introduction by Royal Cortissoz, published by the Grolier Club of New York in 1913. The appropriate bibliographies are not as difficult to ferret out as this one example might lead you to suppose. Any single book on the author should contain references to other works and to the standard bibliographies.

Bibliography A publication containing the systematic description and history of certain books, including information not only on their authorship but their printing, editions, illustration, etc. A bibliography may consist of all the literature of one particular subject or a list of the books of a particular author, printer, area, or country, or for one limited period of history. "A tool for the scholar, a weapon for the bookseller, a suit of armor for the collector"—A. Edward Newton. There are bibliographies in print for a wide range of subjects; see the current issue of *Books in Print.* Among the bibliographies of bibliographies, one of the most highly useful is the *Bibliography of Bibliographies in American Literature,* edited by Charles H. Nilon.

Bibliography of American Literature Not the same as

Charles Evans' *American Bibliography*, this is a major work edited by Jacob Blanck, Volumes I through V covering Adams to Longfellow published 1955–1969, and recently extended with a sixth volume covering Longstreet to Parsons. Abbreviated to B.A.L.

The Yale University Press, which is publishing the volumes as they become ready, estimates that there will eventually be eight or nine volumes containing in all a total of about 35,000 numbered entries by nearly 300 American authors, with the first editions in chronological order and first appearances more briefly cited, and reprints which might be confused with firsts also noted. Volume VI became available at about $30.

Biblioklept   A person who steals books (bibliokleptomaniac).

Bibliolatry   A superstitious reverence, or an excessive and unreasonable admiration, for books.

Bibliomane   A person consumed with a desire for books (bibliomaniac).

Bibliopegist   A collector who specializes in book bindings.

Bibliophile   A lover of books, particularly of unusual, hard-to-get, scarce, or rare books. "An otherwise rational member of the community consumed by a love of books"— Eric Quayle.

Bibliophobe   A book-hater; a person who hates everything bookish.

Bibliopole   A dealer in secondhand books.

Bibliotaph   A person who hides books in boxes, closets, or packing cases, or otherwise squirrels them away.

Bidding at auction   Book auctions generally accept advance bids by mail or phone, as well as bids in person at the time the auction is held. The advance bids are executed by the auction house free of charge, and customarily a winning advance bid is but one increment above the next highest bid, although the house may have been authorized to go higher. Many experienced collectors prefer to have a professional dealer who is experienced at auctions do their bidding for them. For this service the dealer may charge a fee of around 10%. However, today there is also a growing number of small auction houses anxious to cater to the individual collector of moderate means, and at the auctions they conduct the proportion of collectors to dealers will be higher than at the larger and more prestigious houses, where the bidders at some sales are almost all dealers.

Bigmore and Wyman *A Bibliography of Printing, with Notes and Illustrations,* compiled by E. C. Bigmore and C. W. H. Wyman, originally printed in London by Bernard Quaritch in 1884, more recently reprinted by Philip C. Duschnes of New York in 1945; a valuable work, now unfortunately out of print.

Bildnis German for portrait or portrait plate.

Binder's board The kind of thick cardboard-like board used to make the covers of a cased book. The term book board is used in the same sense.

Binder's cloth A cloth binding, used to case a book, which is not the original binding; a substitute or replacement binding, of cloth.

Binder's stamp A die used for stamping or embossing book covers.

Binder's ticket A label which the binder places inside the book as a means of identifying his workmanship. Eighteenth-century binders customarily placed their label on the top inside corner of one of the front endpapers; however by the middle of the nineteenth century this ticket was moved to the back of the book, to the inside lower corner. Binders also print their names in gilt-stamped lettering on the lower inside front dentelle and sometimes on the lower part of the front cover where it may be partially hidden in the design.

Binding A book's binding is its exterior covering, which is of stronger stuff than the sheets (pages). Bindings may vary from the simplest of wrappers or plain undecorated boards to those which are exceedingly elaborate, of expensively tooled leather or of fruitwood inlaid with mosaic. The binding of a carefully made book will be designed to be appropriate to that particular book. Some bindings are highly inventive: one limited-edition book telling the story of the foundering of a sailing ship is bound in a piece of the wood taken from that ship at the bottom of the ocean; a book on swords from Japan has covers fastened with a tiny bodkin shaped like a sword.

Bindings may constitute an issue point, and bibliographies sometimes must spend pages describing all the variants. "Bindings are a constant challenge to bibliography . . . first states of the sheets may exist in half a dozen types of cloth, leather, boards, wrappers, or combinations of these, in various colors. One is designated the 'gift binding'; another the 'special presentation binding' and so on. We know that the 'Autocrat of the Breakfast-Table' with the five 'stars' on the spine is rarer than the copy with only four, but there is no proof that the five 'star' is an earlier state."—Merle Johnson.

Binding copy Any book which serves as a model for binding the edition; or, a used book which needs to be rebound.

Binding edge The folds of the sections of a book through which the binding threads pass.

Bindings, cleaning There are some commercial cleaners on the market for cleaning book bindings, especially those of leather. Washing a cloth binding is not advised, since in the process some sizing may be removed and the color therefore affected. (See also **Preserving old bindings.**)

Bindings, collecting "Bindings" sometimes appears in a book catalogue as a category for the listing of a number of different kinds of books. The implication is that these books are much more interesting for their bindings than their contents. Or, that the bindings, themselves handsome, create the interest in the book. In almost all cases, these bindings are leather, and the books are often sets of books.

Generally speaking, however, there is comparatively little

interest in collecting bindings of various sorts, and less, perhaps, known about the skilled bookbinders than about any of the other artisans connected with book production. Perhaps we can expect an upsurge of interest in American bookbinding. It is thought that the first American bookbinder was John Ratcliffe, who was brought over to America from England for the purpose of binding John Eliot's translation of the Bible for the Indians in 1663. American bindings reached the heights of fancy with the elaborately tooled and gilt cloth bindings of the mid-nineteenth century.

Bindings, secrets of In the earliest days of bookbinding, when materials for making books were scarce, binders sometimes resorted to cutting up the pages of one book— possibly unbound sheets still lying around the shop—to make the binding for another book. In this manner, some books which would otherwise have remained forever unknown to us have come down hidden in a binding until exposed by chance.

Binding variant A book differing in its binding from the original or the usual binding; or simply a different binding from that previously observed.

Black-letter A heavy style of lettering and of type, also called Gothic. The first European books used black-letter type, following the style of lettering of that time. To the modern eye, it appears ornate. Its greatest use now is in allusive typography. "A black-letter dog" has been used derisively to indicate a collector who wants only black-letter books.

Blanck Jacob N. Blanck (1906–74), author who produced a number of important bibliographical works, including the *Bibliography of American Literature*, commonly referred to as B.A.L., which has as its objective the delineation of some 35,000 works by 300 American authors. He is also the author of an authoritative work on children's books entitled *Peter Parley to Penrod*, often shortened in dealers' catalogues to PP to P, or PP to Penrod. Blanck also prepared the revised version of Merle Johnson's *American First Editions*. For sixteen years he was rare-book editor associated with *Publisher's Weekly* and *AB (Bookman's Weekly)*. (See also **Peter Parley to Penrod; Bibliography of American Literature**.)

Blank   A blank is a page which contains no printing. Usually there are one or more such pages at the beginning of a book; this is where the owner frequently writes his name. If a dealer describes a book as "lacks blank" he is referring to one of these front pages. The blank is sometimes torn out to conceal previous ownership.

Blanking   Machine-stamping without the use of ink.

Bleed   If a printed image extends off the edge of the printed page, it is said to bleed or bleed off. Photographs are sometimes made to bleed off; they are printed without blank margins. Bookmen also say that a page is "bled" if it has been trimmed down—whether accidentally or for special effect—to such an extent that some of the text is destroyed.

Blind tooling   The process of stamping without the use of either ink or foil to produce an indentation, often on leather, though sometimes on other materials including cloth. The result is an embossed effect. Blind tooling and blind stamping are sometimes distinguished from each other, the first meaning a hand process, the second by machine.

Blocking   The process of indenting an impression onto a leather cover. The covers of a book are sometimes described as blocked, blocked in blind, or blocked in gilt. The blocking is blind if no ink is used. Gold foil is used to produce blocking in gilt.

Block-printed books   In Europe the use of single-page block prints to produce a book came only slightly before the invention of movable type. Block-printed books date from 1420. Gutenberg himself was probably printing pictures from blocks between 1435 and 1455 during the years he was working on inventing the first printing press. From then on, the development of printing pictures from blocks to illustrate books and printing words from type proceeded in tandem. In

Japan, however, printing from wood engravings had been known since the year 770 A.D. A Chinese, Pi-Cheng, has been credited with having made the earliest use of separate characters for printing, in 1050 A.D.

Blumenlese   German for an anthology.

Blurb   A publisher's statement concerning a book, published on the dust jacket and naturally always highly laudatory in tone, intended to persuade the public to buy the book.

Boards   The stiff material used for the covers of a book. The name is derived from the fact that the earliest bound books were literally bound between two pieces of wood, usually oak. The same expression continues today, although the "boards" are not wood but a thick cardboard. "In boards" means either in the uncovered boards or in boards which are covered with paper.

Boards, pictorial   Boards picturing some scene from life; the picture may be printed directly on the boards or printed on paper which is glued to the boards. Many art books, for example, make a dramatic use of pictorial boards.

Bodoni   Giambattista Bodoni (1740–1813) designed a typeface known as Bodoni, developed from the previous work of Jenson, Caslon, and Baskerville, but more simple than their types. As a printer, Bodoni is much admired for his practically flawless presswork.

Bold   A style of printing type: **thus.** Also known as black face (not the same as black letter).

Book   A collection of sheets of paper fastened together and bound, in wrappers or in covers.

Book Auction Prices   A publication which reports the prices realized at American book auctions, including the smaller auction houses and therefore books of a lower price range than those covered in *American Book Prices Current* or the (English) *Book Auction Records.* Beginning publication in 1973, the first issue covered November, 1973–February, 1974, reporting 5,000 items. The second issue, covering November,

1973–June, 1974, reported 12,000 items. The prices are $5 and $10 respectively, available from the publisher, Albert Saifer, Box 56, Town Center, West Orange, N. J. 07052.

Book Auction Records A publication containing the prices and annotated records of sales made at major book auctions held in London, New York, Montreal, Melbourne, Edinburgh, Glasgow, and other major cities of the world, combined in a single alphabet. Included are the prices paid not only for books but for bindings, engravings, broadsides, maps, charts, and plans. The first issue of *B.A.R.* appeared in 1901. Modestly priced books such as would attract most beginning collectors do not come within the scope of *B.A.R.* The most consistent users of *B.A.R.* are those antiquarian book dealers who handle truly scarce and rare books. The form of shorthand notation used in *B.A.R.* requires some study. *B.A.R.* is published by Dawsons of Pall Mall, Cannon House, Folkstone, Kent CT19 5EE, England. Volume 70, for the auction season ending July, 1973, published in September, 1974, is available at £13.50 plus postage. There are eight general indexes, covering Volumes 1 through 65; the eighth is currently available at £30 plus postage.

Book binder Any type of cover for keeping a collection of papers, pamphlets, documents, or similar materials safely together in one place—neat and clean.

Book club A bonding-together of persons interested in books: in the case of new books, often to buy books and to circulate them among themselves, but in the case of old books, usually for the purpose of discussion only. The clubs are customarily small in membership and fairly select, with each member bringing to the discussion some particular aspect of book collecting which has become his specialty over the years. There is certainly no reason why clubs should not be formed for the mutual education of members new to book collecting, but all the clubs of which we have some knowledge are composed of persons of equally exotic specialties, permitting the club members to savor the delicious aroma of each others' specialties without having to try the recipe. Clubs formed along these lines include the prestigious Grolier Club in New York City, Club of Odd Volumes in Boston, and the Zamorano Club in Los Angeles.

Some successful clubs, which meet infrequently, have a national or even international membership, and conduct most of their business through the mails. They are formed on the basis of a common interest in collecting the works of one author, or of one kind of book. One example of such a club is the International Wizard of Oz Club, a non-profit organization founded in 1957 and now grown to a membership of over 1200 collectors of the works of L. Frank Baum residing in more than ten countries. The Club publishes a journal three times a year and sponsors both regional and national conventions. It is also responsible for the publication of reprints of articles it considers of particular interest to its members.

Book Collector   (See *American Book Collector.*)

Book fair   A public sale of old books, lasting from a day to, in some cases, several days. This type of sale may be organized by a membership organization, such as a church, synagogue, college club, parents' association, or women's organization, for the purpose of raising funds. The books offered for sale are customarily collected from the membership and thus may cover a wide range of types; many are usually of very little value. Dealers are sometimes invited to a "preview" to take first pick, but even so the collector who is following his own special interests may sometimes find books of interest to him at reasonable prices. However, it can be a stunning experience to find 10,000 old books heaped together and only two or three one wants, and those in poor condition.

Book font   A font of type designed for the reproduction of text matter, and designed with legibility, rather than ornamentation, in mind.

Book label   A label or ticket affixed to a book giving the name of the owner of the book *or* of a store which has offered the book for sale. Not, however, the label which is pasted to the backstrip providing information on the title.

The book label is customarily quite small and usually simple in design. Its only decoration may be a geometric border. Whereas the book-plate is usually pasted to the inside front cover, the label often appears at the lower inside margin of the back cover. The book-plate is used to indicate ownership; the book label often indicates source.

Bookman's Price Index   A serially issued reference work of antiquarian books and periodicals, containing entries selected from the catalogues issued by the world's leading dealers in rare books and by many specialist dealers in books. The *Index* consists of a master list of many thousands of books, arranged alphabetically by author with title, place and date of publication, pagination or collation, along with information on each book's condition, and information pertinent to the conditions of its sale, such as the name of the dealer, the catalogue number, and the year. To date, ten volumes have appeared in print, containing a total of close to 420,000 items. The price of each volume is $52. The publisher is Gale Research Company, Book Tower, Detroit, Mich. 48226.

Bookman's Weekly   Popularly known as *AB,* a weekly trade magazine acknowledged as the leading medium for the exchange of information in the field of old books. The full title is *A. B., Bookman's Weekly for the Specialist Book World . . . Including Antiquarian Bookman.* Jacob L. Chernofsky is editor of this specially important medium for communication between book dealers and librarians. It can also serve the individual collector who has the patience to wade through a great deal of possibly irrelevant information to find one item of information for which he is searching. Each issue carries many pages of advertisements for books which are wanted, and a few pages of books for sale. In addition, the editorial matter, sometimes acerbic in tone, contains the gossip of the trade, notices of meetings, reports on conferences, court decisions, sometimes articles by guest authors, and reviews of new books of bibliographic interest. *AB* does not itself buy, sell, or appraise books. Editor Malkin is proud that *AB* is a trade magazine owned, operated, and published entirely independently of any other organization or business. The address is Box 1100, Newark, N. J. 07101. An annual subscription is $20. This includes the two-part *Yearbook*, an important compendium of information which includes an up-to-date directory of old-book and specialist dealers.

Book Market   A publication of that name which calls itself "the books for sale weekly, for antiquarian and out-of-print books." It is available on subscription from 109 Wembley Park Drive, Wembley, Middlesex, HA9 8HG, England.

Book of hours   A manuscript or printed collection of prayers or other devotions.

Book papers   Printing papers, which come in a variety of weights and finishes. Book paper originally came in standard sizes, and from these sizes the names of the standard book sizes were derived.

Book-plate   A label signifying the ownership of a book and usually pasted to the inside front cover of a book. Book-plates are generally of paper, although some are of leather. A book-plate may establish a book as an association copy, or may otherwise advance the price of a book, if, for example, its presence proves that the book was once part of the library of a collector well known for his good taste and discrimination.

On the other hand, evidence in a book that a book-plate was once present and has now been removed will definitely lower the value of the book.

Book scout   Any individual, either self-employed or working for a book dealer or for one or more collectors, who searches for special titles in such places as second-hand stores, auctions, church sales, book fairs, old-book stores, etc.

A successful book scout must have a very broad knowledge of books; this is not a job for an amateur.

Book search service   One of the many varieties of personal services offered to the public by dealers in old books, sometimes offered—most successfully—by persons who operate by mail out of their own homes, and rather infrequently offered by dealers in new books as a kind of side-line for customers looking for books which have gone out of print. Whatever their nature, most search services make no charge for the search but, of course, add their fee to the price of the book when they find it. The most successful book-searchers keep a permanent file of the needs of their most steady and faithful customers. It is not at all unusual for a search service to turn up a truly rare book some ten years after it was first requested; most books, however, are located within a matter of weeks if they are going to be found at all.

Book dealers make extensive use of the pages of *AB (Bookman's Weekly)* to advertise for the books they want (individual persons may advertise books they have for sale in the pages of *AB*, but only dealers may advertise their needs). However, *The Out-of-Print Bookfinder* welcomes ads from anyone to either buy or sell.

Booksellers   Travellers may find the following translations of the word "bookseller" useful:

Danish	Boghandler
Dutch	Boekhandelaar
French	Libraire
German	Buchhändler
Italian	Libraio
Norwegian	Bokhandler
Spanish	Librero
Swedish	Bokhandlare

Books in Print   A major and highly important reference work used constantly by many old-book dealers and equally useful for the collector of old books, as well as for the dealer in new books, for whom it is primarily intended. Its value to the person interested in old books lies in providing information on books still in print, new reprints, and bibliographical sources currently available.

Issued annually, a recent edition catalogued 265,000 titles in print, listed in all 392,000 items, under 63,500 subject headings, with 55,000 cross references. There is a separate volume listing books in print according to authors, and another volume for paperbacks currently in print. Fortunately, any library of any size finds it necessary to have its own up-to-date copies, and they may therefore be readily examined.

Book size   (See **Size categories.**)

Books, stolen   Collectors, public, private, and university libraries from time to time report the theft of important and valuable books and manuscripts. Recently the University of Virginia reported the loss of three first edition books by Edgar Allan Poe, including his first book, *Tamerlane*. The New York Society Library suffered the theft of the double folio edition of John James Audubon's *Birds of America* in four volumes (difficult to tuck under a raincoat, one would think!). But these are special cases, and the books are instantly recognizable when they turn up. The average dealer is more likely to be the victim of pilfering on a small scale, and the small collector to run the risk of purchasing a book which was stolen, whether innocently offered to him or not. Should you be offered the opportunity to buy a book of obvious value which is rather oddly lacking a pedigree, or history of sale, it would be prudent to guard against the possibility, however remote, that you are being offered stolen goods. Ask for the source of the book—names and addresses—and check the veracity of the information. Ask the seller for a document of sale; if he is the rightful owner he will not object. Perhaps it is best to always be wary of the stories spun by strangers about fantastic finds in attics or the amazing find in the old-book stall where the dealer had no idea what he was selling.

Book stamp   Another term for library stamp: an indication of library ownership by stamping the book. Sometimes the front matter of a book is stamped, either blind-stamped or with the use of ink. A library stamp anywhere in a book reduces its value, but any stamp on the title page is tantamount to a defacement.

Bookworm   The larva stage of any number of varieties of beetle. These beetles lay their eggs on the edges or along the spines of books, and when they hatch the larvae tunnel their way through the books they infest, particularly going for the paste and glue used in making up the book. "Although the bookworm is rarely found in temperate climates, it is not to be written off altogether, since it occasionally makes its appearance as far north as Boston."—Lydenberg and Archer, in *The Care and Repair of Books*. Fumigating books which are infected with bookworms is generally considered an effective way of ridding the books of this pest. Bookworms, incidentally, do not actually have an overwhelming preference for books, but are known to also infest the bookshelves, or even walls or floors of the library. Bookworms are not partial to modern books, apparently disliking the alum which is put into the paste. Among the traditional home remedies for getting rid of bookworms are ether, turpentine, and camphor, and even, according to some sources, tobacco.

Bosses   To boss is to decorate in relief, and in book bindings bosses are clasps or metal ornaments which are added to a book cover. The bosses may be any one of a wide variety of shapes, but actually the most frequently used are simple knobs of metal, usually brass, which are fastened to the boards. Although the original purpose of attaching bosses to a book was to protect the cover, their use today is only ornamental. Of course, because of their expense they are rarely added to a modern book.

Bouquin   French for a secondhand book which is probably of slight value. A *bouquinerie* is a small bookstore which deals in old books.

Bowdlerized Expurgated, to remove any reference possibly giving moral offense. So called after Thomas Bowdler (1754–1825), who produced a so-called clean version of Shakespeare's works in 1818, for the edification of children.

Boxed Neatly cased in a container made of wood or cardboard and open at one end to reveal the spine of the book so contained. Books issued by private presses and books issued in limited editions are often boxed, sometimes fancifully, in matching boards, or with an illustrated label.

Bradel The name of the binder who has produced a special, cased binding, almost always in three-quarters or full leather usually elaborately tooled and gilt. The name of the binder is often placed in tiny gilt letters along the inner dentelle of the front cover, although it may appear elsewhere, stamped or affixed to the top of a front blank page or even hidden in the lower part of the design on the front cover.

Bradley Van Allen Bradley, an authority on old and rare books who is a retired newspaper journalist and the author of the best-selling *Gold in Your Attic*, *More Gold in Your Attic*, and *The Book Collector's Handbook of Values*. The first two of these have inspired many people to take up book collecting and to become alert to the possibilities of making rare finds on their own bookshelves and those of friends and relatives. His most recent contribution to book collecting, the *Handbook*, is fine as far as it goes: the information provided may prevent you from thinking that you have a first edition when in fact your book is a second or third, but by not supplying information on all the necessary issue points to make a book really valuable, it may be misleading. The difference between a fifty-dollar and one-hundred-dollar book may lie in a point which the *Handbook* may not have space to mention. For example, for Joyce Kilmer's *Trees and Other Poems*, the *Handbook* states that the first edition, first state, is thus: "Boards, paper labels. New York, no date

(1914). First edition, first state, without 'Printed in U.S.A.' on copyright page." All true—but, the first issue is completely identified by having top edge gilt. Therefore, before coming to a final decision concerning the worth of any book, it is wise to make a further check in the appropriate bibliography. Bradley is, in other words, a wonderful help in tipping you off to the potential value of a book, but, like auction records, should be used with caution. Neither is a final authority on points, and neither necessarily makes clear what was the relation of price to the condition of the particular book.

Bradshaw Henry Bradshaw (1831–1886), considered the father of scientific English bibliography.

Breaker Slang for a book more valuable broken up than preserved as a unit. Book dealers generally want to keep a book together in one piece as long as possible and will tenderly describe a book which is falling apart as "needing rebinding"; on the other hand, art dealers are always on the lookout for just such books, which they have no compunction about tearing apart for the separate sale of any plates, illustrations, or maps.

Break-off A broken piece of type which does not print properly, producing a broken letter in the text.

Bremer The Bremer Presse, a private press established in 1911 in Germany and celebrated particularly for its fine typography and the work of Willi Wiegand.

Bright copy A clean book, unmarred by foxing, smudges, pencilling, or other signs of wear in the pages. In a bright copy, the paper customarily retains its original crispness and glow.

Bristol Roger Patrell Bristol, editor of *An Index of Printers, Publishers, and Booksellers Indicated by Charles Evans in His American Bibliography*. This work, published in 1961, is a valuable source of information for collectors of early Americana. R. P. Bristol is also the author of a supplement to Evans, published in 1970.

Bristol board A thin cardboard which has a fine smooth

finish, unlike the thick cardboard used for the boards to cover the outside of a book. Index cards are one familiar use of Bristol board. Another frequent use is for binding a typescript.

British booksellers Antiquarian Booksellers' Association, 29 Revell Road, Kingston-Upon-Thames, Surrey, England.

Broadsheet Sometimes called a broadside, a large sheet of paper sometimes printed on one side only, often for use as a poster, announcement, or rhyme-sheet.

Broadside A single printed sheet handed out as a free advertising circular. Properly speaking, the broadside is printed on a fully untrimmed sheet of paper, on one side only.

Brochure A short printed work consisting of a few leaves stitched together; a pamphlet. The word brochure is sometimes employed as a more refined term for pamphlet. A brochure is often the medium for advertising, although a brochure may be any publication of just a few pages, thirty-two or less. The term comes from the French word brocher, meaning to stitch.

Broken letter A chipped, inverted, or otherwise incorrect character of type in the text of a work. "The inverted, broken, or wrong letter, like the mole on a human face, he (the bibliographer) is quick to observe, and his warning 'sic' is not so much intended to call attention to error, as it is to mark a distinguishing feature of the edition by which it may be recognized." From the preface to Evans' *American Bibliography*, Volume I.

Issues within editions are frequently identified by the presence of a broken letter. It should not be assumed, however, that the presence of a broken letter is evidence of the book's being an earlier issue. Frequently this is not the case, since a letter which at first is whole wears down or breaks off and after the press is stopped and the faulty character of type replaced, perfect type then appears in the first and the third state, with broken type only in the second state. There can be no way of knowing this without consulting an authoritative bibliography.

Bronze printing Printing of a bronzish or golden appearance; gilt.

Brown, John Carter The library of that name located at Brown University in Providence, Rhode Island, and well known for its extensive collection of early Americana. The Brown University Press makes available, at around $35, the *Catalogue of the J.C.B. Library . . . Books Printed 1675–1700*, listing 1852 books, pamphlets, broadsides, atlases, etc. *A Short-Title List of Additions—Books Printed 1471–1700* is also available, at about $5.

Browned In the case of paper, discolored with age. Browning is an entirely natural process and to be expected in paper which is more than a hundred years old. Unless it is excessive, it may not, therefore, be mentioned in a dealer's catalogue in the description of an old book. Uneven amounts of browning, from page to page, should, on the other hand, always be noted. Browning often starts to occur at the outer margins of the page and works inward.

Buchbinde German for "advertisement-wrapper" or book jacket. Wrapper is *Schutzumschlag*.

Buchdecke German for the cover of a book.

Buchdrucker German for typographer, or printer.

Buchdruckerkunst German for the art of printing, or typography.

Bücher für Weihnachten German for Christmas books, or gift books.

Büchersammler German for book collector.

Büchertrödler German for a dealer in secondhand books.

Buchhändler German for a bookseller or dealer in books.

Buchhandlung German for a bookshop.

Buch kleinsten Formates German for a miniature book.

Büchlein German for a secondhand book of little value.

Buchrücken German for the back or the spine of a book.

Buckram A fairly coarse and heavy fabric used for book

binding. It is particularly tough and long-lasting and is therefore often used for library books and other books expected to receive considerable use. In the description of an old book, a binding of buckram indicates that the book has been rebound, even though this is not specified.

Bumped With the corners of a book worn, wrinkled, or otherwise worn. "Covers bumped" in the description of a book almost invariably means that the corners are dented and damaged, although occasionally the term is also applied to the top and bottom of the spine.

Burroughs Edgar Rice Burroughs (1875–1950), best known for his series of Tarzan books about a white boy raised in the African jungle among wild animals. First edition copies of the Tarzan books are collected, and *AB (Bookman's Weekly)* makes available a special issue on collecting Burroughs, at one dollar. There is also an authoritative *Edgar Rice Burroughs Bibliography and Price Guide* identifying not only first but other editions, available at $3.75 from the publisher, P.D.A. Enterprises, Box 8010, New Orleans, La. 70182.

Butted Butted corners in rule borders are those which are joined flush rather than mitred, thus: ⌐

Byzantine coating A costly type of book binding, usually found only in books of venerable age, in which the covers of the book are heavily encrusted with precious metals and stones, or ornamented with other, semi-precious materials.

C

C   Roman numeral for 100.

Cabinet collecting   Building a small but choice collection. Such a collection may be built around an author, genre, subject, or a particular size of book or type of binding. However, the term is most generally applied to building a collection specifically of miniature books. An outstanding example of a cabinet collector is H. Yates Thompson, who set himself the task of collecting just one hundred, and no more, of the most beautiful illuminated manuscripts which he could afford; as a new manuscript was acquired, he resolutely discarded one less precious. Obviously this type of limited collecting has great advantages for persons who live in small apartments.

Cabinet edition   Any edition of a work which is smaller and cheaper than the fine edition but still handsomely presented.

Cachet   French for the owner's stamp.

Caldecott Medal   A Randolph J. Caldecott Medal has been awarded each year since 1938 to the illustrator of the most distinguished picture book for children published in the United States during the previous year. Its award is made by the Children's Services Division of the American Library Association. First editions of the Caldecott Award books are eagerly collected.

Caldecott Medal Books

1938	*Animals of the Bible.* Lathrop
1939	*Meil Li.* Handforth
1940	*Abraham Lincoln.* d'Aulaire
1941	*They Were Good and Strong.* Lawson
1942	*Make Way for Ducklings.* McCloskey
1943	*The Little House.* Burton
1944	*Many Moons.* Thurber (Slobodkin, illus.)
1945	*Prayer for a Child.* Field (Jones, illus.)
1946	*The Rooster Crows.* Petersham
1947	*The Little Island.* MacDonald (Weisgand, illus.)
1948	*White Snow, Bright Snow.* Tresselt (Duvoisin, illus.)
1949	*The Big Snow.* Hader
1950	*Song of the Swallows.* Politi
1951	*The Egg Tree.* Milhous
1952	*Finders Keepers.* Lipkind (Mordvinoff, illus.)
1953	*The Biggest Bear.* Ward
1954	*Madeline's Rescue.* Bemelmans
1955	*Cinderella.* Brown
1956	*Frog Went A-Courtin'.* Langstaff (Rojankovsky, illus.)
1957	*A Tree Is Nice.* Udry (Simont, illus.)
1958	*Time of Wonder.* McCloskey
1959	*Chanticleer and the Fox.* Cooney
1960	*Nine Days to Christmas.* Ets & Labastida
1961	*Baboushka and the Three Kings.* Robbins (Sidjakov, illus.)
1962	*Once a Mouse.* Brown
1963	*The Snowy Day.* Keats
1964	*Where the Wild Things Are.* Sendak
1965	*May I Bring a Friend?* de Regniers (Montresor, illus.)
1966	*Always Room for One More.* Leodhas (Hogrogian, illus.)

1967   *Sam, Bangs & Moonshine.* Ness
1968   *Drummer Hoff.* Emberly, Barbara (Ed Emberly, illus.)
1969   *The Fool of the World and the Flying Ship.* Ransome (Shulevitz, illus.)
1970   *Sylvester and the Magic Pebble.* Steig
1971   *A Story-A Story.* Haley
1972   *One Fine Day.* Hogrogian
1973   *The Funny Little Woman.* Hearn: retold by Mosel (Lent, illus.)
1974   *Duffy and the Devil.* Zemach, Harve (Margot Zemach, illus.)
        Honor Books:
        Three Jovial Huntsmen. Jeffers
        Cathedral: the Story of its Construction. Macaulay

Caldecott, Randolph J. A noted English illustrator of children's books (1846–1886) for whom the Caldecott Medal was named.

Calendered Paper which is calendered has a smooth and glossy surface which is highly glazed in the process of manufacture. The "calender" is actually a stack of horizontal rollers of cast iron through which the paper passes at great pressure. In German the word is *satiniert,* and in French *satiné,* both highly expressive.

Calfskin A type of leather used for binding, usually designated in old-book dealer's catalogues simply as calf. Although less durable than goatskin (morocco), it is admired for use in book binding because of its suppleness and many decorative possibilities. Calf can be subjected to a large variety of kinds of processing: it may be marbled, sprinkled, diced, or given a basket-weave imprint. It may also be dyed in a wide range of beautiful colors. Many bookmen feel that nothing can rival the plain good looks of the undecorated calf, however.

In old book bindings, it may be difficult to tell a calf

bookbinding from one of sheepskin, although as a rule the sheepskin wears less well and becomes shabby in appearance more quickly. It is a good guess that an early American binding, before 1830, is sheep rather than calf.

Calipers An instrument for taking fine measurements, much preferred over a ruler for measuring the precise size of a book. Such measuring is often done across the top edge, where a difference of an eighth or sixteenth of an inch may be important.

Calligraphy The art of elegant penmanship; the art of writing beautifully by hand, and thus an art closely related historically to the development of handsome type faces.

Cambridge The Cambridge Bibliography of English Literature, abbreviated to CBEL. Published serially, this scholarly work provides dates for first editions, the dates of any other important or significant editions, and other information which may be helpful in identifying editions. It is thus a good all-around reference, although it does not provide all the bibliographical detail which may be available elsewhere for specific works. The entire five-volume bibliography issued to date is available from the Cambridge University Press for about $65.

Cambridge History The Cambridge History of Literature, edited by A. W. Ward and A. R. Waller, in fifteen volumes, and published by the Cambridge University Press between 1907 and 1933.

Cambridge University Library The library complex authorized under the Copyright Act to receive a free statutory copy of any works published for sale in Great Britain.

Cameo printing A style of printing similar to embossing. An image is made to stand up above the surface of the paper.

Canadiana Publications either originating in Canada or concerned with the history of Canada—or both. The recently published *Contributions to a Short-Title Catalogue of Canadiana*, by Bernard Amtmann (Montreal, 1971–73), is available from the author at 1529 Sherbrooke Street W., Montreal 109, Quebec, four volumes for $225 or, interleaved, five volumes, $275.

Canadian Booksellers The Antiquarian Booksellers Association of Canada, abbreviated A.B.A.C., which may be reached at Box 148, Station M, Toronto, Ontario, Canada. Although in the past overshadowed by dealers in the United States, Canadian book dealers seem to be increasingly active, and their Association has in recent years sponsored successful book fairs attended by both Canadian dealers and dealers from other countries.

Canadian Pseudonyms *Contributions to a Dictionary of Canadian Pseudonyms and Anonymous Works Relating to Canada . . . Contributions à un Dictionnaire des Pseudonymes canadiens et des Ouvrages anonymes relatifs au Canada,* by Bernard Amtmann (Montreal, 1973), published at $18, and available from the author (see preceding entry).

Cancel The supplementary leaf which is inserted to correct a leaf of the text which has been found at fault; or, the original leaf which is supplanted. Usually, the meaning becomes entirely clear in context. Also, called a cancelled leaf. A publisher may wish to excise (cancel) a leaf after a book has been printed and made up but is not yet bound. The presence of a leaf which was subsequently cancelled may add a great deal to the value of a book. For example, the original version of Theodore Dreiser's *A Hoosier Holiday,* which was published in 1916, contained a reference to "chasing German-American professors out of Canadian colleges"—this was at the time politically embarrassing and therefore the leaf containing this statement was cancelled and another containing the revised text substituted. A leaf may be cancelled because of bad workmanship as well as in the cause of censorship.

Cancellans A replacement: the leaf which replaces the original leaf in a book.

Cancelled matter Any reading matter—especially appearing in a newspaper—which has been deleted, in the case of a newspaper usually from one edition to the next.

Cancel title An altered title page, most often a title page bearing the name of a publisher other than that in the original edition. There may, also, be other, additional information on the title. Occasionally a publisher has been known to insert a cancel title for the purpose of giving the impression that here there is a new and different book from that first issued. The reason could be that the first had not been selling well. The publisher of Thoreau's *A Week on the Concord and Merrimac Rivers* became desperate when so few copies sold that he was left with almost the entire edition; his solution was to try substituting a new title page to give the impression that he was now offering a new edition of a highly successful book.

Caps The upper case of type. Large or majuscule letters: THUS. In bibliographical works, the precise title of a book is customarily rendered in all caps if it appears on the title page in all caps.

Caption The headline for a chapter of a book or for a section of a book or chapter. Although caption is sometimes used interchangeably with the word legend, legend, not caption, is the correct term for the description which appears beneath or near an illustration.

Caption title A title which appears at the top of the first page of the text of a printed work, rather than on a separate title page.

Caput Derived from the Latin and meaning a heading or the indication of a new chapter.

Card page The page in a book which lists all the other books by the same author. This page customarily, although not always, faces the title page. At times it may serve to identify the edition, since often a second or later edition will list the present work as one among others by the author. It would be imprudent to rely upon this as the only means of identifying an edition, however.

Carter John Carter, author of a book for serious old-book collectors titled *ABC for Book Collectors,* published by Knopf. A revised edition of this 1952 classic was issued in 1963 and is still available at around $5.

Carton French for a cancel leaf.

Cartonnage French for the original cased binding.

Cartoon A comic or satirical drawing, usually depicting an historical event or the current scene, usually political or social.

Cartouche A scroll-like flourish or frame, oval in most cases, frequently employed on maps to set apart the legend. The cartouche was a device used in ancient Egypt to set apart the names of royalty inscribed on papyri.

Case In the process of book binding, the case is the enclosure, often made of boards covered with cloth, into which are fitted the stitched quires.

The term case is also used for the protective box in which a book is stored, or for the envelope in which pamphlets or maps are kept. A case may be the original case provided by a publisher to protect a book or other printed material. A slip-in case is one which is open at one side to show the backstrip of the book which is enclosed.

In printing, however, upper and lower case refers respectively to capital and small letters. The use of the term in this sense comes from the actual cases—boxes—in which type was stored, one case physically above the other.

Cased A book which is cased is one which is glued at the back rather than stitched (bound).

Casing There is a technical difference between binding and casing a book. When a book is bound, the leaves are sewn onto the cords which are a part of the back of the binding. When it is cased, however, the leaves are sewn onto tapes, then a strip of thick paper or thin cloth is glued to this backing, and the ends of the tapes are then glued to the inner edge of the case.

Casing in Pasting a book into its cover, either during the process of its manufacture or possibly when it is being repaired.

Caslon   A style of type face, designed by William Caslon.

Caslon, William   William Caslon (1692–1766) significantly advanced the art of printing in his day and helped make England independent of the Continent with regard to type style for the first time. He began his working life as an apprentice to a designer of gun stocks and the ornaments for book bindings, and when he established his own foundry in 1720 he was thus able to combine a knowledge of the decorative arts with a competence in working metal. The new kind of type face which he developed had a rounded lower-case letter especially elegant in appearance and easier to read than a great deal of the other type then in use.

Cassell   *Cassell's Encyclopedia of Literature*, edited by S. H. Steinberg, was published in London in 1953.

Castlemon   Harry Castlemon was the pseudonym of C. A. Fosdick (1842–1915), who wrote no fewer than fifty-eight novels for boys, many based on his own experiences as a boy and on gunboats during the Civil War. They are divided into four series: Boy Trappers, Sportsman's Club, War, and Western Adventure. A bibliography by Jacob Blanck (1931) is available in reprint from Mark Press, 16 Park Place, Waltham, Mass. 02154, in a limited edition, at $10.

Catalogue   Book dealers' catalogues listing items for sale or for auction have themselves become an important source of information in the world of old books, so that these catalogues frequently come onto the market, often in large lots, to be sold as reference material.

Catalogue de Livres d'Occasion   French for a secondhand book dealer's catalogue.

Catchword   A word which appears below the text matter on a page, at the bottom of the recto (right-hand page), to indicate what the first word on the succeeding page will be; and also at the top of the verso as well. Thus:

Cathedral

Cathedral binding A binding which is decorated with a design of Gothic arches and other related architectural forms.

Caxton Either a book printed by William Caxton, or a style of printing type named after him, or, of course, the man himself. William Caxton (1422–91) is given credit for being the first English printer. He imported his equipment from The Netherlands and established a press at Westminster in 1476. English translations of the Bible had been forbidden by both the church and the state, but Caxton defied the authorities to insert sections from the Bible in some of the other works which he was publishing. One of his most notable achievements was publication of *The Canterbury Tales* in 1478; one of his most popular publications was his *Fables of Aesop*.

Censorship (See **Banned books.**)

Chain lines The characteristically wide-spaced lines which are visible in laid paper. These lines are produced by the mesh at the bottom of the tray in which paper is made by hand; machine-made paper sometimes also contains these lines or the semblance of them in imitation of handmade paper. Although there are exceptions, an old rule for telling book size is by the direction of the chain lines—up and down for folio or octavo, across for quarto or 16mo.

Chalcography The art of engraving on copper.

Chapbooks Historically, chapbooks are the crude pamphlets which were sold in England from door to door by persons called chapmen, itinerant peddlers. First published in London, they became exceedingly popular in the middle- and late-seventeenth century since they were profusely illustrated with woodcuts which often depicted everyday life and were calculated to appeal to persons who had never learned to read. These small paper-covered books were usually published anonymously, and few are dated.

Modern chapbooks (books or pamphlets 16mo or smaller) have become a specialty of a few private presses and are usually employed for poetry or for reporting some subject of specialized bibliographic interest, such as the history of printing. Issued in limited editions, such modern versions as the *Typophile Chapbooks* series remain steadily popular with book collectors.

Chapter head   The title of a chapter or any other material standing before the opening text of a chapter.

Character   A single letter, used in typesetting or in some other form of writing. A character-count is the average number of characters to a line of specified type.

Chautauquan   Pertaining to adult education. So named after the Chautauqua Institution which offered correspondence courses, held an annual summer school in New York State, and published books, issuing a bulletin, *The Chautauquan*, from 1880 to 1914. The term has become generic for the type of programs offered by travelling lecturers.

Cheap edition   Any literary work, in the original edition or in reprint, which is published at a price attractive for readers of little means. Occasionally, but not often, one finds a book which the publisher has candidly labelled "cheap edition."

Cheap reprint   A new edition of a book, almost always on less expensive paper than the original, sometimes cut down to smaller size although employing the same plates (type).

Chemise   French for a folder or a paper wrapper, or a dust jacket.

Children's books   There are well over twenty-five dealers in the United States alone who make a specialty of old children's books. Their offerings include Horatio Alger first editions, miniature books, toy books, Mickey Mouse firsts, award-winning books, horn books, and books illustrated by famous artists such as Rackham, Pyle, Nielsen, and Parrish. Interest in collecting all manner of children's books seems to be rapidly on the rise.

A. Edward Newton once commented that "when it is realized how flimsy, how easily destroyed children's books were, and are, and what destructive tendencies lurk in the little brains and hands of the best trained children, the wonder is that so many books have been preserved." . . . Standards of conditions for old children's books are appreciably lower than for books designed for adults.

Adults are sometimes very much surprised to hear that some of the books they read and enjoyed as children have now become sought after as collectors' items. Books from the Tarzan series may now, for example, bring up to $50 for the first edition in good or better condition, and $200 has recently been the going price for the first issue of *Tarzan of the Apes*—with the acorn device on the spine.

Some collectors of children's books specialize in illustrated books, or collect the works of just certain authors, but others want the titles listed in *Peter Parley to Penrod*, or the first editions of the books which have received either the Caldecott Medal or the Newbery Award. (See **Peter Parley to Penrod, Caldecott Medal, Newbery Award.**)

China paper　A very fine, soft, and absorbent paper which is often used for proofs of woodcuts or engravings. This type of paper was first manufactured in China, from bamboo fiber.

Chipped　With reference to the covers of a book: marred by light gouging, or nicked. The term chipped may indicate a tiny hole or mean that a piece of the backstrip has been chunked out. Leather is particularly susceptible to chipping; cloth, of course, may rarely chip but does frequently become frayed.

Chirography　The art of penmanship.

Chiroxylographic　With illustrations made from woodcuts, and with the text lettered by hand. Offset printing has recently produced something of a renaissance in this style of bookmaking.

Chrestomathie　French, or German, for anthology.

Chromograph　Chromograph, chromo-lith, and chromo-lithograph all refer to the process of reproducing an illustration in color through the lithographic process. Many children's books at the end of the nineteenth century were vividly and sometimes handsomely illustrated by means of this process.

Chromolithography The art of making a lithographic print in colors.

Chronogram A phrase, sentence, or inscription in which certain letters express, through their numerical value, a date—or convey other information which is partially hidden. In the title page of a book, this might be done by printing the key information in bold, the rest of the letters in italic type: *The Miraculous Calligraphic Manual* (1900).

Church E. D. Church: *Catalog of Books Relating to the Discovery and Early History of North and South America.*

Circa Around, or about, a date (Latin). Abbreviated c or c., often in parentheses. c. 1940 may mean either around that time, or possibly of that specific date, although the latter is usually expressed, in book catalogues, by a question mark.

Circuit binding (See **Divinity circuit**; also **Yapp**.)

Clean proof A proof (of a manuscript) in which there are few if any corrections.

Client card The card which is kept by a dealer in old books to record a customer's name and his specific needs. Dealers who conduct search services are usually glad to keep a client card for a regular customer listing long-term as well as immediate needs. Dealer and client both must recognize that locating any one particular volume may take as long as several years.

Clipped A book is clipped when its margins have been trimmed down so excessively that the text has been chopped into and the book mutilated.

Clique, The A weekly journal published in England for the book trade. *The Clique*, 109 Wembley Park Drive, Wembley, Middlesex HA9 8HG, also publishes *The Book Market*, "the Books for Sale Weekly," listing both antiquarian and out-of-print books, as well as an annual directory of booksellers in the British Isles specializing in antiquarian and out-of-print books.

Clog almanack   An early kind of almanac, printed from characters cut from either horn or wood.

Cloth bindings   Most hardcover books published today appear in cloth. Leather is generally now reserved for expensive, limited editions, and paper over boards is customarily used only for small volumes such as books of poetry. William Pickering, an English publisher and bookseller, is credited with having been the first to use cloth to cover boards, in 1821, although there are books rather crudely covered in cloth which date back to the 1760's. These last were school books, and the cloth was so coarse that a label could not easily be made to adhere; students had to resort to inking in the title on the cover, to identify their books for their own convenience. By the 1830's, however, cloth was being regularly furnished to publishers for use in covering books, and cloth-bound books were no longer a novelty. The first cloth-bound book featuring a pictorial cover was published in 1834; published by John Murray, it was titled *Bubbles from the Brunnens of Nassau, by an Old Man.*

Club of Odd Volumes   A club of bibliophiles founded in Boston in the late nineteenth century at about the same time that the Grolier Club was founded in New York and for approximately the same purpose. The Club of Odd Volumes has encouraged the development of excellence in typography and in bookmaking in general.

Coated paper   Paper having a surface coating which produces a smooth finish. The surface may vary, however, from eggshell, which is slightly rough, to glossy, which is slick.

Cockled   In paper, damaged; having an uneven or blistered surface, possibly even curling at the edges.

Codex   A manuscript volume; or, loosely, any ancient manuscript.

Codices   Manuscripts in leaves: not bound.

Cold type A modern method of printing, in which, rather than hot metal, equipment similar to a typewriter produces copy for photographic reproduction.

Collate Assemble in the correct order; or check to make sure that leaves are correctly assembled. Printers collate the signatures of a book when they place the signatures in the proper order to be bound.

The term collate may also be used to indicate the process of checking to make sure that all the original leaves and insertions of a book are still present as published. To collate a book, the best method is to place the first finger of the right hand at the bottom of somewhere along the fiftieth page, crook the finger, and hold the pages firmly between thumb and finger. Then fan out the pages, checking the pages as you flip through them. Repeat throughout the book, handling about fifty pages at a time. If the pages are numbered at the foot, then the leaves must be fanned at the head. Plates and maps which are not numbered must be carefully checked separately, one by one, against the printed list if there is one. Books such as early Bibles in which the pages were not numbered can be collated by checking the serial lettering of the signatures, by carefully comparing individual pages with another copy, or by reference to a bibliographical source. The catchwords, if present, can also be a help, although it is usually wise to read the text as well to make sure pages are not missing.

Collated and perfect All the original pages of the book have been found to be present by someone who has conscientiously collated the book page by page. Abbreviated to c. & p.

Collation The assembly of the pages of a book in the proper order. For example, the following is the collation for the first edition of Frank Stockton's book entitled *Ting a Ling*, published at the Riverside Press in Cambridge by Hurd and Houghton—glazed yellow end paper; fly leaf; title page, copyright notice dated 1869 on verso; dedication, verso blank; text, pages 1–187; blank (p. 188); fly leaf; endpaper.

Collation marks The small printed marks (usually the letters of the alphabet in proper series) added by the printer at the bottom of the sheet to assist in collation.

Collectibles Books not sufficiently old, rare, or interesting to attract the interest of experienced (and often well-heeled) collectors, and yet of some value or interest of themselves. Yesterday's collectibles have a way of becoming today's antiques and therefore escalating in value. Fantasy fiction, for example—magazines, comics, and hardcover books— once scorned by reputable book dealers now has its own specialty dealers, with the prices for some items already ranging up into the hundreds. Book-lovers who follow their own personal whims may end up with a lot of collectibles, but such items may not only cost much less than more prestigious items but also bring as much enjoyment. Any collection of books would probably be strange if it did not have at least one or two just-plain-collectibles tucked in.

Collotype An expensive—but fine—method for reproducing plates for the illustration of a book. The print is made directly in a process using hardened gelatine as the printing surface.

Colonial edition Between the years 1880 and 1910, British publishers often produced a special cheap edition for export to the colonial market. Some of these editions, formerly ignored by collectors, have now become popular collectibles.

Colophon A mark of identification—crowning piece, or finishing stroke—found in a book and furnishing information about the source of the book. In some of the earliest printed books, in which there might be no title page, the colophon was placed at the end of the book to perform somewhat the same function as a title page by supplying the name of the illustrator for the book, and possibly the name of the book's author and the publisher or printer, as well. Later, when books began to become so popular that unauthorized reprints were being published, printers came to see the wisdom of stamping their name, or having it printed, right at the beginning of a book where it would be hard to miss. Some private press books even today continue to place the colophon at the conclusion of the book rather than the beginning, and when this is done it is usually enlarged to contain information on the kind of type used, the paper, the name of the designer and illustrator and possibly even space for the signature of the designer, illustrator, author, and even the publisher.

A charming aspect of the Limited Editions Club books is that its colophon—or emblem—designed by Clarence Pearson Hornung in 1929, depicting three men sitting together reading, has been successively redesigned by a number of the Club's illustrators for a series of later Club books. For *Droll Stories*, for example, W. A. Dwiggins did three giggly monks all with their noses in books.

The most famous colophon of all was not designed for a book, but a tombstone—on which it did not appear, either, as a matter of fact. It was composed by a well-known printer for his own epitaph:

> The Body of B. Franklin,
> Printer,
> Like the Cover of an Old Book,
> Its Contents Torn Out
> And
> Stript of Its Lettering & Gilding
> Lies Here
> Food for Worms.
> But the Work shall not be lost;
> For it will, as he believ'd
> Appear once more
> In a new and more elegant Edition
> Revised and corrected
> By the Author.

Colophon, The A book-collectors' quarterly, which began publication in 1930. Among its most famous contributors were Anderson, Dreiser, Mencken, and Morley, but it is most prized for its articles of bibliographic importance. A complete run of *The Colophon* commands a good price at auction.

Color plates   Illustrations in color. Many old books are valuable chiefly because of their color plates and may command a high price even though they are sold only as breakers.

Color plate wants   Many book dealers and art dealers are anxious to buy handsomely illustrated books—in any condition—simply for their color plates. It is important, therefore, for them to know whether all the plates listed for a particular book are still present in the book and still in good condition. (A little foxing may be washed out with care.) The condition of the text or the binding is of little interest.

Particularly in demand are illustrations depicting the American West, especially plates executed before 1865. Cowboys, Indians, and western landscapes are all extremely good. The artists most in demand include Remington, Russell, Bierstadt, Catlin, Homer, and Harnett.

In addition, floral and botanical plates are always in high demand, again particularly those from before 1865, with those published in Europe or on the Continent most highly regarded. Sporting subjects likewise usually find a ready market, as does anything to do with ornithology—nests, eggs, and the more spectacular plumage. Plates depicting costume also are in demand; there is a good market for a large number of atlases and maps as well.

Column   A succession of printed lines; books which are printed in more than one column have a special interest for many collectors.

Comics   Although many antiquarian book dealers still express considerable dislike for comic books and refuse to handle them, comics do represent an important new source of material for the trade, as well as a new and lively source of income. *AB (Bookman's Weekly)* now regularly carries the advertisements of a number of dealers who specialize in the comics. Recently one traditional book house advertised, in its catalogue, two items one after the other: "(Clemens, S. L.) *Mark Twain's Autobiography.* BAL 3537. $15. (Comics) Collier, Nate. The Kelly Kids. 75 color proofs . . . a fine collection in very good condition. The Kelly Kids are reminiscent of the Katzenjammer Kids in style and action. $115." A first number of Superman has sold for as high as $1800, even though listed in the Comic Book Price Guide for as low as $325. Most comic book items, however, have been selling for 25¢ and up, many at around $3, and with only a few rare first issues commanding over $100.

Among those comics which find a ready market are the earliest issues of *Marvel Comics* and *D.C. Superheroes*, the Disney comics, and E. C. horror items. Particularly sought by collectors are *Thor*, the *Invincible Iron Man, Hulk, Sgt. Fury*, the *Amazing Spider Man*, the *Fantastic Four, Jimmy Olsen, Superman's Pal, Wonder Woman, Flash*, and some *Classics Illustrated*. One comic book dealer attending the recent Comic and Nostalgia Convention held in Chicago was quoted as saying "Collectors buy our comics just like first editions of good literature, or a fine painting. And they are willing to pay a price to get a certain edition that will complete the entire line of that particular comic subject." Since the going price received for the first copy of *Captain America* (1941) is around $250, this would certainly seem to be true. Because comics are printed on such poor quality paper, and because many come into the market badly stained or torn in use, their condition is rarely more than good at best, and dealers often do not bother to specify condition at all.

Commission book A book produced at the expense of the author, who takes all profits over the cost of production.

Commonplace book A record or series of notes kept by an author or a diarist, often never intended for publication; any kind of memorandum book.

Compartment Either a wood-block border around the wording on a title page (also known as a passepartout), or a border in the design of the book's binding.

Compendium A book containing the substance, only, or an abstract, of another larger book or books.

Compilation A book for which the text consists of material drawn from other books.

Complete book Figuring out whether or not you have a complete book, in the case of one which is disbound or clearly lacking pages, can seem a formidable problem if you are lacking an adequate bibliography. However, do not be upset if you discover that the first signature in a modern book is labelled "B" rather than "A," or perhaps "2" rather than "1." The reason for this is that the front matter often will consist of less than one full signature and that this is thus indicated. In an older book, it may be important to check up on the Roman numeral lettering of the front matter, counting backwards toward the front from whatever Roman numeral first appears: IV, III, II, etc. If this is in fact a complete book, you should find the full complement of pages even if they are not all numbered. Often counting back in this manner is the only way to discover whether or not there may be a frontispiece or half-title missing.

Composition The process of setting and arranging type; a book's composition is, therefore, a part of the general process of its production.

Composition à la main French for type set by hand.

Comprint To steal another's written work and print it secretly.

Compte-rendu French for Proceedings. *Pour compte-rendu* means for review, i.e., a review or advance copy.

Concertina fold A multiple fold, whereby a printed sheet may be opened out to several times the size of the book in which it is contained, as is often the case with maps or charts. Also known as an accordion fold.

Condition The state of wear of a book, and therefore one of the major factors in determining its price, or worth. There may be a well-established price for a mint copy of any particular book, yet the price may vary widely for any copy of the book in less than very good to fine condition.

Condition is described in terms of the best—fine, mint, and close-to-mint—down through very good, good, fair, and poor or reading copy. Wise book-buyers may profit from a study of the precise meanings of these terms as they are employed in dealers' catalogues.

Differences in price between books of the same edition but in different condition can make the collecting game particularly interesting. Whereas a copy of the first edition of Harriet Beecher Stowe's *A Key to Uncle Tom's Cabin*, in wrappers, in very good condition, may command up to $50, the same book in wrappers which are spotted and torn and with the title page crudely repaired with tape may be worth no more than $10. Many dealers like to handle—and most libraries like to acquire—only books in very good or better condition. This leaves the field fairly open for those private collectors willing to settle for copies which may be described as only "good."

On the other hand, collectors who are interested in books as investments should invariably seek out the books in the best possible condition, in modern works never settling for anything less than "fine" or "mint."

Condition/rarity The price of any book is usually determined by a balance between its rarity and general desirability on the market, and its condition. A first-edition copy of James Joyce's *Ulysses*, one of several hundred copies signed by the author, may be worth well over $2,000, even though repairs have been made on the (sacred!) title page, even though the covers are badly spotted. Although its condition is barely good, it may be "priced accordingly for one of the rare signed editions." The average book, however, is most adversely affected by poor condition.

Conjugate leaves Leaves which began as part of a single

sheet of paper before it was folded to become part of a book. If one sheet of paper is folded once, the result is two conjugate leaves. It is easy to trace conjugate leaves along the top of a book, in and out of the binding. In an octavo (8vo book), the first and the eighth leaves are conjugate, for example.

Conservation The great libraries of the world are leaders in the conservation of books, and less important libraries similarly exert every possible effort to preserve valuable books. If budget permits, books are stored in rooms where both the temperature and the humidity may be carefully controlled. Even with the greatest care, however, books sometimes require repair, and newly acquired books, of course, often come into a library in need of repair. One of the methods used in libraries is called "aqueous de-acidification": the book is taken entirely apart and each leaf washed separately in pure water, and then treated with chemicals, and at last the book is rebound. Amateurs without specific training in this process—or any of the many other processes used for cleaning pages and restoring bindings—are not advised to tackle repairs themselves, or, at least, to confine any experimenting to books of little value.

Consignment The practice of furnishing a shipment of books to be sold with the understanding that no money will change hands until they are indeed sold and the purchase money received by the vendor. The consignor is the person furnishing the books; the vendor is the person selling them on behalf of the consignor.

In addition, dealers may send books to prospective purchasers on consignment, i.e., on approval. No money changes hands unless the books are approved for purchase. Unless some other specific arrangement is entered into, it is customary for these books to be either approved for purchase or returned within from two to ten days. If the books should not be returned within this period, the assumption is that the sale has been successfully concluded and payment is due.

Postage charges (both ways) are usually met by the purchaser rather than by the seller.

Dealers also sometimes accept books on consignment (deposit) for sale at some agreed-upon commission. Again, no money changes hands until the books are actually sold. Dealers do not accept responsibility for any books sent to them on consignment *without* their previous agreement based on knowledge of what the shipment consists of.

The rates charged by book houses for selling on consignment may vary somewhat, but many houses, including the auction houses, seem to charge a fairly reliable 20% of the value of the books in lots selling at more than $500 but less than $5000. A fee of from 25% to 30% for lots bringing less than $500 total does not seem unusual.

Conte French for story or tale.

Contemporary In the old-book trade, contemporary is in the sense of contemporary with the approximate date of publication. A contemporary binding, thus, is one representative of the period when the book first appeared in print, possibly but not necessarily, in the opinion of the person describing the book, the original binding.

Contenu French for the contents of a book.

Contrefaçon French for a pirated edition.

Cookbooks Collecting cookbooks, as books rather than for the recipes they contain, can be a fairly specialized hobby. To judge by the growing number of old-book stores making a specialty of cookbooks, it is growing in popularity. A good source of information about cookbooks is the *Bibliography of American Cookery Books, 1742–1860: Based on Waldo Lincoln's American Cookery Books.* By Eleanor Lowenstein, it is available at about $15 from the University Press of Virginia, Box 3608 University Station, Charlottesville, Va. 22903.

Copperplate The result of intaglio engraving on copper, for reproduction. Copperplate illustrations, which are often unusually fine in detail, may add considerably to the value of an old book or, indeed, provide the only source of its value. Copperplate engraving, which at first was extensively used in fine books at a time when wood-engraving was considered crude, was largely superseded by steel engraving.

Copy   A manuscript which has been prepared for printing. The "copy reader" checks the manuscript for possible errors. An alert reader can often save the author from an embarrassing error. One such reader pounced on a line which Robert Frost had written—"Her mother's bedroom was her father's still"—and suggested that he make a change.

Copyright Act (English)   The Act of Parliament (1911) protecting the author of any original literary work for a term consisting of the life of the author and for fifty years thereafter.

Copyright date   The date on which a publication was originally granted its copyright permission, and therefore the time from which the publication's copyright time is to be counted. In American books, this date is printed on the verso (back) of a book's title page. Sometimes a series of copyright dates appears, as when, for example, a series of works which were published earlier, separately, are assembled for a new book. In American books, it is important to remember, the copyright date need not necessarily be the same as the date of publication. The American statute, adopted in 1891 and still in force, provides for copyright protection for a term of twenty-eight years and for a single renewal term. The holder of a copyright has the exclusive right to publish, produce, and sell the article which is copyrighted; this may be not only a book but a map, musical composition, or other result of creative artistic effort.

Copyright deposit copy   Under United States law, two copies of each book published must be made available to the Library of Congress for addition to its collection. The Rare Book Division receives one of these two copies, in the following categories: first editions by a selected list of creative writers, a representative selection of children's books from the many produced each year, examples of the output of a limited number of the fine private presses, books which are illustrated with original graphics, and books in some few other categories. Thus, the Rare Book Division of the Library of Congress often finds itself in a unique position to verify authentic copies of first editions of important works, about which there might otherwise be debate. Sometimes the copies placed on deposit at the Rare Book Division differ from those of the "first run" for distribution commercially. In other words, some publishers have deposited copies from an initial run made prior to that first released to the buying public. For example, a copy of Jack London's *Martin Eden* dated 1908, a year in advance of the first published edition of 1909, recently was discovered as one of the two copyright deposit copies, still in its original wrappers, thus, improbably enough, making some firsts more first than others.

Copyright notice   Notice of the exclusive right given by law for a term of years (twenty-eight, and then twenty-eight again) to print and/or publish copies of an original work. Such notice is indicated by the symbol c. or ©.

Coquille   French for misprint.

Corners   Not only the corners of a book in the usual sense (also known as tips), but the printing ornaments used to connect horizontal and vertical sections of a border.

Corrections   Amendments to literary matter: specifically, an author's corrections as they are indicated by the author, or house corrections if made by the printer or publishers. Such corrections are usually made in the proof. Final page proof for a book with the author's corrections showing his final intentions may be even more valuable than the actual first edition.

Corrigenda   From the Latin, for corrections to be made in a book or manuscript, literally signifying to lead straight.

Cottage style   A type of book binding in which the front cover, and sometimes the back cover also, is decorated with a top and bottom panel which are fancifully joined. This ornate style of book binding was once very popular for Bibles and prayer books, and it is still often used for books of religious content.

Counter mark   A second watermark in paper, most often one which incorporates the name or the initials of the manufacturing concern. Such a mark may be of importance in identifying an edition or the special issue of a limited edition.

Counterproof   A reversed impression made from a freshly printed engraving.

Couronné   French for award-winning.

Courtesy book   One which explains the proper rules of conduct. Such books have always had a steady sale in the United States.

Couture   French for the stitching or binding of a pamphlet or book.

Couverture   French for a book cover: *couverture conservée* means in wrappers; and *couverture illustrée* means pictorial wrappers.

Cover paper   A strong and tough paper, suitable for use as the cover or wrappers of a booklet or even book.

Covers   The general over-all term for the covering of a book, including the front and back (called "sides"), the spine with its backstrip, and the endpapers. Thus, in the general sense, the book's binding. Covers is also used in the more limited sense of sides alone. Covers were originally made of wood, often bound together with leather; today, most covers are of board, a kind of thick cardboard, overlaid with cloth or sometimes paper.

Cox   Edward G. Cox: *A Reference Guide to the Literature of Travel, Including Voyages, Geographical Descriptions, Adventures, Shipwrecks, & Expeditions.*

Cracked   Hinges are said to be cracked when the spine of a book is starting to come apart and therefore the cover is beginning to hang loose. The front hinge (joint between the book's cover and the spine), because it is handled most frequently, tends to weaken first. The book may feel "shaken" (wobbly as it is gently moved back and forth), and some of the signatures may be becoming detached. Any book with a cracked hinge cannot properly be described as in very good condition.

Cradle books Incunabula: books printed in the first fifty years of the history of printing, from the publication of the Gutenberg Bible to 1501.

Crimped Fluted, indented, or pinched. The spine of a book which has been pressed or harmed by water might be termed crimped. Not only covers, but sometimes pages and whole sections of pages become crimped, simply from a pervasive dampness.

Critical Dictionary By Samuel Austin Allibone: *A Critical Dictionary of English Literature, and British and American Authors, Living and Deceased, from the Earliest Accounts to the Middle of the Nineteenth Century.* An important bibliographical work, often simply referred to as "Allibone."

Cropped In books, an excessive cutting down of the margins at the bindery, even to the point that the text may be cut into. Such cropping seriously diminishes the value of any book. Cropping sometimes takes place when a book is rebound. Synonymous with shaved.

Crown copyright That copyright reserved to Her Majesty's (British) Government in works issued by it.

Crown octavo (Cr 8vo) A British book size, $7\frac{1}{2}$ x 5 inches.

Crown quarto (Cr 4to) A British book size, 10 x $7\frac{1}{2}$ inches.

Crushed In the case of leather used in bookbinding, leather ironed or rollered to a high polish. Morocco is frequently treated in this manner. Not the same as crimped, and never used to describe the general condition of a book, it is to be hoped.

Cuala Press A private press founded at Dundrum, County Dublin, in 1902.

Cuir   French for leather.

Cuivre   *Gravure sur cuivre:* French for copper-engraving.

Cul de lampe   French for a floral or other type of highly ornamental design used to fill in what would otherwise have been a blank space on a page.

Curiosa   This is the polite term used to indicate books of prurient interest, sometimes those describing specific sexual acts. Sometimes used synonymously with erotica.

Custom-bound   In a book, bound especially to order, with binding material and ornamentation specified.

Cut   An illustration published to accompany a text. As in woodcut: a print from an engraving on wood.

Cut down   Excessively trimmed, so that the pages of a book have smaller margins than is normal for the type of book.

Cut edges   A term used to specify a book in which all three margins have been trimmed in a paper-cutting machine (guillotine). Since most books, and almost all trade editions, are now published with cut edges, this is rarely mentioned. Much more common is a reference to uncut edges.

Cut flush   With the page edges and the cover of a book trimmed level with each other.

Cut-in note   A few words only, set into the text from the left-hand margin, usually in explanation of the text or to demonstrate some facet of it.

Cut-out book   A book for children designed to be cut up with scissors. Obviously, few such books will survive to come into the old-book market. The few which do appear are usually valued simply as curios.

Cut to register   Paper cut so that the watermark appears in the same place on every page; one of the signs of a well-made book.

D

D   Roman numeral for 500.

D̄   Roman numeral for 5000.

Damage from water   Of all the agencies which may cause damage to books, water is probably the worst. Not only does water, from just a few drops of rain to a flood, do the most harm to the most books, but a water-damaged book is often extremely difficult to repair. Among the innovative techniques only recently developed to repair books damaged by water is freezing. When the Connecticut Historical Society in Hartford suffered a plumbing leak in the basement of its headquarters, thousands of old books which had been stored there were soaked. The books were quickly wrapped in plastic and frozen at 10 degrees below zero. The intention was to prevent mildew, and it was planned to return the books eventually to good condition by freeze-drying them. The New England Document Conservation Center received the credit for this resourceful idea.

Damp paper   A particular kind of paper which is of a hard texture and requires dampening to be printed.

Dandy roll   The cylinder on a paper-making machine which imparts a characteristic watermark to the paper.

Day   John Day (1522–1584), acclaimed one of the finest English printers of the sixteenth century. He devised the first Anglo-Saxon type, and is noted for his handsome title pages as well as italic fonts. His printer's mark is a rising sun; his motto: "Arise, for it is Day." (Stephen Daye, printer of the Bay Psalm Book, spelled his name differently.)

Day book   Any type of diary or journal.

Deacidifying   A process which may be required in the repairing of the text block of a book, as distinguished from the book's binding or its covering of cloth or leather. The paper of a book may eventually deteriorate because of its acid content. One remedy is to take the book apart, then rinse the leaves in a bath of water, followed by one of magnesium bicarbonate, which leaves a deposit of salt as a buffer against further acid. Another process uses gas and does not require pulling the book apart. Some book conservors feel, however, that this second method has not proved entirely safe. The most conservative approach to the problem is to make a neat, tight box for the affected book and set it aside, hoping to slow the acid process until some better method for deacidifying will have been developed.

Déboité   French for loose in the binding; disbound.

De Bury   (See **Philobiblon**.)

Déchiré   French for torn, as the pages of a book may be torn.

Deckel aus Pappe   German for the original cased binding.

Deckle edge   In paper, the untrimmed feathery type of edge which occurs naturally in handmade papers and is sometimes imitated by machine. Deckle edges are most often found in press books, where the rough edges often seem particularly suitable to the particular character of the book, or in special editions where an appearance of elegance is considered appropriate.

Décor   French for the decorations in a book.

Decorated boards   Boards may be the ordinary gray stuff, or they may be decorated in so beautiful a manner as to make the book memorable. Private press books are often issued in boards rather than in cloth. "In boards" may mean that the boards are covered with paper; then, to be precise, it is the paper which is decorated, and to indicate this the book may be described as in paper-decorated boards. Although small and regular geometric designs are often favored for paper-decorated boards, fanciful, elaborate, and colorful pictorial representations are not uncommon. Sometimes boards are decorated with a paper label which is pasted to the front cover. Thus, decorated boards may mean any of these arrangements.

Dedicace French for the dedication or dedication-page of a book.

Dedication The inscription of a book, to a relative, friend, or—often—patron. The dedication statement most commonly appears by itself on the recto of the leaf following the title page.

That particular copy of a book which any author gives to the person to whom he dedicates his work always has a special value. It is usually identified by a note in the author's own hand, and in the instance where the author is one who is collected and the person to whom he dedicated his book also notable, the book may attain some value as an association copy.

Today it is usual to dedicate a book to a teacher, wife, or mother. It was originally the practice to dedicate a book to the patron whose financial support had made the book possible. Sometimes there might be more than one patron, and in such a case the author might see that the first edition contained several issues with different dedication pages, and thus manage to keep all his patrons happy.

Dedication copy Specifically, the copy of a book bestowed by the author upon the person to whom he has dedicated the book. Such dedication copies are collected and can form a highly exotic—and expensive—collection. In 1965 the Grolier Club held an exhibit devoted exclusively to dedication copies.

Deep page A page of type or illustrations of greater length than usual in books of the kind.

Defects Even a few minor defects—imperfections—may lower the value of an old book. Standards do vary, however, according to the type of book: children's books, travel guides, almanacs, cookbooks, and other books which normally receive a great deal of wear cannot be expected to be as free of defects as some other types of books. On the other hand, those handsome books published by the private presses, so often works of art in themselves, are expected to come into the old-book market almost perfectly free of any defects resulting from use. A book is considered defective if the covers are badly stained, the binding shaken, the covers loose, or the pages marked up, especially in ink. An owner's signature on the title page is routinely mentioned as a defect by scrupulous dealers. In describing items for sale, most dealers attempt to list each sign of wear in a book which might possibly be considered a defect by a potential purchaser. One of the most serious of defects is a missing title page; in most instances this destroys the value of the book. Inserting xerox replacement pages in a book from another copy or copies may provide a scholar with one complete working copy, but scarcely solves the problem of "preserving" a valuable old book.

Defects, exterior To a certain extent old books are certainly judged by their covers, at least to the degree that price is going to depend upon condition. The commercial value of any book is lessened if its covers are rubbed, bumped, chipped, frayed, torn, or certainly if loose. Even so, a book may be well worth owning so long as it is clean, with a tight binding.

Defects, lack of A lack of observable defects in any old book never means that the book necessarily must have value, whatever its age. A hundred-year-old copy of an American Bible, for example, even if it were in mint condition, would probably have little or no commercial value, with certain exceptions of course. Yet, in the case of a book for which any number of dealers and collectors would be willing to spend money, an absence of any defects in a particular copy can send the market skyrocketing. Any book described as free of defects is expected to have bright and clean pages, an unmarred title page, an unfaded backstrip, and covers which are without blemish. It should be free from any evidence of library use.

Definitive edition   The final and authoritative text of the complete works of an author.

De-foxing   Although foxing may be considered relatively unimportant in the text of any old book, foxing may, on the other hand, seriously mar the beauty of a plate (illustration). Art dealers, who frequently buy old books simply for their plates, have developed a process for de-foxing black-and-white plates. First, the plate is separated from the book and placed in a flat receptacle. Then, with a gentle rocking motion it is soaked for a few minutes in a solution of slightly warm water containing a few tablespoonfuls of ordinary household bleach. The plate, gently supported, is then washed in plain warm water. Any color lost from the paper in this process may be restored by adding a tiny amount of powdered coffee to the rinse water. The plate is then left to dry on a piece of glass, in a warm place. Any wrinkles which develop are removed later with the gentle application of a slightly warm iron. Although good results cannot be guaranteed, the amateur might experiment with this process starting with some plates which are not especially valuable.

Défraîchi   French for soiled.

Delenda   Printed material to be removed, or information to be erased.

Deluxe edition   An especially elegant edition, usually in a fancy binding.

Demand, false   This note is inserted here as a warning to the book collector that he may himself, if he is not careful, create a false demand for books he wishes to purchase, and may unwittingly raise the price. It is always unwise to tell more than one bookdealer at a time about your need for any particular volume. Several dealers inquiring after the same book or even advertising for it creates the impression that a particular book has suddenly become exceedingly popular.

Demi-reliure   French for half-binding.

Demi-toile   French for in half-cloth; with board sides and cloth back. *Demi-veau* is French for half-leather or half-calf; and *demi-velin* means half-vellum.

Demy octavo (Dy 8vo)   A British book size, $8\frac{3}{4}$ x $5\frac{5}{8}$ inches.

Demy quarto (Dy 4to)   A British book size, $11\frac{1}{2}$ x $8\frac{3}{4}$ inches.

Dentelle   Any fine scrollwork or lacy patterns which might be tooled into the leather covers of a book. However, the term is most usually encountered in "inner dentelle." This is the fold of leather turned in around the edges of the covers of a book, often decorated in gilt in a geometric design. The inner dentelle, in a fancy hand binding, may be the source for identifying the binder, who sometimes inserts his name in tiny letters along the inner dentelle at the bottom of the inside front cover.

Dépareillé   French for an odd volume, one of a broken set.

Deposit copy   (See **Copyright deposit copy.**)

Dérelié   French for lacking the binding; disbound.

Derrydale Press   A modern American press collected for its sporting books, always issued in limited edition.

Description, dealers'   Dealers are to be held strictly accountable for the description of a book in any catalogue. If any mistake is noted or omission found, a dealer is expected to accept the return of the book and grant a refund of the purchase price. In the case of inexpensive books offered for sale simply as good or good-to-better, the dealer cannot, of course, be held accountable for details of condition, but in any books offered with full bibliographical description, the utmost care and scrupulous honesty are both routinely expected.

Descriptions, shortened   Sometimes, in a book dealer's catalogue, we may find that a book is not fully described as to condition, size, or general format. Books which are listed thus or, as is often the case, lotted together as one bundle for sale, may be simply listed as "poor to very good." This has saved the dealer time and signals to the prospective purchaser that these books are not worth much of the dealer's time.

On the other hand, some books which are not individually described in detail may be lacking the description simply because it is understood that they conform to the usual size, format and condition for such books. For example, *American Book Prices Current*, which reports the prices paid at auction each year for thousands of literary properties, does not specify size of binding for any book published after 1900 if it is either octavo or duodecimo and bound in cloth, since this is usual with more recent books.

Dessin à la plume   French for a pen-and-ink drawing.

Deteint   French for faded or discolored.

Device   An emblem used on a bookplate. Or, a printer's special distinguishing mark, which is placed either at the beginning of a book, usually on the title page, or, as was done in early printed books, at the end of the book. (See also **Colophon.**)

Devise   French or German for device or motto.

Diaper   A geometrical or otherwise conventional pattern of lines linked in a diamond pattern, with the interstices sometimes filled with dots or some other small design. Such a pattern of cross-hatching may be more familiar in weaving, specifically in an infant's "clout," as it was once called. This type of design is often used effectively on leather bindings.

Dibdinography   The Rev. T. F. Dibdin (1776–1847) was a bibliographer; this, therefore, is a coined word indicating a great passion for books and specifically for collecting volumes which are oddities because of misprints or for some other reason.

Dictionary for the Antiquarian Booktrade   A dictionary edited by Menno Hertzberger and published by the International League of Antiquarian Booksellers, in eight languages: French, English, German, Swedish, Danish, Italian, Spanish, and Dutch. The key language is French, with indexes providing references to words of the same meaning in the other languages. Published in Paris in 1956 and considered by many book collectors and dealers an indispensable aid, the dictionary is sold in the United States at around $12. You might inquire at the Antiquarian Booksellers Association at 630 Fifth Avenue, New York, N.Y. 10020, to see if it is still available.

Dictionary of American Biography A major reference work often found useful in the study of old books, abbreviated *DAB*. The first volume of *DAB* was published in 1928, and the basic twenty had all been issued by 1936. The most recent addition is *Supplement Three*, published in 1973 and covering the lives of eminent Americans who died between 1941 and 1945. As the *New York Times* has said, the *DAB* moves along in its magisterial way. Under the general editorship of Edward T. James, this supplement contains 15,443 entries, the work of 3,527 contributing authors. *The Dictionary of American Biography* is modelled on the British *Dictionary of National Biography*, which was issued between 1880 and 1901, in 66 volumes. The *DAB* style, which has been characterized as "freewheeling scholarship," makes for delightful browsing. The American *Dictionary* is edited by the American Council of Learned Societies, and the full set is available by subscription only, at around $300. *Supplement Three*, in the same characteristic russet binding as the earlier volumes, is available from Scribner's at $35.

Dictionary of National Biography An authoritative reference work, abbreviated to *D.N.B.*, consisting of a compendium of the biographies of eminent British men and women, originally issued in 66 volumes between 1880 and 1901. *D.N.B.* is highly valued by bookmen and considered indispensable by dealers and collectors who specialize in English authors.

Didot Denis Didot was a Parisian printer and bookseller whose son François (1689–1757) as well as his grandsons and

further descendants all became important printers. The
family also included type-founders, papermakers, and publishers. Didot masterpieces of typography and printing
during the eighteenth and nineteenth centuries include some
magnificently showy books, many accepted as models of the
very finest craftsmanship. The Continental system for the
measurement of type was named after one member of this
family, Ambroise Didot (1730–1804).

Dime novel   Any very inexpensive (including 10¢) American book issued to the popular market in the last half of the
nineteenth century; or, more particularly, a type of early
paperback (book in wrappers) published in series for boys.

The first dime novel published was *Malaeska: the Indian
Wife of the White Hunter*, by Mrs. Ann S. Stephens,
published in 1860. The first edition, first issue, in the original
wrappers without a woodcut on the cover may be worth
between $300 and $400—quite a substantial increase in
price!

Directory   A guide book for a specific locality or group.

Direct process   A method of photo-engraving when the
negative is obtained directly from the subject rather than
from a photograph or drawing.

Disbound   Not at present bound, though formerly; lacking the original binding or any other binding. A disbound
book, manuscript, map, etc., is one which has been removed
or otherwise become disengaged from an original binding.
Not the same, therefore, as unbound—which indicates that
there was no binding at all.

Discount   In the old-book trade, dealers in many areas
expect a 10% discount from each other, although this is not
so universal but that sometimes dealers' advertisements
intended for other dealers state the amount of discount.
Discounts are most unusual in this business except between
dealers.

Disneys   Copies of the earliest Disney publications, which
originated in Hollywood in the 1930's. They may now

command good prices. For example, a mint copy of Walt Disney's *The Adventures of Mickey Mouse* in the 1931 first edition—a book in paper boards with illustrations in color on each page—recently brought $50. Another scarce early title, the 1937 *Stories from Walt Disney's Silly Symphony*, may be worth $25; and the *Fantasia* promotion booklet, folio-size, which is very scarce, even more. This does not mean that every early Disney is equally rare or valuable, of course. However, it would be worthwhile to check the going price for any pre-World War II Disney item . . . literary value aside, of course.

Dissected map Any map which has been cut down into sections for insertion into the pages of a book.

Divinity calf A dark brown calfskin used for binding ecclesiastical works and generally undecorated, lacking gilding.

Divinity circuit A flexible binding made of a soft leather, of the kind which has often been employed for Bibles. The extended edges of this type of binding characteristically curve over the text block, or leaves. A British term for this type of binding is yapped. In some of the old books with this type of covering, the corners may be split, producing an even yet more limp effect. Few books are being bound in this fashion today.

Document, signed A document in which the signature, but only the signature, is hand-written. This is therefore not the same as an autograph document, which is entirely written out by hand.

Dog-eared Expressive as this term is, it is rarely used in the old-book trade; books are, instead, called bumped or frayed at the corners, or worn at the tips, but never "dog-eared."

Dolphin The dolphin and the anchor, together, form the famous pressmark of Aldus Mantius. The dolphin has, therefore, become an emblem, or symbol, of fine books.

Dolphin, The An annual about the making of books,

published by the Limited Editions Club of New York between 1933 and 1941, consisting of Volumes 1–4, No. 3, all published. *The Dolphin,* hailed as a major contribution to good printing and the study of sound book construction, was directed to book buyers and collectors rather than to the bookmakers. Contributors to this journal included Frederic W. Goudy, Dard Hunter, and W. A. Dwiggins. It is now available in reprint at $295 from the Greenwood Reprint Company, 51 Riverside Avenue, Westport, Conn. 06880. Copies of the original, though usually quite worn, are still to be found sometimes in the secondhand book market.

Doré French for gilt-tooled or gilt-stamped. In French, *doré sur tranches* means a book with gilt-edges; *dorure en tête* is a gilt top edge. *Dorure à froid,* on the other hand, means blind-stamped, without gilt or other ink.

Dos à dos The French word for the back of a book, its spine, is dos; in a dos-à-dos binding, two volumes are bound together but facing in opposite directions, so that the back cover of one volume serves as the back of the second, and the fore-edges of one are adjacent to the spine of the other. Such a book therefore appears to have two front covers. Some books which customarily go together may be issued in such a binding.

Dos orné French for a book with a decorated back (spine).

Doubled With a design in the binding of a book made more accurate by the use of a finishing tool to correct an impression found to be out-of-register, i.e., out of line.

Double elephant folio A huge book: in American sizes, more than 38 x 25 inches. One of the best-known examples of this size is John James Audubon's *Birds of America.* The American naturalist and artist published his multi-volume work in a limited edition of two hundred copies, of which there are now estimated to be no more than possibly ninety surviving intact.

Double spread An illustration or map (rarely text) which spreads entirely across two facing pages in a book or other publication.

Doublure The inner faces of the boards of a book, usually indicating that they are covered not in paper but, rather, in silk or in leather.

Doves Press An English private press (1900–1916) which turned out work of unusually high caliber. This press originated in the Doves Bindery which was under the direction of T. J. Cobden-Sanderson. Of the approximately fifty publications issued, undoubtedly the most outstanding achievement was the "Doves Bible" which appeared in five large quarto volumes. It was the work of one compositor, J. H. Mason, and was produced on one hand press. The Doves Bible has been compared, as a typographic achievement, with the Gutenberg Bible. The use of this press's type came to a final if rather astonishing end when Cobden-Sanderson consigned the type to the River Thames in a series of stealthy nighttime excursions.

Drop title The title which is placed at the top of the first lines of text, rather than appearing separately on the title page.

Druckvermerk German for a printer's mark.

Drypoint An engraving made from a copperplate, marked with a steel point, and without the use of acid.

Dummy copy A sample volume demonstrating the size of page and sometimes style of binding for a book which is not yet completed.

Duodecimo A book size between sextodecimo and octavo (16mo and 8vo), produced by folding a sheet of paper in any one of several ways to produce twelve leaves, thus twenty-four pages as numbered. A book in this size category may be from seven to eight inches tall. In appearance, it strikes the eye as definitely smaller than the more usual octavo; many paperbacks appear in this size, whereas hardcover novels are usually octavo. Abbreviated to 12mo.

Duplex paper Paper which has its two sides of a different texture or color.

Durant A kind of hard-wearing cloth made in imitation of leather and often used in modern bookbindings.

Durchgesehen German for revised, or corrected.

Dusting books There is more danger to books in dusting than might be supposed. Under some circumstances it might be better to leave books on a shelf undusted rather than have them, let us say, banged about by an unsympathetic or careless housekeeper. If need be, dust can always be removed at some later date, whereas the damage done by careless handling could be permanent. Dusting with a rag simply tends to grind in any dirt which is present; however, the round brush attachment which comes with the vacuum cleaner does an adequate job without the books being moved. Also, a soft camels hair brush is an excellent dusting tool; again, the books need not be moved. There is, after all, a great deal to be said for the old-fashioned glass-fronted bookcase, which does an efficient job of the primary task of keeping dust away from books. Proper air conditioning can help, too, of course.

Dust jacket A removable paper cover placed by a publisher on a book, usually in hardcover, to protect the binding. This dust jacket is often used as a medium for advertising the book to potential buyers. Abbreviated to D.J. or d/j. NOT the same as the wrappers of a book (q.v.).

Dust wrapper This must be considered a mixed term: the terms dust jacket and wrappers mean two different things. However, "dust wrapper" is frequently used in dealers' catalogues, to indicate dust jacket.

Dusty Any dust on the exterior of a book can be flicked off, but the dusty interior of a book means that the book has been neglected, or at the least not stored properly. However, in any book more than two hundred years old, dusty leaves might not be considered a serious defect.

Dutch metal Imitation gold leaf; gilt.

E

Early printed Either books printed before 1700; or, *Early Printed Books in the British Museum with Notes of Those in the Bodleian Library (1896–1906)*, an important bibliographical reference work by Robert Proctor.

Eau-forte French for etching.

Écriture French for writing.

Edge bolt The uncut folds of a sheet of paper as seen in an uncut book.

Edges The external (paper) surfaces of a book; the edges of the leaves. An edge which is left uneven is uncut. It may be termed deckled, or feathered. A smoothly cut (guillotined) edge is sometimes decorated with gilt, or printed in a marbled pattern. An edge may also be fancifully decorated to match the book's covers or endpapers, and sometimes is painstakingly handpainted to represent some scene, not always one associated with the subject of the book. (See **Fore-edge painting.**)

Édité French for edited; "édité" may be used as a synonym for *publié* (published), or—in the sense of the English term edited, prepared by an editor who readies a text for publication. *Éditeur*, in French, is publisher, *not* editor.

Éditeur French for publisher.

Edition The entire printing of one book from one over-all setting of type. ". . . an edition may be defined as including all copies of a book printed from one setting of type. If the type is *reset,* then a second edition comes forth"—Herbert Faulkner West, *Modern Book Collecting.* The first edition of a book is its *first* appearance in print, wherever it may be published. (See also **Issue.**)

Edition binding The usual modern method of binding employing mass production methods to produce a large number of copies all in the same style. This process begins by taking the signatures, consisting of large sheets of paper folded into leaves, and gathering them together for binding along with the endleaves which are placed outside the first and the last signatures. This gathering is then sewn together by machine, and then the entire book is trimmed down in a paper-cutting machine. The sewn edges are then treated with glue, and the book goes through the rounding machine, which gently rolls the backbone to produce a curved spine. The book's covers are readied in a separate process. They come to the book already stamped with the book's title and, sometimes, decorated by the use of metal dies or colored through the use of metallic foils. A casing-in machine applies paste to the endleaves, to glue the book into its covers. Finally, the book must be dried under a hydraulic press. Another name for edition binding is publisher's binding. It should be evident why books so often split at the hinges, a weak point yet the point of greatest wear.

Editio princeps The first printed edition—in the original language, a term applied generally only to early books.

Edition revue et augmentée French for a revised and enlarged edition.

Eggshell A type of paper having a smooth surface, not, however, entirely even; a finish soft, dull, and faintly pebbly.

Einband German for the binding of a book. *Einband fehlt* is German for lacking a binding, or disbound.

Einblattdruck German for a broadside, or a broadside containing a woodcut.

Eingedrückt German for embossed.

Einleitung German for the introduction of a book.

Einzelband German for an odd volume, or one from an incomplete set.

Electroengraving A method of deepening the relief in electroplates.

Electrotyping A means of producing exact copies of either engravings or type, by means of a deposit of copper onto a wax, lead, or plastic mold of the original.

Elephant A size of paper, 20 by 27 inches.

Elephant folio In American book sizing, a book over 23 inches tall. The double elephant folio is larger than 25 by 38 inches.

Emargé French for ripped or cut.

Embellish Add pictorial illustration to a book.

Emblazon Illustrate with heraldic figures.

Emblem book A book in which the text is fancifully embellished with decorations, usually showing heraldic or allegorical emblems. In such a book the text on each page is frequently enclosed within a border. Such books were particularly popular from the seventeenth century on. Emblem books often combine handsome typography with beautiful bindings.

Emboitage French for the slipcase for a book.

Embossed finish In books, the finish in a paper cover over boards which has a raised (embossed) surface, sometimes for the purpose of making the boards resemble cloth or leather. Embossing can also mean, more generally, any kind of blind-stamping, although to be accurate embossing means a raised rather than indented design.

Enamel finish In paper, a very high gloss achieved by coating the paper during its manufacture. Such paper may be used for the reproduction of fine-screen halftones.

Enclosure Anything inserted into the book which is not an integral part of the book. Any enclosure pertinent to the subject of the book or to its provenance (history) is generally left within the book. Many such enclosures add to the value of the book. Examples are letters to or from the author, or press clippings of the same date as the book.

Encollé French for mounted on a page, or pasted into a book.

Endommagé French for damaged.

End papers The sheets of paper added, usually at the bindery, to connect the interior of the covers of a book to the body of the book. The end paper which is next to the cover is pasted to the inside cover, whereas the free end paper is that which is not pasted. Most end papers are of sturdy and strong paper, and many are highly decorative. They may be printed with designs, photographs, maps, or charts. Liners of silk or leather sometimes serve the same purpose as end papers. A bookplate, if it is used, is customarily glued to the inside front cover (end paper).

End piece A decorative device or illustration, usually quite small, placed at the end of a chapter or a section of a book. Also called a tailpiece.

Ends Specifically, the top and the bottom of the spine. The ends of most books are particularly susceptible to wear and often fray or tear while the rest of the book is still in very good condition.

Enemies of books An authority on the preservation of books, H. W. Liebert, of Yale University's Beinecke Rare Book Library, has listed the chief enemies of books as fire, flood, atomic bomb, architects, time, readers, photocopying machines, librarians, cataloguers, library pages and desk attendants, binders, repairers and—last but certainly not least—conservators. According to him, damage through use appears to be the greatest danger. This could pose a nice problem for collectors whose greatest pleasure is in examining and re-examining their treasures. Our advice: go ahead, that's the joy of ownership.

Engraving The process of cutting a surface for the purpose of producing a print. Line engraving is the incision of the polished surface of a metal plate, which may be made of copper, steel, or zinc. In printing this plate, ink fills the channels which have been first cut into the metal. In wood-engraving, on the other hand, the part which is to be printed is allowed to remain raised on the block, as the rest of the surface is cut away. In the old-book trade, the term engraving is customarily used to refer to the first kind of process, or line-engraving, whereas engraving from a wood block is called wood-engraving and the means, a woodcut. Historically, wood was first used, then copper, and finally the use of steel engravings was introduced. Most fine engravings made before 1830, therefore, are copper engravings. Steel, however, had the great advantage in permitting longer runs of better quality for the length of the run.

Ensemble French for together, or all, not necessarily referring to a matched set.

Ephemera Peripheral material, material of lesser importance. Light and frothy stuff, sometimes, as distinguished from more solid and impressive work; or, material of only a passing or temporary interest. In book collecting, ephemera has taken on the meaning of any sort of related material, or fugitive materials. The catalogues furnished by dealers are progressively offering more and more ephemera, including posters, playbills, dance programs, etc.

Epigraph A short quotation or motto at the beginning of a book, head of a chapter, or on the title page.

Epilogue A concluding statement; a prologue is an introductory statement.

Épître dédicatoire French for dedication.

Épreuve d'artiste French for artist's proof. In French, *épreuve d'essai* means trial-proof; and *épreuves corrigées*, corrected proofs.

Épuisé French for out-of-print.

Eragny Press A private printing press founded at Epping in 1894, operated by Lucien Pissarro, and the first to print colored engravings on vellum. The last book issued from this press appeared in 1914.

Ergänzung German for a supplement, or addenda.

Erinnerungen   German for memoirs.

Erotica   Material of specific sexual interest or content. In the old-book trade, erotica, curiosa, exotica, and facetiae may all be used in pretty much the same sense. Pornographica, however, is material of doubtful legality.

Errata   From the Latin: mistakes. The singular form is *erratum*. On a book's errata slip, which is often tipped in, may be listed those mistakes which were caught before the book was released, but too late for corrections to be made in the text. The errata slip is often missing in very old books, from which it may have been torn out, or in books which have been rebound. The careful bibliographical description of a book requires that the presence or absence of the errata slip be noted. Any book which still has its original errata slip is presumed worth more than one without it.

Erscheinen   German for still to be published; thus, one of a series which is not as yet concluded.

Erste Ausgabe   German for *editio princeps:* first edition in the language of the author.

Erster Band   German for the first in a series, thus often appearing on a title page to indicate Volume I.

Erzählung   German for story.

Essex House   The private press, founded in 1898 at Mile End, which became heir to much of the Kelmscott Press equipment.

Estienne   Or, Étienne; or, Latinized, Stephanus. An illustrious family of French scholars and printers who made a major contribution, over five generations, to learning. The head of this family, Henri (d. 1520), published over one hundred books. He was succeeded in business by his son Robert (c. 1503–1559). The son specialized in scholarly works, many of which he edited himself. His Latin dictionary was one of his especially notable achievements. Robert was succeeded by his brother Charles (1504–1564) who added medicine to the other family interests. Joseph Blumenthal, eminent printing historian, has praised the "sustained vigilance which is evident in all the minutiae of the Estienne production," calling Robert the greatest printer who ever lived.

État de neuf   French for new, or as new.

Étiquette   French for book label.

Étoffe   French for cloth, such as might be used in bookbinding.

Étroit   French for narrow or tall, as might appear in a tall 8vo.

Evans   Charles Evans' monumental work, *An American Bibliography*, is customarily simply called "Evans." Evans began in 1903 to prepare a bibliographical work of all the books, pamphlets, and periodicals published or printed in America from the year 1639. At his death, in 1935, he was still at work, on the twelfth volume, only down to the letter "M" at the year 1799. Later editors have brought his work down through the year 1829. A two-volume short-title "Evans," edited by Clifford K. Shipton and James E. Mooney, is available at $45 from the Antiquarian Society of Worcester, Massachusetts 01609. The original thirteen-volume Evans is also available in mini-print from Scarecrow Press, at $39.50.

In the combined Evans-Shipton-Bristol and the Shaw-Shoemaker bibliographies (q.v.) we have a major tool for the research of Americana. These works together contain bibliographical information on more than 50,000 titles, including not only books but also pamphlets, newspapers, journals, and broadsides. Dealers rarely specify that an early item of Americana is to be found in Evans, since it can be assumed to be listed. However, it is worth noting if any certain work does *not* appear in Evans.

Ex dono   A gift from someone.

Exemplaire d'auteur   French for the author's own copy.

Ex-library   Once part of a library, possibly a circulating library, and therefore showing the signs of wear common to such use. The indications of previous use may include a blind stamp on the title page, a label on the spine, a pocket affixed to the inside of the front or the back cover. Whatever the evidence, it should be described for a book of any value offered for sale.

Ex libris   "With the ex libris of . . ." means with the bookplate of a former owner. Since there is another expression—ex-library—to denote former ownership by a library or other institution, it may be assumed that in the case of ex libris, the former owner was an individual. The ex libris, or bookplate, is usually affixed to the inside front cover of a book.

The presence of a bookplate need not always detract from the value of a book. The ex libris may indicate an important tie between the owner of the book and the author, or may prove that the book has come from the library of some well-known collector of fine books or other famous person.

Ex Libris Society   A society which was formed by a few ardent collectors of bookplates meeting in London in 1891. Its original membership numbered only about fifty. The *Ex Libris Journal*, published by this society from 1891 through 1908—eighteen volumes, all published—has become a classic reference book. It is now available in reprint from the Greenwood Reprint Corporation, 51 Riverside Avenue, Westport, Conn. 06880, at $595.

Exotica   One of those general terms or labels, the precise meaning of which is hard to pin down. Literally, the foreign or outlandish, from the Latin. Also, however, anything strangely beautiful or enticing. In the old-book trade, exotica is a term used to indicate the erotic specifically, though also sometimes used interchangeably with curiosa and facetiae.

Exposé   French for synopsis. The same word appears in German.

Extended   In book repair, a page is extended (guarded) when it is strengthened at the inner margin.

Extra binding   The best quality of bookbinding, especially one which is heavily and elaborately ornamented.

Extra cloth   A heavily coated bookbinding cloth, which has, however, a fine finish.

Extra-illustrated   With additional plates incorporated into the book beyond those which were originally issued with the book. The extra plates can frequently be identified because they are not noted in the list of illustrations, whereas the illustrations issued with the book are customarily so listed. Another term for extra-illustrated is grangerized. Any extra illustrations may be either laid in or tipped (pasted) in. (See also **Grangerized; Illustrating.**)

F

Fabriano An excellent kind of handmade paper, sometimes used for fine editions.

Fabrikoid An imitation leather, often used for book bindings but usually fairly easy to tell from real leather.

Face The part of a print character which actually is made to do the printing.

Facetiae From the Latin, meaning literally humorous sayings or witticisms. In common use in the old-book trade, however, this term may be employed to indicate a diversity of books within the genre: vulgar and common chapbooks, various kinds of joke books, non-books, all kinds of curiosa, and comics, as well as sex books which do not take their subject very seriously. The term facetiae may also be used to indicate erotica.

Facsimile The exact reproduction of a work; a reprint from a book's original plates. As a result of the development of the techniques for facsimile reproduction, many books formerly to be seen only in a rare-book collection by the few scholars who might have access to them have now become available to the public, in what one facsimile printer calls "a robust working copy."

Any facsimile should state clearly, somewhere between its covers, that it is a copy rather than the original. Some copies, printed on handmade paper or on paper simulating the original, are very hard for the amateur collector to tell from the original without comparing the original and the copy side by side.

Facsimile copy Facsimile and facsimile copy are two terms often used interchangeably, yet facsimile copy has the specific meaning of a made-up copy, that is, a split-and-hitch job. The leaves of one book, usually itself incomplete, are used to make up a full complement of the pages in another, second, book. Whereas such a practice may be legitimate to form one complete copy where no other exists, no dealer, of course, should try to palm off the facsimile for a pristine original. Any individual facsimile leaves should always be mentioned in a book description. Calling a patched-up copy of this sort a "made-up" copy makes its condition more clear.

Factotum In printing, an ornamental block with a hollow center into which an initial letter may be inserted.

Fair Any book described as in fair condition is one which is well-worn. "Fair" is usually used by dealers to describe a book which is in less than good condition but still better than poor. The book may be missing its dust jacket, have torn or even missing end papers, and the hinges may be cracked, the covers scuffed and stained, the corners bumped. The book should not, however, be missing any pages, especially the title page. As a general rule, collectors are not interested in books in only fair condition, although scholars may, of course, need such books, if they are the only ones available, for their studies.

Fair calf An undyed calf leather, which is buff in color, and is sometimes used for binding books.

Fall-down box A box which is made to enclose a book, and has a double-hinged spine so that the box may be opened out flat. This type of box is particularly useful when it is important that a book should be available for examination without removal from its box. The pages may be turned without the book's cover being touched.

False bands Decorative bands attached to the spine of a book, primarily for the visual effect. Such bands usually have the effect of making a book look more rugged than it actually is. False bands are sometimes also used to impart an antique look to a modern binding.

Family Bible The large Bible used by one family, possibly over several generations and often containing blank pages for the purpose of recording births, marriages, deaths. Usually quite without value on the old-book market. (See **Bible.**)

Fanfare binding A binding elaborately decorated with strapwork, fleurons, etc., such as is frequently found in a book printed before 1650.

Farbig German for in various colors. *Farb-Holzschnitt,* in German, means a woodcut printed in color.

Fasciculus A section of a book which is printed and issued in installments.

Faults escaped Mistakes overlooked in printing; an earlier, and gentler, term for errata.

Faux-titre French for half-title.

Federzeichnung German for pen-and-ink drawing.

Feuille de garde French for endpaper.

Feuilleton French for serial story, or story in installments.

Feuille volante French for broadside.

Figure An illustration, in a book, which is less than full-page and often, though not necessarily so, consisting of a diagram or chart. The figures in a book are often numbered and contained in a separate table of contents. Not infrequently books have plates listed separately from the figures.

Filigrane French for the watermark in paper.

Fillet The decorative, though simple, design rendered on a book binding by the use of a metal disk, consisting of a line or a number of lines.

Finding list An abbreviated list of books which does not provide full bibliographical detail; a rudimentary sort of catalogue, possibly listing only title, author, place and date of publication.

Fine Print A quarterly newsletter for which the first issue appeared in January 1975. *Fine Print* reports "on what the private and specialized presses are doing," and provides bibliographic descriptions of their works. Available at $8 a year, from Box 7741, San Francisco, Cal. 94120.

First edition The first edition of a book consists of the entire first run of the press from the same setting of type. Within the first edition, however, minor changes may be made, thus creating a first, second impression or issue, or even more. A collector of first editions, to paraphrase H. S. Boutell, author of *First Editions of To-Day and How to Tell Them* (now out of print), is really a collector of the first lot struck off the press so long as the content and format remain the same. "A second edition postulates some alteration of text or format." The definition may seem broad, but even so Boutell remarks that "these terms are, unfortunately, not strictly adhered to."

It is sometimes easier to tell if a book is not a first edition than to prove conclusively that it is. If you can inform yourself of the earliest date of the book's publication, then of course the appearance of a later date—anywhere in the book, in the preface, for example, would prove the book is *not* a first. This holds true for any advertisements bound in with the book, also; a moment's thought, however, will make clear that advertisements of a date earlier than might be expected are no evidence of date of publication, since binders often picked up ads which might be dated several years back.

Some publishers do not place any date on the title page of a first edition, but insert a date for subsequent editions. Others place the date on the title page for the first edition and then drop it later.

If there is a date on the title page and it is later than the latest date appearing on the copyright page, on the verso (back) of the title page, then you can be fairly certain that you do not have a first edition. One notable exception is a Christmas, or gift, book copyrighted in, say, 1883 for sale at the end of that year and therefore bearing the date 1884 on the title page.

Also, a series of several dates appearing under the copyright line might possibly rule out the book's being a first edition—unless it is a collection or an anthology, and each of the separate contributions had previously been copyrighted. Or, you might have the "first published edition" of a novel which had previously been serialized in a magazine.

There is, however, a generally accepted policy among publishers, which was once summed up by the Princeton University Press with academic nicety: "Our only way of designating first editions is by negative implication. In other words, our first editions bear no special designation. If, however, a title is reprinted or reissued that fact is set forth on the copyright page."

People who do not themselves collect first editions have a tendency to consider those who do either mad or utterly whimsical. The sober rationale for collecting firsts includes the facts that the first edition of a book is considered to be closest to the author's original intention, and that the plates, in the case of any illustrated book, are at their clearest and brightest during the first run.

First edition points The identifying marks in a book which signify that it is a first edition. The first edition point may consist simply of the date on the title page, or a cluster of first edition points may be so complicated that only an expert bibliophile can be sure that he understands them all. Fortunately for the collectors and would-be collectors of first editions, there are numerous bibliographical works which list and explain the points for the first editions of thousands of authors. At first the collector finds that a general reference work, covering a range of authors, may suit his purposes quite well, but very soon he will need to own the one or more authoritative works on his own particular author.

Along with the *Cambridge Bibliography of American Litera-*

ture and that for *English Literature*, there are a number of standard works on first editions such as Merle Johnson's *American First Editions*, Cutler and Stiles' *Modern British Authors*, and Boutell's *First Editions of Today*. These last three are, unfortunately, all out of print. A proposed four-volume guide, *First Printings of American Authors*, edited by Matthew J. Bruccoli and published by Gale Research Company, will undoubtedly fill a great need. Meanwhile, the catalogues issued by book dealers documenting the first editions they are offering for sale, issue points and all, have been serving as an invaluable reservoir of information. Many new collectors have been tipped off as to firsts by a reading of Bradley's *Handbook of Values*. Useful as this handbook is for identifying first editions, it is not, however, to be relied upon for the much greater detail needed for discovering first issues.

Three additional guides specifically on American authors are Whitman Bennett's *A Practical Guide to American Book Collecting (1663–1940)*, which has some facts not easily found elsewhere, Herbert F. Stone's *First Editions of American Authors*, and, from Mark Press, the reprint of Patrick K. Foley's *American Authors, 1795–1895*.

Aside from checking at the nearest large public library for any reference works on file dealing with the author in whom one is interested, the best way to secure information might be to look under the name of that author in *Books in Print*, which will list any bibliographies currently available. Also, the *Encyclopaedia Britannica* is particularly helpful in listing bibliographies at the end of the information it provides about any author.

First Folio Of the thirty-eight plays which comprise the Shakespeare canon, thirty-six were printed in what has now come to be known as the First Folio. This was the first collected edition of Shakespeare's works, appearing in 1623.

First impression The first run of printed material struck off a press for the first edition of a work. For a short run, therefore, the first edition may consist of no more than a first impression. A second impression is a second run through the press. Distinguishing between a first and second impression may make considerable difference in the value of an old book: the first impression is more highly valued by collectors in almost all instances.

Even earlier than the first impression, it should be pointed out, can be the first revise, the proof which is initially pulled from the press to make sure that all errors which may have been discovered in the galley proof have indeed been corrected preparatory to the actual running of the sheets.

The term first impression is often used interchangeably with first issue.

First issue The first run through the press for an edition. Most collectors want not only the first edition but, within that, the first issue. First issues are identified by "points," variations, often minute and immaterial to the text, often consisting of some printer's error, typographical mistake, or even variation in binding.

It would be idle speculation to attempt to guess whether or not one has a first issue, and, in most cases, a waste of time to attempt the research necessary for an independent judgment. One need only locate the proper bibliography which will furnish all the facts concerning issues and points.

First print An early printed copy of a published work, usually at the proofing stage, when it is not yet ready for general publication.

First-word entry A system of cataloguing books which utilizes the first word of the book's title, dropping any definite or indefinite articles such as "the" or "an."

Flap book A type of book for children which was especially popular at the beginning of the nineteenth century, but has continued to this day. As the name would indicate, each page of such a book generally has a flap, under which is hidden the answer to a question, which may appear above or below. Early examples of flap books, in good condition, are prized; a second edition of *The American Toilet*, published in 1827, a small book, square 16mo, consisting of only twenty leaves, recently sold for $100.

Fleurette   A small floral design, such as might appear in the design of a bookbinding.

Fleuron   A printing or binding ornament in the shape of a flower, possibly quite stylized.

Fleuron, The   A *Journal of Typography* (sub-title), published in London between 1923 and 1930, in seven volumes, all published. It was the intention of the editors to produce one volume a year which would demonstrate that books set by machine could be as beautiful as those set by hand at the private presses. Stanley Morison was editor of the last three numbers. A reprint is available at $565 from Greenwood Reprint Corporation, 51 Riverside Avenue, Westport, Conn. 06880.

Flexible binding   A binding usually made of leather or plastic, so soft that the book may actually be bent or even be rolled up. This term is also used, however, to indicate the type of spiral binding, of plastic or metal, which permits a book to be opened up completely flat at each side.

Florilegium   Latin for collection of flowers, a term used for anthology in German.

Flugblatt   German for broadside.

Flugschrift   German for pamphlet.

Fly leaf   Any blank leaf between the free endpaper and the first of the printed pages at the beginning of a book, or any blank leaf at the end of a book. The fly leaf of a book which constitutes the free endpaper is often the page which is inscribed.

Fly sheet   A tract of only two to four pages; a sheet folded only once or twice.

Fly title   A second printing (repetition) of the contents of the half-title, usually placed before the first pages of the text.

Fold   At the binding, a pair of leaves.

Folded   Two meanings: (1) a technical term meaning that the sheets folded for the pages of a book are ready for stitching but not yet stitched, and (2) also, in the sense that a sheet larger than page size, such as a map, may be folded down to fit among the pages of a book. Folded material is particularly likely to disappear from an old book, and therefore any book which lists among its contents one or more maps should be especially carefully checked to make certain that any maps listed are still present.

Folded to paper   With the sheets folded so that the edges match, even though the matter printed on the sheets may not, as a result, line up properly.

Folded to print   With the sheets folded so that the print matches when the book is held up to the light, even though the edges of the paper may not line up exactly. Many press books, for example, have the text carefully aligned, whereas the uncut edges of the paper may be extremely uneven, often adding, needless to say, to the charm of the book.

Folding case   Also known as an envelope or a wallet-type case, a kind of protective covering for a book. This covering may simply wrap around the book it protects or have a flap which folds over and then is tied or snapped shut.

Folding plates   Illustrations larger than the size of a page in a book and therefore folded down to fit. Maps are often folded thus, and some very large maps are sometimes folded a great many times to fit the book. Among the ultimate in large folding plates are the maps of railway rights published to accompany United States government documents; some of these fold down from a mighty six feet in length to fit into an octavo book.

Foliation   The numbering of the leaves of a book.

Folio   This term has a number of meanings all of which are associated with books: (1) a large sheet of paper which is folded once to form two leaves, or four pages, (2) the simplest form of a book, (3) the largest size of a book.

In American book sizes, a folio is 13 inches tall or taller. The elephant folio is 23 inches, the atlas folio is 25 inches, and the double elephant folio is as much as 50 inches. When the reference is to book size, folio is abbreviated F or F°.

A fourth meaning for the word folio is the page number in a book, for example "The folio is missing from what we assume must be page 20."

Folioed   With the leaves only—rather than each page—numbered.

Following the flag   Abiding by the nationality of an author in collecting first editions of his works, in that case where there are firsts for countries other than the author's native land. Thus, collecting the English first editions for Masefield, the American firsts for Steinbeck. It is not unusual for an author to be published first outside his own country. For example, Galsworthy's English classic, *Forsyte Saga* (1922) was actually published first in America. *The Adventures of Huckleberry Finn* by Mark Twain made its first appearance in England, in December, 1884, followed in a scant three days by the American first edition.

Foolscap   A size of paper for printing, $13\frac{1}{2}$ by 17 inches.

Foolscap quarto (F 4to)   A British book size, $8\frac{1}{2}$ by $6\frac{3}{4}$ inches.

Fore-edge   The edge of the leaves of a book which is opposite the spine. The outer edge.

Fore-edge painting   Any painted decoration on the front (fore-) edge of a book, but, more specifically, a miniature painting executed on the fore-edge and which only appears to view when the pages are slightly fanned out. Such a painting is frequently hidden under gilt and need not necessarily have some relation to the subject of the book. It may, indeed, have been executed some years after the book's publication. Collectors are particularly interested in books with two fore-edge paintings, painted on the same edge but appearing separately as the pages are fanned either to the right or left. A so-called "double" painting need not be of this type, but may have one painting above the other, sometimes quaintly out of perspective to each other. Fore-edge painting has so few modern practitioners that most examples in the market are probably genuinely old. An early example of this type of work will frequently have a binder's imprint stamped on the edge of the front board, to indicate that there is a hidden picture. Fortunately for collectors seeking guidance, there is a definitive work on the subject of this type of painting: *Fore-Edge Painting, a Historical Survey of a Curious Art in Book Decoration* by Carl J. Weber, published by Harvey House at $20.

Foreign words For an understanding of foreign words and phrases used in the old-book trade, there is an excellent reference book, *Dictionary for the Antiquarian Booktrade*, in French, English, German, Swedish, Danish, Italian, Spanish, and Dutch, edited by Menno Hertzberger, and published by the International League of Antiquarian Booksellers at Paris, in 1956, recently available directly from the League; you might write to see if copies are still available. The *Dictionary* can be approached from any one of the eight languages. Another basic work, the *Bibliographers' Glossary of Foreign Words and Phrases*, by Barbara Cowles, was published in wrappers by Bowker in 1935. Although it defines words peculiar to the book trade in no fewer than twenty languages, it has the disadvantage that it lacks the cross-referencing of the later book. Of course, a second and rather considerable disadvantage is that this book is long out-of-print.

Forel A type of parchment occasionally used in book-binding.

Format The general size, shape, structure, and arrangement of a book.

Fortsetzung German for continuation, as in a monthly or weekly serial story.

Forwarding In book publication or repair, a technical term meaning all the processes in binding a book which follow upon the sewing and work preliminary to putting on the final touches such as hand-lettering. Bookbinders thus "forward" a book.

Foxing A discoloration of the paper in a book, consisting of light brown spots. Paper containing iron particles or fungus, or both, may develop such spots with age. Since paper which is of anything less than the highest quality may eventually develop some foxing, this does not necessarily diminish the value of any old book, although a dealer should certainly be expected to mention this condition if offering a book for sale. (See also **De-foxing.**)

Fraktur German for a style of German type, also known as black-letter.

Franklin Benjamin Franklin (1706–1790) established his printing press in Philadelphia in 1730 when he was still a young man; its financial success permitted him eventually to retire from printing and to devote himself to his many other interests. His best-known and probably most-admired typographic achievement is *Cicero's Cato Major* (1774).

Frayed Unravelled at the edges: strictly speaking, only cloth or a cloth binding can become frayed, but one of the idiosyncracies of the old-book trade is that frayed is likewise applied to worn book jackets. Various imitations of leather made from cloth and used for the binding of a book will eventually betray themselves by starting to fray at the edges.

French rule An ornamental dash or line used to divide sections of type, thus: ▼▼▼▼▼

Frontispiece An illustration which faces the title page of a book. It is sometimes the only illustration in a book and frequently the most important one. It is the frontispiece, for example, which customarily carries the portrait of the author of the book.

Frontispiz-Titel German for an engraved title page.

Front matter (See **Prelims.**)

Frotté French for rubbed.

Fugitive material Printed material of only temporary interest at the time of its production. Such material is usually produced in limited quantity, adding subsequently to its interest for collectors. Such material includes theater programs, for example. Also, any text printed in fugitive inks will fade and thus, in a different sense be called fugitive.

Full bound Entirely bound in leather—or maybe, nowadays, leatherette.

Full gilt With every part of the book's binding decorated in gilt.

Full leather In a binding made entirely of leather, as contrasted to one described as one-half or three-quarters leather.

G

Gallery of Ghosts A publication of that title issued by the Modern Language Association of America in 1967 and containing five thousand entries of titles published between 1641 and 1700 known to exist but which have not yet been located in any of the two hundred libraries researched for Donald Wing's monumental *Short-Title Catalogue*.

Garamond Claude Garamond (1480–1561) was one of the earliest designers of type, and highly influential.

Garrison-Morton *A Medical Bibliography of Selected Works*—an annotated check-list of titles illustrating the history of medicine. A third edition, edited by Leslie T. Morton, was published by Lippincott in 1970.

Gathering The process of arranging loose sheets or signatures into the proper order for a book. Or, the cluster of leaves resulting from the printer's having folded the printed sheets to book size.

Gauffered With the fore edge of a book cut into a decorative pattern. Also spelled goffered.

Gebräunt German for with the pages browned.

Gedruckt German for printed.

Gekritzelt German for scribbled in, as a child might do.

Gemischte Schriften German for miscellaneous works.

General title In the case of a book which is published in parts, the over-all title for the work as a whole. This title is generally repeated in the several parts or volumes of the whole. In some books published serially, there may be discrepancies between the various titles for the parts, including, sometimes, the general title.

Genre Belonging to a category of works descriptive of domestic and everyday life. Or, sort or kind.

Geographies (See **Atlas** or *National Geographic.*)

Gesamtkatalog der Wiegendrucke A German reference work on incunabula, published at Leipzig between 1925 and 1938, considered possibly the most comprehensive of its kind as far as it has been completed; Volumes 1–7 (all published) extend down the alphabet only as far as "Eig."

Geschenkexemplar German for presentation copy.

Gesner Konrad von Gesner (1516–1565), considered by many the father of bibliography.

Gestochener Titel German for engraved title page.

Gift book A book designed primarily to be presented as a gift and thus often elaborately printed, frequently with greater emphasis on illustration and binding than on content. Such books reached a height of popularity in the United States in the middle of the nineteenth century.

Gilding The decorative application of gold color to the sides, back, or edges of a book. The application of gilt (gilding) is said to help protect the edges of a book from dust or dirt.

Gilt Made golden in color, particularly with regard to the edges of books or decorative bindings.

Glassine A transparent paper covering used to protect the printed covers of a book. Rarely mentioned in dealers' catalogues except perhaps as "original glassine," to indicate that the covers of this book have been protected ever since the book was first issued.

Glossary A dictionary limited to a selection of technical or otherwise specialized and possibly generally little-known terms, with their definitions. A collection of glosses.

Glossy In paper, glossy is synonymous for polished, lustrous, smooth, and slick. Glossy paper is often used for art books, for example.

Gnawed Usually by mice, although squirrels will also chew on books if given the opportunity.

Golden Cockerel A press founded in 1920 by Harold M. Taylor; vehicle, under Robert Gibbings, for a renaissance in the use of wood-engravings in book illustration.

Gold in Your Attic A book by Van Allen Bradley, to which can be given the credit for having sent thousands of people to their attics, closets, garages, and basements to scout for old and possibly valuable books. The sequel is *More Gold in Your Attic*. Both books have recruited many people to the hobby of book collecting. Since they include estimations of the value of the books described, it is a good idea to get hold of the latest editions. Bradley's *The Book Collector's Handbook of Values*, published in 1972, is a marvelously handy directory of old books which frequently come into the market, with recent prices listed.

Goldschnitt German for having gilt edges.

Good In describing a book's condition, the term good means better than fair but still short of being very good. A book in good condition is missing no parts and has no major defects. Probably most of the books on your own bookshelves could be accurately described as in good condition, if not better. They look as though they had been read, but they have not been abused. They may show some slight shelf wear, but the interiors are bright and clean. Most of the books which are sold in secondhand book stores seem to be in good condition, except of course for those on the bargain tables if there are such.

Goudy Frederic W. Goudy (1865–1947), an influential American type designer, the proprietor, with his wife Bertha, of the Village Press in the early 1900's. Goudy is considered by many to have contributed more, individually, to type design than almost any other man in history.

Gouge A simple curved line of decoration in a bookbinding.

Gouges Nicks and holes in the cover of a book, or in its back (spine), and therefore a serious type of defect in any old book. Books with gouges can be presumed to have been seriously mistreated. In a truly rare book, however, it might be necessary to overlook such a defect as gouging. In cheap books, never.

Government documents The most usual type of government documents which come into the old-book market are the individual House and Senate reports which are seventy years old or older. Prices for the more recent material have been ranging between $6 and $35, depending upon the subject and thus historical significance, with the oldest documents, dating back to the days when Congress had not yet adopted a system for numbering its various documents, commanding, of course, a great deal more. Some of the flimsiest and most tattered of these early documents may command the most money if they deal with hostilities or the conclusion of a war, Indian disputes, or western expansion.

There is considerable interest in government documents dealing with the forced migration of Indians West, the Mormon settlement in Utah, frontier military exploits, the adjustment of mail claims, the establishment of mail routes, Indian captivities, and accounts of individual heroic deeds. Documents setting forth the details of the admission of a new state to the union are particularly prized. A rare and valuable document is the first code of laws printed for the Oregon Territory, in 1853. The 1854 edition is almost as rare, since most of the copies, which had been printed in the East and shipped West by boat, went down with the ship off the coast of southern California, leaving just a few copies to make it through all the way by overland mail.

Some government documents, of course, have a great scientific interest, and various national and state reports on natural history have become collectors' items because of their plates, often in color. One greatly prized document is the 1854 report titled *Report of the Superintendent of the U.S. Coast Survey*. It contains the first known engraved plate by the artist Whistler—a vignette of two flights of wild fowl, apparently just added for scenic effect.

Grabhorn A San Francisco press operated by Edwin and Robert Grabhorn between 1919 and 1965. Among its publications, which are noted for their lively style as well as excellent workmanship, is the 1930 edition of *Leaves of Grass.*

Grangerized Extra-illustrated: with added pictures, letters, documents, or other associated items and memorabilia either laid in or, more usually, tipped in. In 1789 James Granger published a biographical history of England, in which he purposely left blank pages into which the reader was invited to paste any related illustrative material which might strike his fancy, much as a bibliographical work may leave blank pages for additional notes.

Gravure The process of printing from a depressed, or sunken, surface. Letterpress, on the other hand, utilizes a raised surface; and offset, a flat surface. In gravure, the image which is to be reproduced is etched below the surface, and ink is flooded into the tiny wells which are the source of the image which is to be transferred to the paper. Examples are steel-engraving and copperplate-engraving.

Gravure (French) Print, or engraving: *Gravure sur acier* (steel-engraving); *gravure sur bois* (wood-cut); *gravure sur cuivre* (copper-engraving); *gravure en taille douce* (copperplate etching).

Gregynog A Welsh private press founded in 1922 by the Misses G. E. and M. S. Davies and noted for the fine work accomplished throughout the 1920's and thereafter.

Griffonné French for scribbled, as by a child.

Grolier Jean Grolier de Servieres (1479–1565), an early French collector of fine books, who owned one of the best libraries of his day. When he travelled to Italy as French ambassador, he met Aldus Manutius, a famous scholar and member of an eminent family of printers. He was so impressed that books subsequently became his passion. His collection, which reached three thousand volumes, was huge for its day. Many of his books were especially bound in morocco or calf for him, and fancifully decorated in gold and color. One interpretation for the inscription he had placed in his books—Jo. Grolieri et amicorum—is that he intended thus to make it known that all his books were to be shared among his friends. The Grolier collection stayed in the same family for years until it was finally dispersed. Someone has ventured the guess that there may still be about 500 books in the world definitely identifiable as having once belonged to this great man's library.

Grolier Club A club founded in New York City in 1884 by a group of bibliophiles, for the study of literature, the promotion of book collecting, and the study of the art of bookmaking. It continues today as a private club of book and print collectors and maintains its own library which consists mostly of rare volumes and also includes an extensive collection of booksellers' and auction catalogues. From time to time the Grolier Club sponsors exhibits and publishes books in limited edition in the areas of its special interests.

Grolieresque Said of a binding which is elaborately and beautifully embellished with geometrical and floral designs after the special bindings developed for the book-collector Grolier.

Grolier Lists Among the many other publications of the Grolier Club, there are two important and highly influential lists, each frequently consulted by book collectors, upon which many collections have been built. The first is a list of the most influential American books, and the second is a list of the most famous books in English literature. There are one hundred titles on each list. A first-edition copy of any of these titles is sure to have value.

Grolier List of Books That Influenced America

1640   *Bay Psalm Book.* Cambridge.
1644   Williams, Roger. *The Bloudy Tenent of Persecution, for Cause of Conscience.* London.

1649 *Platform of Church Discipline.* Cambridge.
1662 Wigglesworth, Michael. *Day of Doom.* Cambridge.
1682 Rowlandson, Mary. *Narrative of the Captivity and Restauration of.* Cambridge.
1702 Mather, Cotton. *Magnalia Christi Americana.* London.
1717 Wise, John. *Vindication of the Government of New England Churches.* Boston.
1727 *New England Primer* (earliest known). Boston.
1736 Zenger, John Peter. *Brief Narrative of Case and Trial.* New York.
1751 Franklin, Benjamin. *Experiments . . . on Electricity.* London.
1754 Edwards, Jonathan. *Freedom of the Will.* Boston.
1757 Franklin, Benjamin. *Almanac for 1758.* Philadelphia.
1768 Dickinson, John. *Letters of a Pennsylvania Farmer.* Philadelphia.
1776 Paine, Thomas. *Common Sense.* Philadelphia.
1776 *Declaration of Independence.* Dunlap broadside, Philadelphia.
1783 Webster, Noah. *A Grammatical Institute.* Hartford.
1787 *Northwest Territory Ordinance.* New York.
1787 *Constitution, The.* Philadelphia.
1788 Hamilton, Madison, and Jay. *The Federalist.* New York.
1789 *Bill of Rights, The.* New York.
1791 Franklin, Benjamin. *Autobiography.* Paris.
1792 Thomas, Robert. *Farmers' Almanac for 1793.* Boston.
1794 Rowson, Mrs. Susanna. *Charlotte. A Tale of Truth.* Philadelphia.
1796 Washington, George. *Farewell Address.* Philadelphia.
1802 Bowditch, Nathaniel. *The New American Practical Navigator.* Newburyport (Mass.).

1804   Marshall, John. *Marbury v. Madison.* Washington.

1806   Weems, Mason. *Washington.* 5th ("cherry tree") ed. Augusta (Ga.).

1809   Irving, Washington. *A History of New York.* New York.

1810   Thomas, Isaiah. *History of Printing in America.* Worcester.

1814   Lewis, Meriwether and Clark, William. *History of the Expedition to the Pacific Ocean.* Philadelphia.

1819
–20   Irving, Washington. *The Sketch Book.* New York.

1821   Bryant, William Cullen. *Poems.* Cambridge.

1823   Monroe, James. *Annual Message, Dec. 2, 1823* (The Monroe Doctrine). Washington.

1826   Cooper, James F. *The Last of the Mohicans.* Philadelphia.

1827   Goodrich, Samuel. *Peter Parley's Tales About America.* Boston.

1828   Webster, Noah. *An American Dictionary.* New York.

1830   Smith, Joseph. *The Book of Mormon.* Palmyra, New York.

1833   Beaumont, William. *Experiments and Observations on the Gastric Juice.* Plattsburg, New York.

1834   Crockett, David. *Crockett Almanack for 1835.* Nashville (Tenn.).

1835   Simms, William Gilmore. *The Yemassee.* New York.

1836   Gray, Asa. *Elements of Botany.* New York.

1836   McGuffey, William. *The Eclectic First Reader.* Cincinnati.

1837   Hawthorne, Nathaniel. *Twice-Told Tales.* Boston.

1837   Emerson, Ralph Waldo. *American Scholar.* Boston.

1840   Dana, Richard Henry, Jr. *Two Years Before the Mast.* New York.

1840
—44   Audubon, John James. *The Birds of America.* New York and Philadelphia.

1841
—44   Emerson, Ralph Waldo. *Essays.* Boston.

1842   Longfellow, Henry W. *Ballads.* Cambridge.

1843   Prescott, William. *History of the Conquest of Mexico.* New York.

1843   Fremont, J. C. *Report on Exploration of Country Lying Between the Missouri River and the Rocky Mountains.* Washington.

1843   Holmes, Oliver W. *The Contagiousness of Puerperal Fever.* Boston.

1844   Moore, Clement. *Poems* (with The Night Before Christmas). New York.

1845   Cushing, Luther. *Rules for Proceedings and Debate in Deliberative Assemblies.* Boston.

1845   Poe, Edgar Allan. *Tales.* New York.

1845   Poe, Edgar Allan. *The Raven and Other Poems.* New York.

1845   Herbert, Henry W. *The Warwick Woodlands.* Philadelphia.

1848   Lowell, James Russell. *The Biglow Papers.* Cambridge.

1849   Parkman, Francis. *The California and Oregon Trail.* New York.

1850   Hawthorne, Nathaniel. *The Scarlet Letter.* Boston.

1851   Melville, Herman. *Moby-Dick.* New York.

1852   Stowe, Harriet Beecher. *Uncle Tom's Cabin.* Boston.

1854   Arthur, T. S. *Ten Nights in a Bar Room.* Boston and Philadelphia.

1854   Thoreau, Henry. *Walden.* Boston.

1855   Longfellow, Henry W. *The Song of Hiawatha.* Boston.

1855   Whitman, Walt. *Leaves of Grass.* Brooklyn.

1855	Bartlett, John. *Familiar Quotations.* Cambridge.
1855	Bulfinch, Thomas. *The Age of Fable.* Boston.
1857	Taney, Roger (and others). *Dred Scott v. Sandford.* Washington.
1858	Holmes, Oliver W. *The Autocrat of the Breakfast Table.* Boston.
1860	Stephens, Mrs. Ann S. *Malaeska.* New York. (The first Beadle dime novel.)
1862	*Emancipation Proclamation.* (Sept. 22, 1862) Washington.
1863	Lincoln, Abraham. *Gettysburg Address.* Washington.
1866	Whittier, John G. *Snow-Bound.* Boston.
1868	Alger, Horatio, Jr. *Ragged Dick.* Boston.
1868	Alcott, Louisa May. *Little Women.* Boston.
1870	Harte, Bret. *The Luck of Roaring Camp.* Boston.
1872	First Mail-Order Catalogue. Sears, Roebuck, Chicago.
1875	Eddy, Mary Baker. *Science and Health.* Boston.
1876	Clemens, Samuel. *Tom Sawyer.* Hartford.
1878	Green, Anna Katherine. *Leavenworth Case.* New York.
1879	George, Henry. *Progress and Poverty.* San Francisco.
1880	Wallace, Lew. *Ben-Hur.* New York.
1881	Harris, Joel C. *Uncle Remus.* New York.
1881	Holmes, Oliver W., Jr. *The Common Law.* Boston.
1881	James, Henry. *The Portrait of a Lady.* London.
1884	Lincoln, Mary. *Mrs. Lincoln's Boston Cook Book.* Boston.
1885	Howells, Wm. Dean. *The Rise of Silas Lapham.* Boston.
1885	Clemens, Samuel. *Huckleberry Finn.* New York.
1886	Burnett, Frances H. *Little Lord Fauntleroy.* New York.
1888	Bellamy, Edward. *Looking Backward.* Boston.

1890   Mahan, Alfred T. *The Influence of Sea Power on History.* Boston.

1890   James, William. *Principles of Psychology.* New York.

1890
-91
-96   Dickinson, Emily. *Poems.* Boston.

1891   Garland, Hamlin. *Main Travelled Roads.* Boston.

1891   Bierce, Ambrose. *Tales of Soldiers and Civilians.* San Francisco.

1893   Turner, Frederick Jackson. *The Significance of the Frontier in American History.* Madison (Wis.).

1894   Holt, Luther. *The Care and Feeding of Children.* New York.

1895   Crane, Stephen. *The Red Badge of Courage.* New York.

1899   Veblen, Thorstein. *The Theory of the Leisure Class.* New York.

1899   Markham, Edwin. *The Man With the Hoe.* San Francisco.

Grolier List of 100 Books Famous in English Literature

c. 1478   *The Canterbury Tales.* Chaucer
1473   *Confessio Amantis.* Gower
1485   *Le Morte d'Arthur.* Malory
1549   *The Booke of the Common Prayer and Administration of the Sacramentes* (Church of England)
1550   *Vision of Piers Plowman.* Langland
1577   *The Chronicles of England, Scotland, Ireland.* Holinshed
1559   *A Myrroure for Magistrates.* Baldwin et al.
1559   *Songes and Sonettes.* Howard
1570   *The Tragidie of Ferrex and Porrex.* Norton and Sackville

1580	*Euphues. The Anatomy of Wit.* Lyly
1590	*The Countesse of Pembrokes Arcadia.* Sidney
1590	
–96	*The Faerie Queene.* Spenser
1598	*Essaies.* Bacon
1598	
–1600	*Principal Navigations . . .* Hakluyt
1616	*Whole Works of Homer.* Chapman
1611	*Holy Bible* (Royal or King James version)
1616	*The Workes.* Jonson
1621	*Anatomy of Melancholy.* Burton
1623	
–32	
–64	
–85	*Comedies, Histories, & Tragidies.* Shakespeare
1623	*The Tragedy of the Dutchess of Malfy.* Webster
1633	*A New Way to Pay Old Debts.* Massinger
1633	*The Broken Heart. A Tragedy.* Ford
1633	*The Famous Tragedy of the Rich Jew of Malta.* Marlowe
1633	*The Temple.* Herbert
1633	*Poems.* Donne
1642	*Religio Medici.* Brown
1645	*The Workes.* Waller
1647	*Comedies and Tragedies.* Beaumont and Fletcher
1648	*Hesperides.* Herrick
1650	*The Rule and Exercises of Holy Living.* Taylor
1653	*The Compleat Angler . . .* Walton
1663	
–78	*Hudibras.* Butler
1667	*Paradise Lost.* Milton
1678	*The Pilgrim's Progress.* Bunyan
1681	
–82	*Absalom and Achitophel.* Dryden
1690	*An Essay Concerning Humane Understanding.* Locke
1700	*The Way of the World.* Congreve

1702

–03

–04   *The History of the Rebellion* . . . Clarendon

1710

–11   *The Lucubrations of Isaac Bickerstaff (The Tatler).* Steele

1711

–12   *The Spectator.* Steele and Addison

1719   *Life and Strange Surprizing Adventures of Robinson Crusoe.* Defoe

1726   *Travels into Several Remote Nations of the World.* Swift

1733

–34   *An Essay on Man.* Pope

1736   *The Analogy of Religion.* Butler

1765   *Reliques of Ancient English Poetry.* Percy

1747   *Odes.* Collins

1748   *Clarissa.* Richardson

1749   *The History of Tom Jones.* Fielding

1751   *Elegy Wrote in a Country Church Yard.* Gray

1755   *A Dictionary of the English Language.* Johnson

1757   *Poor Richard Improved: Being an Almanack . . . for . . . 1758.* Franklin

1765

–69   *Commentaries on the Law of England.* Blackstone

1766   *The Vicar of Wakefield.* Goldsmith

1768   *A Sentimental Journey through France and Italy. By Mr. Yorick.* Sterne

1788   *The Federalist.* Hamilton and Madison

1771   *The Expedition of Humphrey Clinker.* Smollett

1776   . . . *Wealth of Nations.* Smith

1776

–88   *The History of the Decline and Fall of the Roman Empire.* Gibbon

1780   *The School for Scandal.* Sheridan

1785   *Poems.* Cowper

1786	*Poems.* Burns
1789	*The Natural History and Antiquities of Selborne.* White
1790	*Reflections on the Revolution in France.* Burke
1791	*Rights of Man.* Paine
1791	*The Life of Samuel Johnson.* Boswell
1798	*Lyrical Ballads.* Wordsworth and Coleridge
1809	*A History of New York.* Irving
1812	*Childe Harold's Pilgrimage.* Byron
1813	*Pride and Prejudice.* Austen
1816	*Christabel; Kubla Khan, a Vision* . . . Coleridge
1820	*Ivanhoe.* Scott
1820	*Lamia, Isabella, the Eve of St. Agnes, and Other Poems.* Keats
1821	*Adonais.* Shelley
1823	*Elia.* Lamb
1825	*Memoirs . . . comprising his Diary.* Pepys
1826	*The Last of the Mohicans.* Cooper
1836	*Pericles and Aspasia.* Landor
1836 –37	*Posthumous Papers of the Pickwick Club.* Dickens
1834	*Sartor Resartus.* Carlyle
1836	*Nature.* Emerson
1847	*History of the Conquest of Peru.* Prescott
1845	*The Raven and Other Poems.* Poe
1847	*Jane Eyre.* Brontë
1847	*Evangeline.* Longfellow
1847	*Sonnets.* Browning
1848	*Meliboeus-Hipponax. The Biglow Papers.* Lowell
1847 –48	*Vanity Fair.* Thackeray
1849 –61	*The History of England.* Macaulay
1850	*In Memoriam.* Tennyson
1850	*The Scarlet Letter.* Hawthorne
1852	*Uncle Tom's Cabin.* Stowe

1851
–53   *The Stones of Venice.* Ruskin
1855   *Men and Women.* Browning
1856   *The Rise of the Dutch Republic.* Motley
1859   *Adam Bede.* Eliot
1859   *On the Origin of the Species.* Darwin
1859   *Rubáiyát* . . . Fitzgerald, transl.
1864   *Apologia Pro Vita Sua.* Newman
1865   *Essays in Criticism.* Arnold
1866   *Snowbound.* Whittier

There is available a bibliography of the above Grolier Club List for English Literature: *Bibliographical Notes on 100 Books Famous in English Literature*, edited by Henry W. Kent, and published by Kraus Reprint Corporation at $35.

Grösses   German for dimension, size, or format. In German, *grösses papier* means in large-paper format.

Grotesk schrift   German for black-letter script.

Guarded   Repaired by a process of reinforcing the inner margin of a page. To accomplish this, a strip of lightweight paper of high tensile strength is pasted in.

Guinea pig   Slang for a bulky and cheap book, especially applied to the *Catalogue of Books* published by Henry George Bohn in 1841. This work, which became a standard reference work with book dealers and collectors in England, was unusually thick; furthermore, its price was one guinea.

Gutenberg   The term may be a reference to the Bible which was the first European book to be set and printed from type, to the press which produced this book, or to the man, Johannes Gutenberg, who invented the first movable type and was thus able to print the book. Gutenberg press is sometimes used facetiously to mean any old-fashioned or out-of-date press.

Gutenberg Bible   Although undated, the Gutenberg Bible was probably published in 1455 or possibly 1456, at Mainz, Germany. The first book to be printed in Europe, the history of modern printing dates from its publication. It is also known as the forty-two-line Bible, from the number of lines to each page; and as the Mazarin Bible, since the first copy to be located in the eighteenth century was found in the library of the Cardinal Mazarin, in Paris. In 1973 there were known to be forty-seven surviving copies of this work. One page alone is considered a great treasure, not only because of its great historical importance but because of its great beauty, the continued whiteness of the paper, deep color of the ink, and typography outstanding in any century.

Gutenberg, Johannes Little is known of the personal history of Johannes Gutenberg (c. 1400–1468) who is credited with the invention of movable type and the publication of the first book from this type. He was born in Mainz, Germany, and between 1435 and 1440 he was apparently involved in various experiments to develop a type mold and press; he may have kept his experiments secret since others were also at work on the same idea. The process of papermaking had been known for 200 years, and viscous inks were already in use to print from woodblocks, but Gutenberg's contribution was assembling single letters to form words and then locking these compositions into a form for printing. He was also, incidentally, the first to realize the commercial possibilities in printing. In 1455 he published his 42-line (Gutenberg) Bible. At the time he was in partnership with Johann Fust. There is a possibility that the 32-line Bible published at Bamberg in 1458 may also have been his work, as well as the *Catholicon*, an encyclopedia-dictionary published at Mainz in 1460, without, as it explained, "the help of reed, stylus or pen but by the marvelous agreement, proportion, and harmony of punches and type . . . to extol the glory of the Church."

Gutter The blank space between the printed text and the binding of a book. In other words, the inner margin of the page.

H

Halbband German for a half-binding. *Halbleder* means half-calf; *halbleinen*, half-cloth.

Halbjährlich German for semi-annual.

Half-bound Bound so that the back (spine) of the book is covered with leather, but with the rest of the binding in either cloth or boards.

Half-cloth With just the back of the book (spine) bound in cloth.

Half-leather With the back (spine) of a book generously bound in leather, extending sometimes as much as half way across the sides of the book. It is never, however, exactly measured.

Half-title According to those who wish to be exact, the first printed page of a book after the front end papers. Or, any one of the front pages on which there is printed an abbreviated version of the title which appears in full on the title page.

In a list of the pages which make up the preliminary pages of a book, however, the half-title is customarily listed last, since it often simply repeats the main words of the title just before the text begins. In the most common use, the half-title is simply any appearance of the title in brief among the pages which constitute the front matter.

Halftone An illustration produced by means of a screen which is used to break up the image into a series of minute dots for reproduction. In contrast, a line engraving utilizes the solid opposition of strong black and white areas.

Halkett Samuel Halkett and John Laing: *Dictionary of Anonymous and Pseudonymous English Literature.* The first edition of this work, in four volumes, appeared in 1882–88. A seven-volume edition is still in print, available from Haskell at about $100. As compendious and authoritative as this work is, it still cannot be expected to solve every mystery of real authorship.

Hamer Philip M. Hamer: *A Guide to Archives and Manuscripts in the United States.*

Hamiltonian Bearing a translation of the original text between the lines of the original, after the practice of James Hamilton (1769–1831).

Handbook of Values The Book Collector's Handbook of Values, a one-volume reference work published in 1972 at $17.50 by G. P. Putnam's Sons. By Van Allen Bradley, this work contains listings of over fifteen thousand scarce and rare books, with the most important points for each and the most recent prices paid at the time the book was published. The *Handbook* is a particularly useful guide for collectors with limited funds, since it reports many nineteenth- and twentieth-century books, both American and English, which are valued as low as $25 and which, furthermore, are fairly likely to appear again on the market. It is not, however, a complete reference work and should be used with caution: it can serve to eliminate some books by demonstrating where they would not qualify as first editions, but does not always furnish sufficient information to prove that a book may be, for example, a first edition.

Hand-colored With the illustrations colored, though not necessarily by the artist himself. There have been a few studios specializing in hand-coloring illustrations for books, mostly in the recent years for the fine presses which are the only ones which can afford their work. Such hand work adds greatly to the cost of any book. Obviously, it must today be confined to limited editions. Perhaps this is why we particularly value some books, such as books on sports or botany, or gift books, which were colored by hand over a hundred years ago. The work in these old books is frequently fairly crude.

Handsatz   German for type set by hand.

Hanging indentation
A style of type composition in which the first line is full out to the left but succeeding lines are indented, sometimes to accommodate a subhead (as appears in this paragraph).

Harleian   A style of binding, of red morocco with a wide tooled border and a lozenge-shaped inner panel, so named after the kind of binding used for books in the library of Robert Harley, Earl of Oxford (1661–1724).

Harvard   The Harvard University Press, at Cambridge, Massachusetts, is the oldest continually operating press in the United States. When the Widow Glover married President Dunster of Harvard, she brought along the press her previous husband had owned. This was the press used to produce the first book printed in America, the *Bay Psalm Book*, in 1640. The press was thereafter used in close association with the college.

Hatching   The crossed lines sometimes used for decorative effect in the binding of books.

Headband   The narrow strip of cloth which is glued to the spine of a book in the process of rounding and backing a book (forwarding). The purpose of the headband is to strengthen the book and to protect it from careless handling. In some old books you will see that this headband was sometimes made of elaborate material, such as embroidery. Occasionally today it appears in a contrasting color or stripes, again purely for decorative effect. The headband, incidentally, appears at both the head and the foot of a spine.

Head/foot   The top and the bottom, respectively, of the spine or the backstrip; not, properly, used in reference to the sides or the entire book.

Head margin   Any space which is left above the text on a page.

Headpiece   The decorative detail inserted at the top of a page which starts a chapter. The book's designer may specify headpieces, or the illustrator feel they suit the book's style, but it is occasionally the printer who adds it on his own initiative.

Heard   J. Norman Heard: *Bookman's Guide to Americana*, by Heard and Jimmie H. Hoover. The sixth edition is available at $10 from Scarecrow Press.

Hebdomadaire   French for weekly.

Hebraica   Literature pertaining to, or related to, the Hebrew people. (See also **Judaica**.)

Heft   German for pamphlet, booklet; or part, issue, or section.

Henty   George Alfred Henty (1832–1902), an English journalist primarily known as the author of books for boys. His tales of adventure were as popular in America as in England, and they are now widely collected. *A Henty Bibliography*, by Robert L. Dartt, is available from Dar-Web, 33 Franklin Street, Cedar Grove, N. J. 07009, at $12.

Heraldic   Displaying a coat of arms, as might be done by the cover of a book.

Herausgeben   German for edit (*not* publish). *Herausgeber* means editor or publisher.

Heritage Club Books   For several decades now the organization known as Heritage Club has been issuing the classics in editions of some merit. They are produced in sturdy bindings, handsomely printed, and well illustrated. Club books are issued in slipcases, and there is a steady flow of them into the old-book market, as a result, in close-to-mint condition. Prices may range from $8 to $20 and higher.

Hermetics   Books dealing with alchemy.

High Spot   In the old-book trade, "High Spot" has the specific meaning of one of those books selected by Merle Johnson for inclusion in the list which he titled *High Spots in American Literature* and published in 1929. He intended to give the public "a practical bibliography and brief literary estimate of outstanding American books." Since many

collectors of American books have been guided to some
extent, at least, by Merle Johnson's list, many of the books
listed have remained in the public eye long after they might
otherwise have been forgotten. The books on the list were
selected on the basis of the acclaim of their readership in the
1920's, as well as the critical judgment of the day. Merle
Johnson also admitted to being guided by some of his own
personal prejudices.

Merle Johnson's book is now available in reprint at about
$9 from the Pemberton Press, Box 2085, Austin, Tex. 78703.
The book itself furnishes detailed bibliographical information including the points on first editions, but the following
short-title list may prove helpful in indicating the taste of
that period and explaining why some of these books are still
collected.

High Spots of
American Literature

1900	*Fables in Slang.* Ade
1868	*Little Women.* Alcott
1869	*Little Women, Part Second.* Alcott
1871	*Little Men.* Alcott
1870	*Story of a Bad Boy.* Aldrich
1901	*Flute and Violin.* Allen
1895	*Kentucky Cardinal.* Allen
1896	*Aftermath.* Allen
1919	*Winesburg, Ohio.* Anderson
1921	*Triumph of the Egg.* Anderson
1924	*A Story Teller's Story.* Anderson
1918	*Jungle Peace.* Beebe
1888	*Looking Backward.* Bellamy
1891	*Tales of Soldiers.* Bierce
1832	*Collected Poems.* Bryant
1891	*"Short Sixes."* Bunner
1886	*Little Lord Fauntleroy.* Burnett
1895	*The Purple Cow!* Burgess

1906	*Are You a Bromide?* Burgess
1871	*Wake-Robin.* Burroughs
1906	*Pigs Is Pigs.* Butler
1857	*Nothing to Wear.* Butler
1919	*Jurgen.* Cabell
1879	*Old Creole Days.* Cable
1873	*Farm Ballads.* Carleton
1918	*My Antonía.* Cather
1876	*The Adventures of Tom Sawyer.* Clemens (Twain)
1885	*Adventures of Huckleberry Finn.* Clemens (Twain)
1894	*Tragedy of Pudd'nhead Wilson.* Clemens (Twain)
1826	*Last of the Mohicans.* Cooper
1895	*Red Badge of Courage.* Crane
1899	*War Is Kind.* Crane
1856	*Prue and I.* Curtis
1840	*Two Years Before the Mast.* Dana, Jr.
1899	*Old Chester Tales.* Deland
1914	*The Single Hound.* Dickinson
1867	*Hans Brinker.* Dodge
1921	*Three Soldiers.* Dos Passos
1900	*Sister Carrie.* Dreiser
1911	*Jennie Gerhardt.* Dreiser
1925	*An American Tragedy.* Dreiser
1898	*Mr. Dooley.* Dunne
1871	*Hoosier School-Master.* Eggleston
1883	*Hoosier School-Boy.* Eggleston
1841	*Essays.* Emerson
1889	*Little Book of Western Verse.* Field
1889	*Little Book of Profitable Tales.* Field
1894	*Honorable Peter Stirling.* Ford
1908	*Trail of the Lonesome Pine.* Fox, Jr.
1896	*In the Valley.* Frederic
1896	*The Damnation of Theron Ware.* Frederic
1914	*North of Boston.* Frost
1922	*A Pioneer Mother.* Garland
1891	*Main-Travelled Roads.* Garland

1865	*Man Without a Country.* Hale
1881	*Uncle Remus.* Harris
1870	*Luck of Roaring Camp.* Harte
1871	*Poems.* Harte
1850	*Scarlet Letter.* Hawthorne
1837	*Twice-Told Tales.* Hawthorne
1871	*"Jim Bludso" in Pike County Ballads.* Hay
1887	*Some Chinese Ghosts.* Hearn
1890	*Two Years in the French West Indies.* Hearn
1906	*The Four Million.* Henry
1917	*Three Black Pennys.* Hergesheimer
1923	*The Presbyterian Child.* Hergesheimer
1858	*Autocrat of the Breakfast-Table.* Holmes
1861	*Elsie Venner.* Holmes
1922	*The Covered Wagon.* Hough
1885	*The Rise of Silas Lapham.* Howells
1890	*A Boy's Town.* Howells
1898	*A Message to Garcia.* Hubbard
1819	*The Sketch Book of Geoffrey Crayon, Gent.* Irving
1884	*Ramona.* Jackson
1879	*Daisy Miller.* James
1904	*The Golden Bowl.* James
1890	*Aztec Treasure-House.* Janvier
1900	*To Have and to Hold.* Johnston
1914	*Trees and Other Poems.* Kilmer
Nd.	*Hans Breitmann's Party.* Leland
1897	*Wolfville.* Lewis, A. H.
1920	*Main Street.* Lewis
1922	*Babbitt.* Lewis
1903	*Call of the Wild.* London
1907	*Before Adam.* London
1913	*John Barleycorn.* London
1847	*Evangeline.* Longfellow
1855	*Song of Hiawatha.* Longfellow
1916	*Men, Women and Ghosts.* Lowell, Amy
1848	*The Biglow Papers.* Lowell

1916	*Casuals of the Sea.* McFee
1899	*Man with the Hoe.* Markham
1915	*Spoon River Anthology.* Masters
1851	*Moby-Dick.* Melville
1917	*Renascence.* Millay
1871	*Songs of the Sierras.* Miller
1850	*Reveries of a Bachelor.* Mitchell, Donald G.
1897	*Hugh Wynne.* Mitchell, S. Weir
1844	*Poems.* Moore
1899	*McTeague.* Norris
1903	*Epic of the Wheat: The Pit.* Norris
1887	*In Ole Virginia.* Page
1917	*Susan Lenox.* Phillips
Nd.	*The Raven and Other Poems.* Poe
1845	*Tales.* Poe
1892	*Men of Iron.* Pyle
1906	*The Way of an Indian.* Remington
1883	*Old Swimmin'-Hole.* Riley
1904	*Watchers of the Trails.* Roberts
1899	*"Where Angels Fear . . ."* Robertson
1920	*Smoke and Steel.* Sandburg
1916	*Poems.* Seeger
1898	*Wild Animals I Have Known.* Seton
1906	*The Jungle.* Sinclair
1891	*Colonel Carter.* Smith
1884	*Lady, or Tiger?* Stockton
1886	*The Casting Away . . .* Stockton
1888	*Dusantes.* Stockton
1852	*Uncle Tom's Cabin.* Stowe
1899	*Gentleman from Indiana.* Tarkington
1900	*Monsieur Beaucaire.* Tarkington
1914	*Penrod.* Tarkington
1916	*Seventeen.* Tarkington
1854	*Walden.* Thoreau
1849	*A Week on the Concord.* Thoreau
1897	*First Christmas-Tree.* Van Dyke

1901	*The Ruling Passion.* Van Dyke
1921	*Story of Mankind.* Van Loon
1880	*Ben-Hur.* Wallace
1873	*Fair God.* Wallace
1898	*David Harum . . .* Westcott
1911	*Ethan Frome.* Wharton
1913	*Gold.* White, S. E.
1915	*Gray Dawn.* White, S. E.
1920	*Rose Dawn.* White, S. E.
1899	*Court of Boyville.* White, Wm. A.
1906	*In Our Town.* White, Wm. A.
1855	*Leaves of Grass.* Whitman
1866	*Snow-Bound.* Whittier
1913	*Bunker Bean.* Wilson, H. L.
1915	*When a Man Comes to Himself.* Wilson, W.
1902	*The Virginian.* Wister

This is the conclusion of Part I of High Spots, some, obviously, judged by succeeding generations as more deservedly "high" than others. Included in Merle Johnson's Part II were titles he thought "a bit more debatable than those of the first group."

Hinge The interior junction of the spine and the sides of a book. The exterior junction, on the other hand, is properly called the joint . . . even though it is often referred to as the hinge! The hinges of any old book are likely to crack: split and start to come apart, usually the front hinge before the back one, since in normal use it will receive more wear.

A second use of the word hinge is to describe the stub, in a bound book, which permits the free movement of a bound-in map, illustration, or other insert made into the binding of a book.

Hinges cracked Hinges are termed cracked when the endpapers covering the hinge are split or splitting and the cover starts to wobble. In other words, the book is in essence beginning to come apart. The word "starting" is sometimes used by itself to indicate a weakness in the hinges.

Hinweis   German for reference.

Historiated   A rather awkward term, having in fact less reference to history than to art, and meaning fancifully decorated with figures of men and other animals. Historiated also has the specific meaning of decorated with illuminated initials.

Holland   A linen fabric of a type which originated in the Province of Holland, the Netherlands. Holland cloth and Holland boards both refer to place of origin.

Hollow back binding   A method of binding books whereby a hollow tunnel is created down the spine of the book, enabling it to lie flat when opened. The history of its origin is explained by Douglas Cockerell in his book *Bookbinding, and the Care of Books* (Fourth Edition, 1924): "Leather was doubtless first chosen for covering the backs of books because of its toughness and flexibility; because, while protecting the back, it would bend when the book was opened and allow the back to 'throw up' . . . When gold tooling became common, and the backs of books were elaborately decorated, it was found that the creasing of the leather injured the brightness of the gold and caused it to crack. To avoid this the binders lined up the back until it was as stiff as a block of wood . . . This was all very well for the gold, but a book so treated does not open fully, and indeed, if the paper is stiff, can hardly be got to open at all.

"To overcome both difficulties the hollow back was introduced, and as projecting bands would have been in the way, the sewing cord was sunk in saw cuts made across the back of the book."

Hollow back binding has now become standard, even though Cockerell pointed out that the hollow back may result in "the production of worthless bindings with little strength, and yet with the appearance of better work" since it "throws all the strain of opening and shutting on the joints, and renders the back liable to come right off if the book is much used."

However that may be, the hollow back has not been improved upon.

Holograph A manuscript, letter, or other document which is completely written out by hand, usually by the person in whose name it appears. This may also be termed a holographic manuscript.

Holywell Pornographic literature, such as was sold in Holywell Street at Aldwych.

Holzdeckel German for wooden boards.

Holzschnitt German for woodcut.

Horae The Latin plural for *hora,* meaning hour: a manuscript or printed collection of prayers or other devotions.

Horn book An early type of book designed for children. A tablet, usually of wood, contained a recessed sheet of paper which was protected by a thin sheet of horn. This see-through piece of horn protected the little booklet underneath from the hands of children. Children studied their lessons from horn books well into the first decades of the nineteenth century.

Horn Book A number of books about children's books are published by the Horn Book, Inc., which also publishes a bimonthly journal containing reviews of new books for children. Among the books are *Newbery Medal Books, 1922–1955,* edited by Bertha Mahony Miller and Elinor Whitney Field ($10) and *Caldecott Medal Books, 1938–1957,* also edited by Miller and Field ($10). A sequel to these two volumes is *Newbery and Caldecott Medal Books, 1956–1965,* edited by Lee Kingman ($10). Three books on illustrators of children's books, all by that title, cover the years 1744–1945, 1946–1956, and 1957–1966, respectively, with various editors ($20 each). A catalogue of these and other publications is available from the Horn Book, 585 Boylston Street, Boston, Mass. 02116.

Hors commerce   French for not-for-sale. Sometimes rendered as *hors de commerce*. As may appear, for example, in the limitation of a press book.

Hot metal   A casting of an entire line of type or of individual characters of type.

Household pests   Books may be attacked by any number of household pests, including cockroaches, mice, termites, and silverfish. The glue and paste which are used in the manufacture of books attract them. Bookworms cause considerably less damage to books than the pests already mentioned.

An occasional close inspection should be made of any valuable books to make sure that they have not become infested. Some experts advise periodic fumigation whether or not evidence of pests has been found.

House proof   An early proof pulled simply for editorial use.

Howes   Wright Howes: *U.S.Iana*, a major reference work in the field of Americana, covering the years 1650–1950 and considered close to invaluable by many book dealers and collectors in this field. Howes codes the prices received for books in recent years, but his information is too out-of-date to be a great deal of help. *U.S.Iana* covers nonfiction; American fiction over substantially the same period is covered in Wright (q.v.). Howes is a singularly good one-book reference for books and documents relating to American history before the Civil War; after that his emphasis, understandably enough, shifts to the story of American western expansion, so that practically anything published in the West has a chance of being in, to the neglect of the type of eastern material previously admitted to the book.

The 1962 second edition of Wright Howes was published by Bowker at $27.50; no longer available, secondhand copies have recently been purchased at auction for as much as $70.

Hundred best   There is apparently quite a fascination in getting up a list of the "one hundred best books." The first such list we know of was compiled by Sir John Lubbock; it appeared in print as the fourth chapter of a book of essays he published in England in 1887. He made up his list from an examination of the books which he had found to be most frequently mentioned with approval in the course of his extensive reading—but he also later confessed that he had sneaked in just a few of his own favorites as well. This list, which had first been delivered as a lecture at the London Workingmen's College, started something of a fad for making up lists. A list offered by Lord Acton was criticized by Sir John as too specialized, but that compiled by a Mr. Shorter seemed rather frivolous. Among the other people who later made up and published their own lists are Somerset Maugham, Arnold Bennett, and Sir Winston Churchill. Since many of the earlier lists were intended as guides for self-education, few novels were included. A. Edward Newton broke the mold by offering a list of one hundred books exclusively made up of novels.

Although none of the lists was offered primarily as a guide to book collectors, this was precisely what they each became. A few avid book collectors even accepted the challenge posed by Dickinson's list of not one hundred, but one thousand best books. The most famous lists, which stand as the greatest challenge to modern book collectors, are the Grolier Lists and Merle Johnson's list of High Spots (q.v.).

Hunter Dard Hunter (1883–1966), the great American authority on paper and its manufacture. Hunter traveled throughout the world studying methods of making paper by hand and wrote extensively on the history of papermaking. Among the books which he printed on his own private press were a biography and a treatise on papermaking—both now collectors' items. Even the trade editions of Dard Hunter's books, now out of print, command steadily high prices.

Huntington The library established by Henry E. Huntington at San Marino, California, to house his magnificent collection of books from all over the world.

Huntsup Slang for a hunting song, ballad, or thus by derivation a book on sporting. Supposed to have come from the first words of the song to rouse sleepers: "The hunt is up . . ."

I

Idem Latin for the same. Used in a book catalogue to indicate that an author's name or book title is the same as for the previous entry.

Illumined (Illuminated) In the old-book trade, the meaning is not bright but decorated, although if gold and bright colors are used the effect can be bright indeed. But in general its meaning is to embellish, as with letters, scrolls, or other fanciful designs, often in gold, and sometimes in red or, less frequently, other colors such as green and blue.

Illustrating Collectors and bookbinders occasionally take a hand in illustrating books which they feel could be made more handsome with some further kind of embellishment. This process is also called extra-illustrating or grangerizing.

Illustrating a volume, in this sense, means inserting or binding in additional portraits, landscapes, sketches, or what have you, supposedly somehow related to the content of the book. Material so bound in can often be identified since the illustrations published with the book are listed in a table of contents whereas those added are not. Furthermore, the added illustrations are often on a heavier paper than the original illustrations, and frequently on a variety of different papers, in different styles, and different mediums. Although some book lovers consider the finished product a mutilation, some collectors make a specialty of books so treated. John Hill Burton, an eminent book-hunter as he termed himself, declared: "The Illustrator is the very Ishmaelite of collectors

158

—his hand is against every man, and every man's hand against him. He destroys unknown quantities of books to supply portraits or other illustrations to a single volume of his own; and as it is not always known concerning any book that he has been at work on it, many a common book-buyer has cursed him on inspecting his own last bargain, and finding that it is deficient in an interesting portrait or two. Tales there are, fitted to make the blood run cold in the veins of the most sanguine book-hunter, about the devastations committed by those who are given over to this special pursuit." Thus, the endeavor to enhance one book sometimes leads to another book's being cannibalized, and it is a wise buyer who carefully checks each plate (illustration) in any expensive book he is thinking of buying.

Illustrators: Bibliographies Two eminently worthwhile bibliographies of American book illustrators are: *A Practical Guide to American Nineteenth Century Color Plate Books*, by Whitman Bennett (New York, 1949), now out of print, containing identifications of more than three hundred and thirty selected American color-plate books, each of which has at least three full-page plates colored by hand or by lithography; and *American Book Illustrators*, by Theodore Bolton, consisting of a bibliographic check list of one hundred and twenty-three artists (New York, 1938), now also out of print.

Illustrators in magazines Many illustrators of books have also made extensive appearances in magazines, not only illustrating articles and stories but in advertisements. In some cases, book illustrators have even designed magazines. Therefore, any truly comprehensive collection of the works of such an illustrator would have to include his various appearances in periodicals. There is now a growing number of magazine bibliographies available for quite a few modern artists.

Illustrierte Ausgabe German for illustrated edition. *Illus-*

trierter Buchumschlag, in German, means pictorial wrappers.

Imperfect   Lacking leaves.

Imperial folio (Imp Fol)   A British book size, 22 x 15½ inches.

Imperial quarto (Imp 4to)   A British book size, 15 x 11 inches.

Imposition   The placement of pages to be printed in the correct order on a sheet of paper so that they will appear in proper sequence when the sheet is folded to constitute a signature. Books are generally printed so that eight pages or multiples thereof are laid out for printing on one side of a large sheet of paper.

Impressa littera Venetiana   Fine printing, after that achieved in the city of Venice between 1470 and 1520.

Impression   Called the kiss of the ink on paper: actually, (1) the process of printing with ink on paper, (2) the printed copy which is thus produced, or (3) a single run of the press from one setting of type, without alterations, changes, or corrections. When people in the old-book trade speak of impression, they generally mean it in the last sense. "The first impression has a misspelling which was subsequently caught and corrected for the rest of the run." (See also **Issue**.)

Imprimatur   Literally, let it be printed, from the Latin. The imprimatur is a license to print, an authorization granted by either the church or the state. Many sixteenth- and seventeenth-century books have an imprimatur leaf at the beginning of the book stating that permission has been granted for this particular book to be published and that, therefore, there will be no penalty attached to being caught reading it.

Imprimé   French for printed matter. *Imprimerie,* in French, means a printing office.

Imprint   The information which is customarily contained in a book identifying its source: publisher's name and place and date of publication. This information is usually to be found at the bottom of the title page, on the copyright page, or sometimes at the end of the book. The history of printing in America can be studied through a series of successive imprints.

By association, imprint can also mean any printed work. In this sense, for example, early imprints are collected. And, in an interesting combination of the two meanings of imprint, first imprints of particular towns, territories, or states are frequently collected.

Im selbstverlag Erschienen   German for privately printed. "Not for sale" is *nich im Handel.*

Incunabula   Books printed before 1501, or, roughly, during the first fifty years after the invention of printing and the publication of the Gutenberg Bible, in 1455. The literal meaning of the term is swaddling clothes. During the seventeenth and eighteenth centuries, collectors might refer to these books as fifteeners. In spite of the fact that any book from this period must have considerable interest for us, not all are equally valuable, and by now most of the truly valuable books have disappeared into the great private collections which have in turn become for the most part the foundations of great library collections. The term incunable is sometimes used to refer to a single book of this period.

Index   An alphabetically arranged list of the names and subjects occurring in a book, customarily placed at the end of the book and containing page references. Not the same as a table of contents, which usually is placed among the front matter of a book and contains a list of subjects as they appear. Within the Roman Catholic Church, index has the particular meaning of a list of prohibited books.

One specific meaning of index is the five-year Index to *American Book Prices Current*, which is published by the Columbia University Press. This is a priced summary of literary properties sold at auction in the United States, Canada, and England during five successive seasons. The most recent *Index*, to August, 1970, has been issued in two volumes, at $100.

India paper   An especially thin paper sometimes called Bible paper, often employed for books with thousands of pages, such as a dictionary. India paper is also used for pulling proof on engravings. Sometimes engravings on India paper are mounted in well-wrought books, and the paper is so fine that its presence seems no more than a breath of color; a bold fingernail may identify it, however.

Informal layout   A pattern or arrangement of type, or type and decoration together, in which an approximate balance is achieved by the free distribution of the elements around an imaginary pivot—rather than through a one-to-one balance.

Inhalt   German for contents. *Inhaltsübersicht*, in German, means the list of contents, as does *Inhaltsangabe*.

Inhaltsübersicht   German for list of contents.

Initial   Not simply the first letter in the first word in a paragraph, but this letter set in type larger than the rest of the body type. It is made larger not so much for emphasis as for decorative effect, is sometimes fancifully embellished or illuminated, and sometimes in limited-edition books is hand-lettered and hand-illuminated. Such an initial letter may be called a rising letter or an inset initial.

Inlaid   With decorative inserts in the binding. Sometimes a leather of a different type or color is laid into the binding. Even a different substance, such as ivory, can be used. The result, if there are many pieces inlaid, can be a mosaic binding. Sometimes the word inlaid is used to indicate that a pictorial paper label is set in.

In losen Bogen   German for in sheets, not yet bound.

Inner dentelle   (See **Dentelle**.)

Inner joint   The place where the spine of a book is joined to the body of the book, allowing the cover to swing; more properly called the hinge.

In paper   With paper wrappers rather than a book in hard cover. These paper wrappers are an integral part of the book, not a dust jacket which, although also made of paper, is simply an external wrap-around. A book in a dust jacket is not properly called "in paper."

In parts Published serially. Many novels in Victorian England, for example, were published in parts. Charles Dickens' *The Posthumous Papers of the Pickwick Club* was published in twenty parts, in nineteen sections, between 1836 and 1837. As long ago as 1939 a collector's set in mint condition brought almost $30,000; today even a badly defective copy might be worth several hundred.

Warning: any book which was published in parts is likely to have more points than a dog has fleas . . . particularly if the author is Dickens—one bibliography devotes forty-two pages to describing the hundreds of points just for the English first edition.

One of the ways of detecting a book which was originally issued in parts and then bound is to look carefully at the inner margin, where the original stabholes for stitching can sometimes still be seen after the original wrappers and stitching have been removed and the parts assembled for binding.

In print Copies still available for sale, from the publisher even if nowhere else.

In quires Folded into sections for a book but not yet bound.

Inschrift German for inscription.

Inscribed copies, collecting A simple and ingenious way of collecting inscribed copies from living authors has been described by Frederick W. Skiff in his *Adventures in Americana* published in 1935. In 1916 he had been looking over his fairly extensive collection of Americana when it occurred to him that the collection would be vastly more interesting if he had inscribed copies; he took the chance of mailing books to their authors, with requests that they sign them. To his delight, almost without exception he got his books back, signed, in a few instances with a few extra books as well.

Since then, however, authors have become more wary, their publishers more protective. Perhaps the only way to systematically collect inscribed copies is to follow the book auction sales, where these books frequently turn up.

Inscribed copy   A copy of a book which its author has signed. Not all inscribed copies are necessarily of any particular value. Some authors, as a matter of fact, John Galsworthy, for example, seem to have signed literally thousands of copies of their own books. Charles P. Everitt, who wrote about old books, once said that whereas an inscribed copy of George W. Childs' *Recollections* might be worth in the neighborhood of $1.50, he himself would be willing to pay considerably more if ever he found that rarity, a copy which its author had *not* inscribed.

The value of the author's signature increases in proportion to the warmth of the sentiment with which he inscribes the book. "Good wishes" can hardly be compared to "In memory of that wonderful night."

Book catalogues usually make the careful distinction between signed and inscribed, the latter meaning not only signed but also with a personal message. A presentation copy is one which is inscribed to someone in particular; a book signed for an autograph party would not qualify.

Inserted leaves   Usually, pages of advertisements added to a book after it was printed but before it was bound, although inserted leaves could contain any type of printed matter. Inserted leaves often provide important bibliographical information and make it possible to trace the publication of a book through an edition from issue to issue. Great confusion can arise, however, since leaves of advertisements which are inserted are frequently dated, as it is quite possible for a printer to pick up a batch of earlier ads to insert rather than the latest off the press.

Inside margin   Also known as the gutter; the edge of the page toward the binding. Also, on a book which is covered with leather, the inside margin may be the edge of the front and back covers where the leather is turned over around the sides.

In slip   Type matter which is assembled but not yet made up into pages.

Insurance   In the old-book trade the risk of the transport of books is customarily assumed by the sender unless specified otherwise. However, it generally is so specified. Usually the purchaser of books who desires to have them shipped to him will be asked to pay not only for the shipping costs, but for the cost of packaging for shipment and for the insurance for mailing. Information on this may be contained in the fine print of a book catalogue—so be sure to check. These costs can add considerably to the expense of buying a set of twenty-four volumes, an encyclopedia, or a long run of a magazine.

Intagliography   A method of printing which is the opposite of letterpress: the design to be printed is incised below the printing surface rather than raised.

Investing in books   Recent articles have indicated that there is a growing interest in buying books—old and rare books—for investment. Economic authorities have pointed out that old books have been consistently escalating in value at the rate of 10–20% per year—potentially not a bad rate of return for capital invested! However, there are several snags. The books which constantly increase in value are those with "a certain eternity," and many of those already command a very high price to start. Many of the most popular authors and subjects already have their coterie of highly experienced collectors who are way ahead of the amateur just beginning to be interested in book collecting. However, there are new fields which are entirely open and should be attractive to those who have an interest in books qua books as well as in finding relatively safe investments. Some authorities believe that children's books will become much more important in the future, and that relatively recent authors such as Dr. Seuss and a wide variety of other illustrators will be eagerly collected. Science fiction is another category of rapidly growing interest. Comic books already have their own passionate collectors, and prices for first editions of early classics are beginning to range up into the hundreds. Industrial and commercial materials of all sorts are now being snapped up: an advertising brochure for the Auburn, instructions for operating a new type of loom, a salesman's sample book, early advertisements, brochures, catalogues. But the one firm caveat in buying old printed material of any sort is to insist upon very good to fine condition—that is, if you are buying for investment; and to make sure that it remains in the same good condition.

Ironed morocco   A kind of smooth leather.

Issue   A term which is used to differentiate between the first part of an edition (first issue) which is then followed by the second issue. The two issues may be different by no more than a broken comma, or there may be dozens of issue points involved. According to Herbert Faulkner West in *Modern Book Collecting*, "An 'issue' may be defined as all copies of an edition which are put on the market at one time, if differentiated by some substituted, added, or subtracted matter from those copies of the same setting of the type which were put on the market at other times. Copies must actually have been issued before the word can be used." Issues may be differentiated not only by typographical changes but by changes in binding, printer's imprint, or inserted advertisements.

Issue point   Any change made in the process of publishing a book which helps to identify a particular issue. It may occasionally happen that most of the copies of an old book which are ever seen are first issue, whereas it is the second or even third issue which is rare and therefore valuable. The only way to know for sure is to check the appropriate bibliography.

Italics   Cursive type, characterized by letters slanting to the right, *thus*. This is a style of type which was developed for economy's sake, in part. The earliest books, set in black letter, which took up a great deal of space on the page, were fairly large, cumbersome, and also expensive. Aldus Manutius, around 1500, cut a new font of type which more clearly resembled the informal handwriting of his day than the heavy type which was then used for books. It was fairly easy to read, and more words could be squeezed into the same amount of space, making possible a reduction in the size of books. The new style was an important breakthrough for its day, quickly bringing more reading material, more conveniently, to larger numbers of people.

J

Jacket A loose paper wrapper for a book which is not, however, an integral part of the book but may be removed. Also known as a dust jacket, book jacket, and dust wrapper. (See also **Wrappers**.)

Jahrbuch German for yearbook or annual. *Jahrgang*, in German, is year of publication. *Jahrbuch der Auktionspreise* is book auction records.

Jansenist Simple: referring to a book binding, a style simple to the point of severity, popular in the late seventeenth century in France.

Japanese paper A fine paper, light and strong, sometimes used for fine etchings.

Japanpergament In German, Japanese vellum.

Japon Japanese vellum: a smooth, glossy paper, buff in color, which since it looks like vellum is frequently used for de luxe editions and limited editions. It has, however, the very considerable disadvantage that it is almost impossible to remove any marks.

Jenson Nicolaus Jenson (c. 1420–1480), a Frenchman (in spite of that name) who developed a kind of type face which was different from that used by Gutenberg and other of the earliest printers. The original face had been based on Gothic hand-lettering; Jenson, working in a printshop in Venice in the 1470's, produced a new shape of character which was closer to the Roman style of lettering. This style has been called Venetian; and the books in which Jenson first demonstrated its use are today considered models of simplicity and beauty. According to the eminent printing historian Joseph Blumenthal, "His type has great clarity and liveliness, and at the same time an element of divine repose."

Joe Miller   A Joe Miller is a joke book.

Johnson, Merle   An influential figure in the history of book collecting, Merle Johnson (always known by his full name rather than simply his last) is the author of *High Spots in American Literature*. This was first published in a limited edition of 750 copies in 1929 and has since provided an important checklist for collectors and dealers. Merle Johnson is also the author of a book on American first editions, a bibliography of Mark Twain, and a checklist of the works of James Branch Cabell. (See **High Spot,** *American First Editions*)

Joint   The exterior junction of the spine and the sides of a book. In the construction of a book, the groove made at the edge of the back to receive the ends of the millboard which constitutes the covers. Hinge, on the other hand, is the interior junction. In a cloth, leather, or paper-covered book the joint may show wear without necessarily meaning that the hinge has as yet become weak.

Joint author   The co-author of a work.

Judaica   Printed works dealing with the history of the Jews or with some particular aspect of Jewish culture. Judaica is sometimes defined extremely broadly, to include, for example, such items as the first few lines in Hebrew to appear in print in the United States—in the works of the early Protestant divine Cotton Mather, some believe. A standard work on Judaica is *An American Jewish Bibliography*, published in 1926, by A. S. W. Rosenbach, and now available from Kraus Reprint at $14.

Justification   In printing, arranging exactly for an even margin. "Is that copy justified (lined up properly)?"

Juvenile   A book written expressly for children.

Juvenilia   The output of a youthful author. Many mature authors have wished that their juvenilia might be forgotten.

K

Kalbleder German for calfskin, used for bookbinding.

Karton German for a cancel leaf: a supplementary leaf inserted to correct a printed text.

Keepsake A type of gift book which was especially popular in the United States during the first half and into the middle of the nineteenth century. Such books were usually elaborately illustrated, often in color, fancifully printed, and decoratively bound. Unlike the more recent coffee table book of somewhat similar purpose, they were mostly octavo in size. A keepsake which proved particularly popular might then become an annual publication. Although the keepsakes were a particular type of publication specifically aimed at the ladies' market—containing sentimental tales illustrated with plates showing ladies in fashionable dress or floral arrangements—there were also keepsakes which were publications simply commemorating some special event.

Kelmscott The first of the modern private presses to be concerned with book production per se and with the book itself as an art form. The press was established by William Morris in 1891, and in the brief seven years during which it functioned it became well-known for its handsomely designed books with their characteristically wide margins, decorations furnished by Morris himself, and the illustrations by Burne-Jones. The Kelmscott *Chaucer* has been hailed as one of the greatest triumphs of English typography. In the seven years, only fifty-two works, in sixty-seven volumes, were produced.

Key A book containing the answers to problems or puzzles, or the source material for another book, as the *Key to Uncle Tom's Cabin*, which documents the sources for the book by Harriet Beecher Stowe.

King James The authorized Anglican Bible of 1611.

Kleine Schrift Pamphlet in German.

Kompilator Compiler in German.

Kopfgoldschnitt In German, top edge gilt. *Kopfschnitt* is top edge.

Kopftitel Title, or heading, in German.

Kostümwerk In German, costume plates, or other illustrations showing costumes.

Kunst In German, fine arts.

Kupferstich In German, copper engraving.

L

L Roman numeral for 50.

Labels Small strips of paper or leather affixed to the covers of a book. Paper labels, which have been in use since about 1790, have been rendered actually unnecessary since it is now possible to stamp a book's title directly onto a cloth binding. However, both leather and paper labels are still sometimes used for decorative effect, usually on the more expensive trade edition books or on the books issued by a private press. In any old book, the label is very likely to be chipped or worn, and although this should be mentioned if the book is to be sold, it can scarcely ever be considered a serious defect.

Lacing The cords, in bookbinding, which help attach the boards to the back of a book.

Lacuna A break or gap in text caused by damage to the book. Plural, lacunae.

Laid Laid paper is distinguished by the parallel lines which have been watermarked into it. The general effect may be compared to ribbing. Laid stock, on the other hand, may be paper which is manufactured to look like a handmade paper. In handmade paper these characteristic lines are unavoidable.

Laid in Inserted into a book but not attached to the book in any way. Old letters, clippings, and personal notes are sometimes found laid into old books. Such ephemera need not necessarily add to the value of the book—give a sigh, and toss away the pressed pansies, the locks of hair. However, occasionally some piece of writing laid in will prove to be a letter from the author, or a comment by some famous person on the book. Never throw away anything you discover laid in without first examining it!

Landkarte German for map.

Lantern land An imaginary country.

Lapped Lapped covers are those with an overhang at the edges, such as are found in Bibles of the traditional type.

Large copy A large copy—or large-paper copy—is a book with extra-wide margins, not necessarily a physically large volume, since it is possible to have a 32mo large-paper edition. A large-paper edition is usually from the same plates as the original edition, if there was an earlier one. The overall effect of the type on the page is more generous and therefore more elegant. Private press books are frequently issued in large paper, for example.

Large crown octavo (L Cr 8vo) A British book size, 8 x 5½ inches.

Larned J. N. Larned: *The Literature of American History: a Bibliographical Guide.* This important basic work was published in 1902 and is still available, from Ungar, at about $12.50. It was published under the auspices of the American Library Association.

Law binding A plain sheepskin binding, which was once extensively used for law books in the United States. Law bindings, unfortunately, do not wear as well as other types of leather bindings.

Layout A design for typographic arrangement.

Leaf The bibliographer's term for what is commonly considered a single "page" in a book. A leaf consists of two pages numbered odd on the recto, even on the verso. The leaf's recto is its top when the book is lying open; the underside is the verso. Leaf is abbreviated l, and leaves ll.

Leaf book A book which contains a few or possibly many leaves inserted from some early printed work.

Leaflet A small printed statement, either a single sheet unfolded or folded once only. Modern advertising throw-aways are often in the form of leaflets; in the old-book business, however, the value of a printed work need have no relation to its size or expected durability, and a leaflet published at Philadelphia stating a pacifist position during the American War for Independence may be more valuable than a book published the same year.

Leather, artificial   Often hard to tell from the real thing, especially when the artificial leather is manufactured by engraving the impression of real leather onto a plastic surface. Some scrupulous book dealers, in a quandary as to whether a book is indeed covered by real leather or not, will state it is "leatherette" assuming that it must be imitation. With any modern book except the most expensive, this is probably a realistic assumption, since the cost of leather has recently become prohibitive. Bindings made of cloth in imitation of leather are considerably easier to detect. Check the wear-points on the binding: if cloth, it will eventually start to fray or show the telltale interlacing pattern of the cloth.

Leather bindings   Some collectors are interested only in books which are bound in leather. Book dealers and auction houses cater to this with listings under the general term "bindings" rather than author or subject, but such a subject heading is generally the tipoff that the elegance of the binding may be the sole selling-point.

Leather, because of its variety and many decorative possibilities, the pleasant feel of it in the hand, its great durability—and its great expense—has always been favored for luxury bindings. The leather which is most customarily used for bookbinding comes from sheep, goat, and calf, although sealskin and pigskin are occasionally used also. (See also the various kinds of leather listed under **Morocco, Calf, etc.**)

Leather bindings, care of   The first rule in the care of leather bindings, all experts seem to agree, is that some sort of regular treatment is vastly better than no treatment at all. Plain Vaseline may be applied to leather to keep it soft and pliant, although it should be thoroughly rubbed off so that only the slightest residue remains, otherwise the book may become gummy. The exercise of the greatest care in applying Vaseline or any other preparation is necessary to prevent smearing the edges of the book. An excellent book on the care and repair of books, including leather bindings, is Carolyn Horton's *Cleaning and Preserving Bindings and Related Materials*, second edition, revised, published by the Library Technology Program of the American Library Association of Chicago in 1969, at $4.50. The broad overall advice this book has for the amateur, however, is to seek the help of a professional unless one can make a careful study of the particular problem at hand before trying to salvage any worn or damaged leather binding.

Leatherette Cloth, paper, or plastic made to look like leather—and sometimes very hard to tell from real leather.

Leather spine labels Now sufficiently rare that they deserve special mention. Very few modern books are issued with leather labels, and any old books which still have their original labels in good condition are especially attractive to collectors. Leather labels chip easily.

Lebensbeschreibung In German, biography.

Legend The explanatory or descriptive material which accompanies a book illustration and is usually placed near it.

Leg-o'-mutton school That class of authors who, in return for patronage, praise their patrons in extravagant terms in their works.

Leinen German for cloth.

Letterpress The oldest method of printing: ink is applied to a raised surface on a block of wood or metal, and the image is transferred directly from the surface of this block to paper, under pressure. Most of the books which enter the old-book trade have been printed by letterpress. The offset method of printing did not go into production on a large scale until shortly after 1900, and letterpress, still the darling of the private presses, has continued to be used.

Levant A kind of morocco, made of South African or Cape goatskin. Tough and hardwearing, it is characterized by a fairly coarse grain. It may be dyed a variety of colors, and is often used for large books. Purists may say "levant-morocco."

Libraire French for bookseller. *Libraire antiquaire* is an old-book dealer.

Library binding A type of cloth binding which has been customarily ordered by libraries for books which will receive hard wear in circulation. Library buckram is the same thing.

Library edition An edition which is intended for library circulation; or an edition which is printed in large and eminently readable type.

Library gilt Top edge gilt.

Library stamp The mark made by a library in a book to indicate that the library is the owner. This is sometimes a purple rubber stamp, sometimes an embossed stamp made without ink. A library stamp on a title page diminishes the value of the book.

Lichtdruck German for photoengraving.

Lieferung German for part or issue, or section.

Limited edition One definition of a limited edition is an edition of no more than 4000 copies. For many private presses, however, this seems absurdly large, since it is two, or in some cases twenty, times the number of copies issued in limited edition. Therefore, a more comprehensive definition might be any edition of anywhere from a few to several thousand copies. Whereas the very small presses, particularly those where the books are set and printed by hand, cannot physically print more than a few copies, many of the large commercial presses arbitrarily decide to issue a limited edition, or several, perhaps in different bindings, along with the trade edition. A modern limited edition carries a statement of the number of copies run. This statement is sometimes to be found among the front matter, but just as often at the very back of the book. In examining any handsomely presented book it is wise to search carefully for any statement of limitation, which is, of course, proof of the exclusiveness of the book and therefore important. Furthermore, many limited edition books not only state the limitation but number each copy, and frequently, as well, the author or the illustrator or both sign the book.

The history of limited editions goes back as far as possible—to the Gutenberg Bible, which came out both on paper and, in more limited edition it is presumed, vellum. Some of the most beautiful books in the world have come out in limited edition; some collectors would say all, in limited edition.

Yet John T. Winterich, an eminent connoisseur and authority on old books, once pronounced the issuance of books in limited edition "a genteel racket." He thought that the practice was intended more to line the pockets of the publishers than to increase the public's enjoyment of good books. In this connection it is probably worth noting that some publishers have been thought to run their so-called limited editions through the presses more than once; the only protection the buyer has is to know his publisher's reputation.

Limited Editions Club Books A series of books made available by subscription by the Limited Editions Club, beginning in 1929. In editions of no more than 2000, these are re-issues of the classics and notable for their handsome illustrations, the excellence of their typography, the quality of their paper and bindings. Some of the illustrations in these books are hand-colored, and most are signed by the artists. The books were originally available by subscription only, but there is now a steady small flow of them through the old-book market. Limited Editions Club books, which were issued boxed, are expected to be in close-to-mint condition. Prices for some few individual books may be as low as $20, but many are valued at $35, $50, or a great deal more.

The first Limited Editions Club book to appear was *The Travels of Lemuel Gulliver* by Jonathan Swift. The book was designed by George Macy, the prime mover of the Club, and coincidentally appeared on that October day in 1929 when the stock market crashed. The second publication was Walt Whitman's *Leaves of Grass*, a not entirely successful combination of the delicate typography of Frederic Warde with the robust text. The third was something of a prank: *The Travels of Baron Munchausen* which carried an introduction by Carl Van Doren condemning lying, and, surprisingly enough, illustrations by John Held, Jr., famous for his flappers. By the end of its first ten years of publication the Club had produced one hundred and seventeen books, seven "special publications," and a thirty-seven volume Shakespeare. This is the basic collection of Limited Editions Club books.

However, there are, in addition, later publications attractive to collectors, including the 1944 *Aeneid* in covers of brocaded cloth, the Bruce Rogers *Aesop's Fables*, the Hans Christian Andersen, Confucius (in a wooden box with inlaid title), *The Call of the Wild* bound and slip-cased in lumbermen's shirting, and *The Dolphin*, Numbers One-Three, the third in particular, a history of the printed book.

Among the Limited Editions Club books commanding the most money today are Joyce's *Ulysses*, illustrated by Henri Matisse; *Conquest of Mexico* by Bernal Diaz del Castillo, illustrated by Miguel Covarrubias; a copy of Aristotle with twenty portraits in line by Leonard Baskin; the *Canterbury Tales*, illustrated by Arthur Szyk; the *Journals of Lewis and Clark*, in two volumes; and *Aristophanes' Lysistrata* with Picasso illustrations, but this is not an exhaustive list.

Limitierte Auflage   Limited edition, in German.

Limp   A highly descriptive term for a kind of leather binding which is not based on boards. Once popular for slim volumes of poetry, limp leather is today considered something of an affectation.

Lined In bindings: having a ruled line running around the edge of the covers of a book.

Line engraving As differentiated from half-tone engraving—a method of photoengraving used when the image consists only of lines, type characters, and other solid black areas, without grey or in-between tones. For example, pen and ink drawings.

Liners End "papers" not made, however, of paper, but of silk or leather. (See also **End papers.**)

Linotype A machine which sets type from a keyboard similar to that of a typewriter. Keyboard linecasters assemble type automatically when actuated by the keys of the linotype machine.

Literaturangabe German for bibliographical reference.

Lithography A method of printing by "writing on stone." The process consists of sketching a design on stone with a greasy substance, wetting the entire surface of the stone with water (the greased surface resists the water), rolling on an ink which then coats the design but does not spread to the moist blank area, and finally taking an impression by pressing a sheet of paper onto the surface of the stone. Currier and Ives were among those who demonstrated the possibilities in this process. Offset lithography—which was apparently discovered quite by accident—is a widely used modern printing process by which an image is lithographed onto a rubber blanket and from there transferred to the paper.

Little magazine The little magazine is primarily a phenomenon of the twentieth century, although it was anticipated as early as 1840–44 by the publication of *The Dial*, edited by Margaret Fuller and Ralph Waldo Emerson. A renaissance of the little magazine dates from 1910, but it received its full impetus from publication of *The Little Review*, published by Margaret Anderson from 1914 through the spring of 1929. These magazines, many of tiny circulation and most of them very short-lived, are now enthusiastically collected. One reason is that many authors who later became well-known made their start on the pages of some little magazine.

A good source book on this subject is *The Little Magazine: A History and a Bibliography*, by Frederick J. Hoffman, Charles Allen, and Carolyn F. Ulrich, published by the Princeton University Press in 1946. The various kinds of little magazines have included, according to the editors, those founded by "editorial barkers" who announced the wonders to be found inside their tents, and those founded to announce that "the world is going this way or that and that therefore a new literature must be founded to celebrate tendencies or to hasten the advent of a new dispensation." A third type, however, is eclectic, exhibiting "a smiling generosity to many types of literary novelty" yet discreetly noncommittal as to their ultimate worth.

Livre   French for book. *Livraison* is part or issue; or section of a larger work. In French, *livre de raison* is a diary; *livre d'occasion*, a secondhand book; and *livre minuscule*, a miniature book.

Local collection   A collection of books all on the subject of one locality, such as a city or a county, territory, or state.

Log book   A diary for recording information day-by-day, especially for a ship at sea.

Longitudinal title   A type of backstrip title for a book especially popular at the end of the seventeenth century, in which the title of the book is printed on a separate leaf and then cut out and pasted along the spine rather than across it. Occasionally, though not often, such longitudinal titles are still found intact in old books. However, today the meaning of this term has somewhat altered to indicate any book title which runs the length of the spine rather than across.

Loose   The hinges of a book may become loose and when this happens the book itself, its covers, or its binding may all then be described as loose. A book which is loose will wobble in the hand as it is moved gently forward and back. However, some old-book catalogues employ the word "loose" in the sense of detached rather than weak or becoming detached. A front or back cover described as loose may in fact, therefore, have entirely parted company from the spine. Any book described as having a loose back may in fact have a backstrip which has become at least partially unglued.

Lose German for unsewn.

Lose im Einband German for shaken; loose in the binding.

Lot A single item in a book dealer's or auctioneer's catalogue. There may be as many as one to several to even a hundred books included in the one sale number; it all, however, constitutes only one lot.

Lowndes W. T. Lowndes: *Bibliographer's Manual of English Literature.* A basic reference work, in four volumes, published in London in 1864. The first and, in some respects, still the only comprehensive conspectus of rare books of English origin.

Luxuseinband German for a deluxe binding. *Luxus-Ausgabe* is a deluxe edition.

Lydenberg Harry Miller Lydenberg and John Archer: *Bookbinding, and the Care of Books.* Lydenberg and Archer are also the authors of a second book: *The Care and Repair of Books.* Both are classic treatises of their subject. However, they are both also unfortunately out of print.

M

M One thousand.

M̄ One million.

Machine direction The direction in which the fibers lie in a machine-made paper.

Machine finish A specific kind of finish in paper: not as coarse-textured as paper which is said to have an antique finish, but still too coarse for fine art work. Such a paper has been subjected to no surface polishing.

Macy George Macy, under whose direction the Limited Editions Club books—beginning in October, 1929—pioneered in a printing venture to bring fine editions of the classics to new readers. Each book issued would utilize the talents of a different designer working with any number of fine printing houses in a number of countries, and would utilize the talents of an artist or artists most suitable for the particular book. Macy himself designed the first book, Swift's *Gulliver*. Macy hopefully thought that this might be the first adult edition of *Gulliver's Travels* ever produced. About its illustration, he said "In 1929 . . . the world was unbearably rich and beautiful and we turned to our illustrated books for stark and ugly pictures. Alexander King was the arch-priest of this 'cult of ugliness,' and he gave our first book a set of fierce, savage pictures which would have made Dean Swift roar with pleasure." (See also **Limited Editions Club books.**)

Magazine A literary publication issued at intervals, often monthly or quarterly. An alert collector can sometimes locate the magazine first of the work of some note which preceded its appearance between hard covers. For example, *The Man Without a Country* by Edward Everett Hale made its first appearance in print in *The Atlantic Monthly*, in 1863, two years before publication of the first edition, first issue, in terra cotta wrappers, which today may command about $350. Yet the magazine may still be picked up for about $20—in fine condition—if one is lucky enough to find it.

The magazines which were published in America during the early years of the Republic had almost as hard a time of it as their twentieth-century counterparts. Few copies of the early and often sporadic and short-lived journals have survived. Most are now tucked away in library collections.

However, bound copies of mid-nineteenth-century periodicals are still around, and even some unbound copies, in various conditions. Any volumes for the years of the Civil War find a particularly ready market. There is, furthermore, a continuing brisk market in copies of *Harper's Weekly* up to 1870. The value of individual issues or runs may be very much influenced by the authors and illustrators included.

The trade in twentieth-century magazines is also brisk, especially for the years of World War I, or II, turn-of-the-century fashion magazines, and science fiction and movie magazines from the twenties and thirties. There is a demand for comic magazines issued before 1950, and for the newspaper Sunday comics. Collectors particularly prize early issues of those magazines (such as *Collier's*) which ceased publication some time ago. The first publications of any author who later became well-known are bound to be valuable.

There is a large group of magazines about fifty years old for which the going price is about $3 per issue, although it may be as high as $10. The first issue of any magazine brings more money. (See also **National Geographic** and **Comics**.)

Mainz Psalter An early book printed by Johannes Gutenberg (died c. 1468) and thought by some scholars to be the first printed rather than Gutenberg's Bible (1455) which is generally credited with having been first.

Maioli   Thomas Maioli, a sixteenth-century bibliophile, whose beautiful bookbindings have become prized collectors' items.

Marbled edges   The edges of a book which have been first cut and then decorated with a marbled pattern in colors, often to match boards and endpapers.

Marbled paper   Book paper patterned in color to resemble the veining in marble. The effect is achieved by swirling the ink.

Märchen   German for tale, or story.

Marginal   In or on the margin of a book; rarely, in the old-book trade used in the sense of less than desirable.

Marginalia   Hand-written notations in the margin of a book alongside the text. Even such marginalia as the single word "No" or a wavy line or an arrow should always be mentioned in the description of a book of any value. Marginalia in ink, obviously, constitute more of a defect than in pencil. But of course it may all depend on who did the scribbling: George Bernard Shaw or Susie Q.

The impulse to comment on an author by writing in the margins of a book goes back in history to the invention of printing and even before, to a time when manuscripts were being transcribed by hand. Thus, in the fourteenth century Richard de Bury complained "impudent youths . . . be uncouth scribblers on the best volumes, and, where they see some larger margin about the text, make a show with monstrous letters, and if any other triviality whatsoever occurs to their imagination their unchastened pen hastens at once to draw it out. There the Latinist and the sophister and every unlearned scribe proves the goodness of his pen; a thing which we have seen to be too often injurious to the best of books, both as concerns their usefulness and their price." And as de Bury said back then, well before Gutenberg, books with scribbled comments in their margins are desecrated vessels of learning—and in almost all cases worth a great deal less.

Margined figures Or, marginal figures. Numerals used to indicate the sequence of lines in a printed work or, sometimes, the number of words to a line. Marginal figures may be employed, for example, in counting off lines of poetry. Such figures are sometimes cited in identifying the location of edition or issue points.

Margins As a matter of aesthetics, wide margins are often preferred in a book. Limited edition books, art books, and other specially designed books frequently will have margins which have been not at all cropped or only slightly cropped.

The inner margin of a page, toward the spine, is the gutter; the others are the outer margins.

Maroquin A leather made from goatskin.

Mechanical binding A coil or ring binding in distinction from a binding which is sewed or glued. Two examples of mechanical binding are the wire coils used on school notebooks and the plastic rings sometimes used on how-to manuals. A dealer in old books has, at least up to the present, never handled books in mechanical bindings. Now, however, collectors are increasingly interested in souvenir programs, advertising matter, instruction manuals, etc., in just this kind of binding which are less than fifty years old.

Medium octavo (M 8vo) A British book size, $9\frac{1}{2}$ x 6 inches.

Medium quarto (Med 4to) A British book size, 12 x $9\frac{1}{2}$ inches.

Mélanges French for miscellaneous works.

Memorabilia Literally, things worth remembering, or noteworthy things, from the Latin. In the book trade, such memorabilia may include documents commemorating an event or other fugitive material. Books classified as memorabilia often contain surprises: for example, a collection of the speeches and poems delivered at a formal state occasion in Boston may contain the first publication of a poem by none other than Oliver Wendell Holmes.

Merle Johnson   (See **Johnson, Merle.**)

Metallic paper   Paper with one or both sides covered with gold or silver foil.

Meynell   Francis Meynell was the proprietor of the Nonesuch Press which in the 1920's broke away from private press tradition to employ commercial printers and binders when deemed advisable, to produce books of superior quality and individualized design in editions as large as 1500 copies, rather than the small number of 300 or so which had been possible when the entire book was handcrafted.

Mezzotint   A print taken from a copperplate, engraved by hand and with even gradations produced by lightly rubbing. The general effect is soft and may be somewhat similar to lithography.

Mildew and mold   Both are the signs of damage wrought by dampness. The combination of dampness and a high temperature creates an environment particularly favorable to the development of these two dangers to books. Books should always be stored in a well-ventilated room which will remain consistently fairly dry. Ideally, the temperature should be maintained at between 65 and 70°F, and the relative humidity should not be over 60%. Unfortunately, this may not be possible under natural climate conditions in many parts of the country. Air conditioning may be the only answer. Some collectors of expensive books maintain their libraries at so cool a temperature, for the sake of their books, that they must bundle up if they intend to spend any time reading in the library.

Both mold and mildew appear as that furry, whitish growth of minute fungi we have all observed at some time on the covers of books stored improperly. Books should not be stored in a basement, or, for that matter, in a garage, in most climates.

Millboard   A strong kind of pasteboard which may be used for the stiff covers of a book. These covers may be enclosed in paper, cloth, or leather.

Mint   A book in mint condition is as fresh, crisp, and bright as the day it was published. The book itself should be free of all signs of use, and if it came with a dust jacket, not only must this still be present but must also show no sign of wear. The price cannot even be snipped off the flap. Of course, there can be no bookplate or inscription. In other words, the book must be just as it came from the binder. Such a book may open a trifle stiffly; it may have the faint odor of a new book still. Very few books come into the old-book market in mint condition; most of those which do are remainders.

The average book collector will probably have few opportunities to see and examine a mint copy of an old and rare book. Such books are generally found in the glass cases of the great museums and libraries. Occasionally close-to-mint copies come into the market; if at auction, the price paid may be extraordinarily high for the particular book.

Mis à jour   French for revised or updated.

Misbound   A book is misbound when a leaf, leaves, or gatherings have been incorrectly placed within the book. A misbound book may be a curiosity, but misbinding seldom increases the value of an old book. Such oddities as pages upside down, or signatures repeated, or a cover misprinted may provide amusing curiosities but they do not mean that the book is worth more.

Mit Gebrauchsspuren   German for worn. *Mit der hand* is German for by hand; *mit-Verfasser* means co-author. *Mit Deckelvergeldung* means with gilt sides (front and back covers decorated in gold color).

Mockup   A layout which is prepared during the early stages of book production to show how the finished book will look. Such mockups practically never survive to come into the old-book market.

Modern British Authors   Title of a book which is subtitled "Their First Editions," compiled by B. D. Cutler and Villa Stiles and published in New York in 1930, since out-of-print.

Still, a fine source to this day of some of the lesser-known authors. "Modern" has of course become something of a misnomer.

Modern first   A first edition published within the last fifty years. Collectors usually demand that a modern first be entirely clean, preferably still with its dust jacket if it was issued with one, and that the jacket also be in very good to fine condition. Many collectors limit their activities to just the first issue of the first edition. Collecting modern firsts has the great advantage that copies of the wanted books are still coming into the market, as people die and their libraries are dispersed, or as old books are simply discarded from home shelves to make room for new ones. The collector of modern firsts can make quite a game of haunting thrift shops, rummage sales, and those often huge book sales held for the benefit of various clubs.

Monograph   A treatise usually of less than full-book length, on one particular subject or aspect of a subject, often highly technical.

Monotype   The Monotype, a machine, casts individual pieces of type (monotype), rather than a line at a time as does the linotype. These characters may then be assembled into lines by hand. Invented by Tolbert Lanston, the Monotype was first produced commercially in 1897.

Montreal Book Auction Records   Released in 1974, a compilation of Canadian auction records for 1967–71 issued in limited edition at $35 by Bernard Amtmann, editor and publisher, 1529 Sherbrooke Street W., Montreal 109, Quebec.

Morison   Stanley Morison (1889–1967), an authority on printing and typography, whose writings, according to Roderick Cave (in *The Private Press*), helped make "typography into an acceptable subject for after-dinner conversation." With Oliver Simon, he published *The Fleuron*, acclaimed as "the greatest of all English typographical journals."

Morocco   A type of leather made from goatskin tanned with sumac. The name comes from its origin in Morocco and the Barbary States. Today, however, it is widely produced and the name is only of historic significance. Morocco has always been a favorite leather with bookbinders, since it is not only extremely durable but supple and easy to work.

Morris William Morris (1834–1896) is considered by many experts in the field of fine books to be the father of modern presswork. A poet and an artist as well as a printing craftsman, Morris entered upon a new career when in his fifties, founding the Kelmscott Press, which issued its first trial page in 1891. The very handsome books which came from this press in the scant seven years of its operation led the way to a strong revival of interest in printing as an art. Morris believed in the sanctity of work done by hand, and his publications combined loving presswork with handsome ornamentation and illustration. "William Morris at the Kelmscott Press not only inaugurated a new era—he created it"—Will Ransom in *Private Presses.*

Morris margin The arrangement of type on a page so that the fore-edge margin is appreciably wider than the inner margin, and the margin at the head of the page much deeper than the margin at the foot. From the practice followed by William Morris.

Mosaic A binding inlaid with other leathers or materials.

Mosher Thomas Bird Mosher (1852–1923) has been acclaimed as the first American to maintain a consistent program of high quality in book publishing. Operating a press at Portland, Maine, he took advantage of a lack of copyright laws to publish pirated editions of living English authors, many of whom are said to have forgiven him because of the high quality of his work.

Mottled calf A light-colored calf for bookbinding, in which a spotty decorative effect has been achieved by splashing with acid.

Mouillé French for damp-stained.

Movable type Type which can be used for printing, first invented in China and apparently used in Korea during the half century before it was independently invented in Europe by Gutenberg. Related devices, used for stamping out impressions in clay—seals and simple stamps—had been used before. "The first dated printing from movable types in Europe is a papal indulgence, printed at Mainz in 1454. The first dated book printed from movable type was a Psalter printed by Fust and Schoeffer at Mainz in 1457. The Mazarin Bible, completed at Mainz not later than 1456, is believed to be the first book printed in Europe from movable type. Gutenberg is believed to have been the printer"—*The Columbia Encyclopedia.*

Mull   A soft cloth, a kind of muslin, used for casing books.

Mutton thumper   A clumsy bookbinder.

Mystery fiction   There is a handbook for collectors of detective-type fiction: *Corpus Delicti of Mystery Fiction: a Guide to the Body of the Case,* by Linda Herman and Beth Stiel, issued by Scarecrow in 1974 at $6.50. This is a handbook for the private collector of detective fiction and for new readers who simply want to know more about the genre. It includes a checklist of reference works, author checklists, and comments, as well as general information. There are fifty authors dealt with in depth.

N

Nachdruck German for a pirated edition. *Nachschlag-werk*, in German, means reference book; *Nachträge*, addenda; and *Nachwort*, epilogue.

Narrow book One of a width which is less than three-fifths of its height.

Nash John Henry Nash (1871–1947) was a book designer and printer who was associated with a group of collectors and printers in California in the early part of the twentieth century. He is especially admired for his four-volume *Dante*, published in 1929.

National Geographic Possibly the one magazine which is most assiduously collected in the United States. It started publication in 1888, going through five different formats for the cover until settling on the now highly familiar bright-yellow border, in 1911. Bound volumes for the years up to 1904 may be worth as much as $50 per year, and any single issue brings at least $10. Volume I, No. 1, could be worth more than $1,000, and certain issues before 1920, in good condition, up to $100. A complete run of the *National "Geog"* would be worth many thousands. Collectors and dealers must be very wary, however, since many issues proved so popular that they came out in reprint, and of course the reprints do not have the value of the originals.

Special issues are collected, as well as runs, and among the specials most eagerly sought are the "Old Russia" issue of November, 1914, that on dogs for March, 1919, on horses for November, 1923, and on shells for July, 1949. The pictorial supplements which were issued along with the magazine between 1903 and 1958 also are collected. N. C. Wyeth was among the artists to be employed on these supplements.

A Collector's Guide to the National Geographic—itself issued in limited edition—is available at $26.25 postpaid from Edwin C. Buxbaum, Box 465, Wilmington, Del. 19899. Its five hundred pages list and evaluate each issue and provide information on the most valuable.

Near-fine   In close-to-fine condition. Some cautious book dealers prefer to use the term close-to-mint and eschew mint; near-fine is used in much the same sense. It seems better to err on the side of understatement than to overpraise.

Neat   In the book trade: of a simple and agreeable appearance.

Nebentitel   German for sub-title.

Neuausgabe   German for a new edition, or a re-issue.

Neudruck   German for reprint.

Neue Umschlag   German for in new wrappers; or in replacement wrappers.

Newbery Award   The John Newbery Award for excellence in children's literature has been made annually since 1922 to the author of the most distinguished contribution to children's books published in the United States during the previous year. The medal is bestowed by the Children's Services Division of the American Library Association. Some collectors of children's books prefer to limit themselves to those books which have won the award or been a runner-up.

Newbery Medal Books

1922	*The Story of Mankind.* Van Loon
1923	*The Voyages of Dr. Dolittle.* Lofting
1924	*The Dark Frigate.* Hawes
1925	*Tales from Silver Lands.* Finger
1926	*Shen of the Sea.* Chrisman
1927	*Smoky, the Cowhorse.* James
1928	*Gay Neck, the Story of a Pigeon.* Mukerji

1930	*Hitty, Her First Hundred Years.* Field
1931	*The Cat Who Went to Heaven.* Coatsworth
1932	*Waterless Mountain.* Armer
1933	*Young Fu of the Upper Yangtze.* Lewis
1934	*Invincible Louisa.* Meigs
1935	*Dobry.* Shannon
1936	*Caddie Woodlawn.* Brink
1937	*Roller Skates.* Sawyer
1938	*The White Stag.* Seredy
1939	*Thimble Summer.* Enright
1940	*Daniel Boone.* Daugherty
1941	*Call It Courage.* Sperry
1942	*The Matchlock Gun.* Edmonds
1943	*Adam of the Road.* Gray
1944	*Johnny Tremain.* Forbes
1945	*Rabbit Hill.* Lawson
1946	*Strawberry Girl.* Lenski
1947	*Miss Hickory.* Bailey
1948	*The Twenty-One Balloons.* du Bois
1949	*King of the Wind.* Henry
1950	*The Door in the Wall.* de Angeli
1951	*Amos Fortune, Free Man.* Yates
1952	*Ginger Pye.* Estes
1953	*Secret of the Andes.* Clark
1954	*And Now Miguel.* Krumgold
1955	*The Wheel on the School.* Dejong
1956	*Carry On, Mr. Bowditch.* Latham
1957	*Miracles on Maple Hill.* Sorensen
1958	*Rifles for Watie.* Keith
1959	*The Witch of Blackbird Pond.* Speare
1960	*Onion John.* Krumgold
1961	*Island of the Blue Dolphins.* O'Dell
1962	*The Bronze Bow.* Speare
1963	*A Wrinkle in Time.* L'Engle
1964	*It's Like This, Cat.* Neville
1965	*Shadow of a Bull.* Wojciechowska

1966   *I, Juan de Pareja.* de Trevino
1967   *Up a Road Slowly.* Hunt
1968   *From the Mixed-Up Files of Mrs. Basil E. Frank-weiler.* Konigsburg
1969   *The High King.* Alexander
1970   *Sounder.* Armstrong
1971   *Summer of the Swans.* Byars
1972   *Mrs. Frisby and the Rats of NIMH.* O'Briend
1973   *Julie of the Wolves.* George
1974   *The Slave Dancer.* Fox
1974   Honor Book: *The Dark Is Rising.* Cooper

New endpapers   The presence of new endpapers in a book is an almost sure sign that the book has been either rebound or recased. Perhaps, then, at the same time that new endpapers are discovered, the book should be examined to make sure that it has not been "made perfect" by the addition of leaves which were not originally with the book, or that some pages have not been dropped out. (Book dealers and collectors learn to be suspicious.)

Newspapers   Individual copies of newspapers reporting great events are collected to some extent. Collecting old newspapers is particularly hazardous because not only have important issues of the papers been saved—but they have also been widely and sometimes very cleverly duplicated. The duplicate may be extremely hard to tell from the original, even down to the paper on which it is printed. There are, for example, over sixty known duplicates which have been issued for the January 4, 1800, issue of the Ulster County *Gazette*, in which the death of George Washington was announced. The Library of Congress has one of the originals, but the likelihood of another showing up now seems pretty remote, although quite a few people may think that their copy is one of the first. Probably almost without exception the truly valuable early newspapers have been gathered up into the big libraries. Meanwhile, the business of duplicating early newspapers and newspaper accounts has reached such proportions that there are now bibliographies for the reprints. A list of the historic issues of newspapers which are most often reprinted—and thus perhaps most often mistaken for the real thing—is available free from the Library of Congress.

Newton   Alfred Edward Newton (1863–1940), American bibliophile and author of numerous books, including *The Amenities of Book Collecting and Kindred Affections* (1918).

Nibbled   By mice, usually.

Nicht im Handel   German for privately printed; not for sale.

Niger   A kind of morocco (goatskin) used for binding books. Niger has an unobtrusive grain and can be dyed handsome colors such as red, orange, and deep green. Another name for Niger is oasis.

Nom de plume   French for pen-name.

Non-book   A pejorative term signifying something dressed in the shape of a book but without substantial reading content. This does not necessarily mean, however, a book which is poorly designed; on the contrary, the chief selling-point for a non-book may be its presentation.

Nonesuch   A British press founded by Francis Meynell with others, to promote excellence in book production. During the 1920's the Press both commissioned books from commercial publishers and produced its own fine examples of presswork.

No place, no date   No place of publication indicated; and no date stated. When the date of publication, or less frequently the place, is not to be located within the book itself, this information is customarily indicated within parentheses. Abbreviated n.p., n.d.

Note   A brief printed comment, often set in smaller type than the body of the work and sometimes appearing at the bottom of the page.

Notizbuch   German for notebook.

Not sold at auction   This comment may appear in a book dealer's catalogue and usually is taken to mean that the book to which it refers has not appeared in the book auction records consulted for the last ten years.

Numbered copies   In limited editions, the total number of copies issued is specified, and it is customary for each individual copy of the book to be numbered in sequence.

Nummer des Bandes   German for volume number.

Nummeriertes Exemplar   German for numbered copy.

O

Oasis In a book which is bound in leather, the oasis is a panel or lozenge set into the cover, sometimes serving as a setting for the title. Or, Niger (q.v.), a kind of goatskin used for bookbinding, a soft leather available in a wide range of colors.

Octavo The most usual size for a book: from an overall size of 5 x 8 inches to 6 x 9 inches. Most hardback novels these days come out in octavo. Octavo (8vo) is one step smaller than quarto (4to) and one larger than duodecimo (12mo). There is also an octavo size in British book measurements: $6\frac{1}{2}$ x $4\frac{1}{2}$ to 11 x $7\frac{1}{2}$ inches. (British sizes are more precise than American.) The literal meaning of octavo is eight leaves, or, the result of folding a single sheet of paper three times to produce eight leaves, or sixteen pages.

Oeuvre French for publication, or work. *Oeuvres complètes* means the complete works.

Offprint A section of a book taken from another publication. An offprint is, thus, an extract; it may be given new pagination even though the text itself is from the original setting of the type.

Offset A page of a book is said to be offset when it bears the print of the page opposite. Illustrations often offset onto the page opposite. The primary function of a tissue guard is to prevent this happening. The fact that a frontispiece illustration has offset onto the title page should be mentioned in the description of the book. Other offsetting, although not as important, probably also should be called to the attention of any prospective buyer.

Offset lithography In distinction from letterpress or gravure printing, printing from a flat surface. The offset printing process was accidentally discovered when an impression was conveyed from a press cylinder onto the rubber blanket of the cylinder and then a sharp image "offset" onto the next piece of paper to be run through the press. The first offset press went into operation in 1904, at Nutley, New Jersey.

Ohne Orte und Jahr German for no place, no date.

Ohne Remissionsrecht German for with all faults; sold as is, not subject to return.

Old/rare Many old-book dealers handle books which are at once both old and rare, but many old books are not rare or even scarce, much less of any value. Old and rare are by no means the same. Most old schoolbooks—spelling, grammar, rhetoric, Latin—have little value in the old-book market; it would, of course, make a difference if a particular book were so rare as to be the only copy in the world—*and* someone wanted it. On the other hand, some fairly recent books are already rarities and thus worth a great deal of money. One example is Sylvia Plath's *Million Dollar Month*, published in 1971 in a first edition limited to 150 copies.

Oldstyle Oldstyle Roman, a group of type faces based on the earliest styles of type. Examples are Caslon and Garamond.

Olla podrida Spanish for a miscellaneous collection of literary odds and ends.

Omnibus A volume containing a large selection of literary works related in some manner to each other.

On approval Sending books on approval is one of the little courtesies in a business justly famous for its many courtesies. Books are generally to be returned within a few days to ten days if not approved. Since many collectors buy by mail, they have no opportunity to examine any books before they actually arrive. However, dealers may quickly tire of any customer who appears to be taking advantage of this privilege to do an excessive amount of browsing at home. Elbert Hubbard once said that he thought a more appropriate term for "on approval" might be "on suspicion."

Onionskin A strong, opaque, paper.

Onlay A decorative device used on the cover of a book. For example, in a leather or imitation-leather binding, other colors or other kinds of materials may be applied, generally by pressure, for their effect.

Ooze leather Split sheepskin which is finished on the flesh side; calf with a velvety finish. Such soft-textured leather is occasionally used for bindings.

Opened edges Edges which have been opened by hand; the sheets slit to open out the pages. Alas, it is all too often done clumsily, resulting in torn pages. A sharp letter-opener is the best instrument for the purpose.

Opening leaves To open the leaves of a book when they are as yet uncut, either a letter-opener or a thin, long knife with a sharp blade but round point should be used. Hold the blade between the pages parallel to the edge to be opened, and cut by pushing the blade forward rather than using a sawing motion. Hold the book steady with your other hand.

However, unless for some very special reason you find it necessary to cut the pages to examine the book more closely, it is better never to "open" the book at all.

Any book which is uncut and unopened may possibly command more money in the old-book market than one which has been opened, however carefully. This is especially true of first editions, which are worth more the closer they are to their original pristine condition, and certainly also true of all press books.

Open-sheet folio A folio-size broadside designed to be read as a double-spread.

Ordinary pages Those in which the depth of the body of type is greater than its width.

Originalausgabe German for first edition.

Original boards The boards in which a book was published. These boards may be uncovered or covered with paper. They may be printed or adorned with a paper label. In an old book, it is often extremely difficult to be sure whether boards which are worn and of old appearance are in fact the original ones or a replacement added some years later. Dealers in doubt about this may prefer to call such boards "contemporary" rather than commit themselves to calling them original.

Original cloth The cloth binding in which a book was published. In nineteenth-century books, the original cloth is often to be vastly preferred, since many of these bindings are fancifully blind-stamped and decorated in gilt.

Original leather The leather binding in which a book was first bound. The original leather could, of course, be sheep, calf, morocco, or some other. When offering an expensive book for sale or auction, a dealer will usually ascertain which kind of leather is used in the book; the use of the term "original leather" may therefore signify that although it is original, it is not in very good condition.

Original-Umschlag German for the original wrapper.

Ornamental dash A line with a filigree center, thus: ⬦

Ornamental type Type adorned with embellishments, thus: 𝒜

Ornamentation The decoration of a printed page by means of special type, ruled lines, fanciful borders (sometimes thick with foliage, fruit, flowers, birds), or the use of initial letters. Many book fanciers prefer the austere beauty of a well-proportioned page without any adornment. However, it is hard to fault the graceful appearance of a handsomely ornamented book such as Howard Pyle's *King Arthur*, and it is undeniable that ornamentation generally adds a great deal to the value of an old book. Some books become collectors' items simply on the basis of their ornamentation, after all.

Ortskunde German for a local history.

Out-of-print No longer available from the publisher. Some books which have apparently recently gone out-of-print may still be secured by writing directly to the publisher.

Out-of-Print Bookfinder A publication addressed to the world of book collecting and available at $20 per year (first class mail, domestic delivery) from P.O. Box 1660, Newark, N. J. 07101. Like *AB* (*Bookman's Weekly*), it runs advertisements for books wanted and books for sale. A special feature is the listing of prices recently realized at auction. Established in 1973 and therefore a newcomer compared with *AB*, it differs from *AB* in that its columns are open to collectors on the same basis as dealers, for search as well as for the advertisement of books for sale.

Out of register The blurry effect which results when the colors in a multicolor print do not line up properly.

Overhang cover A cover of boards in which the boards are somewhat larger than the body of the book which they enclose. Most boards are cut to have a slight overhang, but not too much, since too great an overhang results in the corners being bumped (damaged).

Oxford Oxford University Press, sometimes referred to as the most venerable press in the entire world. Its direct predecessor was established in 1585, and it has been in continuous operation ever since.

Oxford India An excellent printing paper, made for Oxford University Press.

P

Page   One side of a leaf of paper. Abbreviated p.; plural, pp. Or, the assembled type for printing one side of a piece of paper.

Page proof   The sample impression of a page of printing. It is customary to run off a sample impression so that a final check can be made to see if there are any printing errors. A page proof may actually consist of a single sheet of paper with several pages printed on it.

Pagination   The numbering of the pages in a book. Customarily the pagination runs straight through a book, with the exception of the preliminary pages which bear Roman numerals rather than Arabic numbers and, sometimes, the pages on which full-page illustrations appear. The pages with illustrations may be designated by the number of the page opposite.

In a book which constitutes a collection such as five or six plays, each piece in the collection may have a separate pagination. In a book which runs into several volumes, the pagination sometimes continues from one volume to the next. However, since this is not invariably the case, a careful check should always be made in buying a set of books to make sure that they are all present.

Occasionally books which were published before 1820 or so were made up of two or even more separate works. This fact will not appear in the first title page to appear, at the front of the book, but a quick check of the numbering of the pages will show that there must be several works bound in one.

Painted edges   (See **Fore-edge painting.**)

Palimpsest   A paper or parchment prepared for writing and then with the writing wiped off, as on a slate; or, a paper which has been erased and written over. Unscrupulous book dealers have been known to rub out later dates in books or the indication that there should be more than one volume, etc. Holding the page to the light is usually sufficient to expose the attempted fraud.

Pamphlets   Old pamphlets, booklets, advertising brochures, and in fact almost any material over fifty years old and in printed wrappers as issued may have some value in the old-book market. Often such material was ephemeral in nature, and because no one at the time it was issued thought it important, it is now a scarce item. Such material does not always have to be in very good condition. The more specialized and concentrated a collection of such materials, the more valuable.

In general, any material in wrappers printed in one of the eastern states before 1800, or in one of the western states before 1860, will probably have some value. Some of the newer subjects which interest collectors of this type of material are western exploration and the equipment for the move West, the establishment of new industries, fashions in clothes, domestic products, furniture, and china, as well as bicycles, automobiles, airplanes, and cameras.

Paper   A substance made by grinding, beating, and even by boiling vegetable fibers until they become a pulp, then draining out the water to permit this mush to mat together. In more technical terms, paper is a homogeneous formation of primarily cellulose fibers which are held in water suspension on machine wire and bound together by weaving the fibers and with the use of bonding agents. Wood is the basic material from which most paper is made.

If a book contains mention of the kind of paper used, it can be assumed that there is something unusual about it; and it is usually handmade.

Paper is made by hand by the following process: Rags are reduced to a pulp by tearing them into strips and then mixing them with water. Shallow trays which have bottoms made of interwoven wires are then dipped into the vats containing the pulp. When the trays are slowly lifted out, the surplus water drains off, leaving a thin wet sheet of the mash, which is then dried on a woolen blanket. Finally, size is applied, and the paper which results is then ready for use. If you hold a piece of handmade paper up to the light, you will see a number of widely spaced lines in it, crossed by others which are much closer together; you are looking at the pattern which has been created by the wires at the bottom of the papermaker's tray. Paper with these characteristic lines is called laid paper. The wide-apart and thicker lines are the chain-lines, and the thinner lines are called wire-lines. Handmade paper may also have a faint or semi-transparent design which is the insigne of the maker; or the maker may leave an imprint of his name. This is the watermark, and it is formed by incorporating the design into the pattern of wires at the bottom of the tray. The watermark may sometimes incorporate a date, furnishing another reason why it may be important to check the watermark. This date may help establish the fact that a book is a first edition. Many limited-edition books specify the kind of paper used for two runs, one more limited than the other, and the only way of telling whether one has one copy out of ten or one of 500 may be to hold the pages to the light and check the watermark.

Parts (See **In parts.**)

Passepartout An ornamental mat which serves as a frame for a photograph. This mat may be cut out of a page in order to serve this purpose. The arrangement is familiar in photograph albums.

Another meaning of passepartout is the engraved title

which is heavily decorated with an elaborate border which serves for several books, such as a series of musical works all by the same composer or a series of children's books with the title pages the same except for the individual titles in the series.

Pasted-in label Any label which is pasted inside the covers of a book. Such a label is usually designed to show ownership, or to indicate the name of the binder of the book, or perhaps to show the source from which the book was purchased.

Paste-down The outer endpaper, both at the front and at the back of the book, which is pasted to the interior of the cover.

Pell A roll of parchment.

Pencilling Scribbling in a book is generally frowned upon—but not invariably. A great deal depends on who was holding that pencil. Any notes found in a first-edition copy of a book, in the author's own hand, possibly made in preparation for a new edition, would sky-rocket the value of that book. However, question marks and other such doodles by an unknown hand depreciate a book's value.

Another kind of pencilling is that made by some dealer to indicate how much he thinks a book may be worth, whether or not it is a first issue, etc. These jottings appear somewhere in the front matter. The wise book-buyer will take a skeptical attitude.

P.E.N. Club An international society for authors of recognized merit: poets, playwrights, essayists, editors, and novelists.

Perfect "A book is perfect when it retains every scrap of paper, printed or without print, which formed part of the sheets on which it was originally printed, excepting only such part as was cut off by the printer or publisher before the book was issued to the public"—Iolo Williams.

Perfect binding A binding held by a flexible adhesive (glued) rather than stitched. This type of binding was developed to cut the cost of sewing. It is the type of binding now most often used on less expensive books, particularly paperbacks. Occasionally pages have been known to work loose from this so-called "perfect" binding.

Pergament   German for vellum.

Permanent wants   The long-term needs of specialist dealers and collectors, who may advertise for such diversified wants as local histories, science-fiction paperbacks, signed books, dog books, books on the occult, books with color plates, diaries and journals, signed Rockwell Kents, etc. A great deal of the business of the old-book trade is based on the exchange of information about permanent wants. Persons with books to sell may do best by seeking out people who have advertised that they "permanently want" the type of book they have to sell. (See also **Dealers, specialist.**)

Persian   A leather made of the skin of a certain hairy East Indian sheep which is actually called a Persian goat. Thus, it is sometimes erroneously thought to be a kind of morocco (goatskin). Persian is noted for its fine grain.

Peter Parley   Under the pseudonym of Peter Parley, a Boston publisher named Samuel Griswold Goodrich, beginning in 1827 with *The Tales of Peter Parley*, published a series of more than one hundred tales of moral instruction for children. His stories, moreover, broke away from the then prevailing mode of religious didacticism and were instrumental in setting a new style in writing for children.

Goodrich's Peter Parley has become widely known through its incorporation into the title of Jacob Blanck's authoritative book on the history of popular children's literature in America, titled *Peter Parley to Penrod* (see below). Blanck reported in his book that the only copy of Goodrich's pioneer work that he had ever seen was in the collection at Harvard University.

Peter Parley to Penrod   A bibliographical description of the best-loved American juveniles, compiled by Jacob Blanck, published in 1938 by R. R. Bowker and now available in a reprint of the 1956 edition, published by the Mark Press of 16 Park Place, Waltham, Mass. 02154, at $15. Blanck's book spans the period from publication of Griswold's *Peter Parley* in 1827 to Booth Tarkington's *Penrod* in 1914, and actually somewhat beyond (yielding something to the delights of alliteration). The last book in the series reviewed is actually Will James' *Smoky the Cowhorse*, which was published in 1926. This extension permitted the inclusion of such recent favorites as *The Story of Dr. Dolittle* by Hugh Lofting, and *Rootabaga Stories* by Carl Sandburg, as well as *Tarzan of the Apes* by Edgar Rice Burroughs. Blanck also provides a list of what he calls "border-line selections." Most important, full bibliographic information is provided for all of Blanck's first-line choices, and therefore this slim book has become a prime resource for identifying first-edition copies of American juveniles.

The following titles are those appearing in Blanck's *Peter Parley to Penrod*. Author's names are given as they appeared on the title page, except where parentheses are used to indicate the author where no name appeared.

"Best-loved American Juvenile Books"

1827	*The Tales of Peter Parley.* Goodrich
1834(?)	*Rollo: Learning to Talk.* Abbott
1851	*The Wide, Wide World.* Warner (Wetherell)
1852	*A Wonder-Book for Boys and Girls.* Hawthorne
1852	*Queechy.* Warner (Wetherell)
1852	*Robert and Harold/or The Young Marooners.* Goulding
1853	*Tanglewood Tales, for Boys and Girls* Hawthorne
1854	*The Lamplighter.* (Cummins)
1855	*The Boat Club.* Oliver Optic (Adams)
1855	*The Age of Fable.* Bulfinch
1859	*The Age of Chivalry.* Bulfinch
1860	*Seth Jones; or, the Captives of the Frontier.* Ellis

1861	*The Seven Little Sisters Who Live on the Round Ball that Floats in the Air.* (Andrews)
1863	*Faith Gartney's Girlhood.* (Whitney)
1864	*Cudjo's Cave.* Trowbridge
1864	*Little Prudy.* May (Clarke)
1865	*Helen Lester.* "Pansy" (Alden)
1865	*Little Prudy Series/Dotty Dimple.* May (Clarke)
1865	*The Man Without a Country.* (Hale)
1866	*Hans Brinker; or, the Silver Skates.* Dodge
1867	*Elsie Dinsmore.* Farquharson (Finley)
1867	*The Gun-Boat Series/Frank on the Lower Mississippi.* Castlemon (Fosdick)
1868	*Stories of the Gorilla Country.* Du Chaillu
1868	*Ragged Dick; or, Street Life in New York with the Boot-Blacks.* Alger, Jr.
1868	*Little Women.* Alcott
1869	*Elm Island Stories/Lion Ben of Elm Island.* Kellogg
1870	*Ting–a–Ling.* Stockton
1870	*An Old-Fashioned Girl.* Alcott
1870	*The Story of a Bad Boy.* Aldrich
1871	*Little Men . . .* Alcott
1871	*Tattered Tom; or, the Story of a Street Arab.* Alger, Jr.
1871	*Jack Hazard and His Fortunes.* Trowbridge
1873	*What Katy Did.* Coolidge (Woolsey)
1874	*The Young Moose Hunters, a Backwoods-Boy's Story.* Stephens
1875	*Doings of the Bodley Family in Town and Country.* (Scudder)
1876	*The Adventures of Tom Sawyer.* Twain (Clemens)
1876	*Helen's Babies.* (Habberton)
1877	*The Boys of '76.* "Carleton" (Coffin)
1877	*The Boy Emigrants.* Brooks
1880	*Zigzag Journeys in Europe.* Butterworth
1880	*The Peterkin Papers.* Hale
1880	*The Boy Travellers in the Far East.* Knox

1880	*Five Little Peppers and How They Grew.* Sidney (Lothrop)
1881	*Uncle Remus . . .* Harris
1881	*A Family Flight through France, Germany . . .* Hale and Hale
1881	*Toby Tyler or Ten Weeks with a Circus.* Otis (Kaler)
1881	*Phaeton Rogers.* Johnson
1881	*The Floating Prince . . .* Stockton
1882	*What to Do and How to Do It/the American Boys' Handy Book.* Beard
1882	*The Story of Siegfried.* Baldwin
1882	*Diddie, Dumps, and Tot . . .* Pyrnelle
1882	*The Prince and the Pauper.* Twain (Clemens)
1883	*Peck's Bad Boy and His Pa.* Peck
1883	*Three Vassar Girls Abroad.* Champney
1883	*The Hoosier School-Boy.* Eggleston
1883	*The Merry Adventures of Robin Hood.* Pyle
1885	*Adventures of Huckleberry Finn.* Twain (Clemens)
1886	*Davy and the Goblin.* Carryl
1886	*Ten Boys Who Lived on the Road from Long Ago to Now.* Andrews
1886	*Little Lord Fauntleroy.* Burnett
1886	*The Bow of Orange Ribbon.* Barr
1887	*The Flamingo Feather.* Munroe
1887	*The Brownies: Their Book.* Cox
1887	*The Story of the Golden Age.* Baldwin
1887	*The Birds' Christmas Carol.* Wiggin
1888	*Jack Hall or the School Days of an American Boy.* Grant
1888	*Editha's Burglar.* Burnett
1888	*Two Little Confederates.* Page
1888	*Juan and Juanita.* Baylor
1888	*Otto of the Silver Hand.* Pyle
1890	*A Boy's Town.* Howells
1890	*Betty Leicester . . .* Jewett
1891	*Captain January.* Richards

1891	*Little Smoke* . . . Stoddard
1892	*The Admiral's Caravan.* Carryl
1893	*Jenny Wren's Boarding-House.* Otis (Kaler)
1894	*Cadet Days/a Story of West Point.* King
1894	*War of 1812 Series/the Search for Andrew Field.* Tomlinson
1894	*Beautiful Joe.* Saunders
1894	*The Fur-Seal's Tooth* . . . Munroe
1896	*"Cosie Corner Series"/The Little Colonel.* Fellows-Johnston
1897	*Master Skylark/a Story of Shakespere's Time.* Bennett
1898	*The Hollow Tree.* Paine
1898	*Wild Animals I Have Known.* Thompson (Seton)
1899	*The Half-Back/a Story of School.* Barbour
1899	*The Court of Boyville.* White
1900	*Goops/and How To Be Them.* Burgess
1900	*The Wonderful Wizard of Oz.* Baum
1901	*Mrs. Wiggs of the Cabbage Patch.* Hegan (Rice)
1901	*The Snow Baby* . . . Peary
1902	*Barnaby Lee.* Bennett
1902	*The Flight of Pony Baker.* Howells
1902	*The Real Diary of a Real Boy.* Shute
1903	*The Call of the Wild.* London
1903	*Rebecca of Sunnybrook Farm.* Wiggin
1906	*White Fang.* London
1908	*Anne of Green Gables.* Montgomery
1908	*The Hole Book.* Newell
1908	*The Young Alaskans.* Hough
1909	*Miss Minerva and William Green Hill.* Calhoun
1910	*The Varmint.* Johnson
1911	*The Tennessee Shad.* Johnson
1912	*Daddy-Long-Legs.* Webster
1913	*Pollyanna.* Porter
1914	*Penrod.* Tarkington
1914	*Tarzan of the Apes.* Burroughs

1916	*Penrod and Sam.* Tarkington
1917	*Understood Betsy.* Canfield
1920	*The Story of Doctor Dolittle.* Lofting
1922	*Rootabaga Stories.* Sandburg
1922	*Daniel Boone/Wilderness Scout.* White
1923	*The Dark Frigate.* Hawes
1926	*Smoky the Cowhorse.* James

And, in addition, there is a selection of "border-line" titles. Obviously, many of these titles would have probably been forgotten long ago had they not been included on his list. All of these books were, however, extremely popular in their day and most went into numerous editions; it is therefore wise to investigate the book for issue points before assuming that one may have a "find."

Phillips John C. Phillips: *A Bibliography of American Sporting Books.*

Phillips P. L. Phillips: *Atlases, Maps in the Library of Congress.*

Phillips Sir Thomas Phillips (1760–1851), an early nineteenth-century book collector who, in fifty years of attending auctions, managed to amass a now legendary collection of sixty thousand manuscripts and fifty thousand scarce and rare books.

Philobiblon The first book, it is thought, to be written on the subject of book collecting. Richard Aungervyle, better known as Richard de Bury, Bishop of Durham, completed this book in 1345—over one hundred years before the invention of the printing press in Europe. It first achieved publication in 1473, in the original Latin; the first English version appeared in 1832. Richard de Bury wrote: "No dearness of price ought to hinder a man from the buying of books, if he has the money demanded for them, unless it be to withstand the malice of the seller or to await a more favourable opportunity of buying."

Photocomposition A method for "setting" reading matter by the use of a camera rather than printers' type.

Photographic material In recent years, interest has steadily grown in collecting many kinds of photographic material, including books. There are now a number of dealers who specialize in this area. They report a demand for any books on photography written before 1900, and for examples of the earliest use of photography to illustrate books, especially with the actual photograph mounted on the page (tipped in). Among the magazines devoted to photography, one of the most eagerly sought is *Camera Work*, edited by Alfred Stieglitz and published between 1903 and 1917. In addition to photographic journals, the operating manuals and manufacturers' catalogues for all manner of photographic gear also find a ready market.

In addition to the books, journals, and manuals, some book dealers now also handle old photograph albums. Today, collectors and dealers are particularly interested in collections of photographs which appear to have some historic interest, whether mounted or not, photographs of famous people, and photographs by "name" photographers.

Collectors of photographic material are rarely interested in the over-all condition of a book or in its binding. It is the photograph alone which is important.

Photogravure A form of intaglio printing which does not employ a screen. Light is projected between minute granules of resin to produce the image.

Photo-illustrated Illustrated exclusively or primarily with photographs.

Pigskin A tough leather, of rugged appearance, sometimes used in book bindings and considered most suitable, because of its coarseness, for books of large size. Unfortunately, pigskin has a tendency to dry out and crack with age.

Pinchbeck Collectibles. The term is used in the sense of the opposite of treasures or great finds. Sometimes, cheap merchandise.

Pirated A pirated book is one printed without the specific approval of the author. Thus, it is printed without proper recompense paid to him.

Plagiarism The reprehensible act of stealing literary ideas.

Planography Printing from a flat surface, as in lithography.

Plantin Christopher Plantin (1514–1589), who founded a press at Antwerp in 1555. A good businessman, Plantin eventually employed 160 men in his plant and kept 20 presses busy, publishing 2000 books in his lifetime. In addition to issuing new editions of the classics, he published the works of his contemporaries on medicine, geography, and cartography, botany, the other sciences, and music. His Polyglot Bible (1572), a mammoth eight-volume edition with four languages to each page—Greek, Latin, Hebrew, and Aramaic—is considered one of the all-time masterpieces of printing. Although not himself a book-designer, Plantin employed the best available talent to produce books of a style and elegance still much admired. The familiar device of the Plantin Press was a hand holding a compass, wreathed around in a ribbon bearing the motto "Labore et Constancia."

Plate In the printing process, the plate is a flat and smooth substance, possibly of metal, used to create a printing surface. In offset printing, however, this so-called plate may be of paper. The result of printing from this plate is also called a plate: "This book has twenty plates by Remington." A plate in a book is often a full-page illustration, such as a frontispiece portrait, but a plate need not necessarily be full-page. If, however, all the plates are full-page or even double-page, and if the value of the book lies chiefly in its plates, it may be referred to as a plate book.

Plate book A book more valued for its plates than any other feature. Such a book is sometimes called a breaker, since it is more valuable if it is broken up and the plates sold separately.

Plate paper   A fine, soft-sized paper suitable for printing plates.

Point   The means of identifying a particular issue within one edition of a book; sometimes also called issue point. A point may consist, for example, of an error made in the initial printing run through the press for a book's first edition. The presses are stopped and the error corrected. However, we now have a means of identifying the first issue . . . or point.

The points for the first issue, first edition, of Thomas Hardy's *Tess of the D'Urbervilles* include an incorrectly numbered chapter and, on page 198 of Volume III, the word "road" where "load" should have been. Any copy of the first edition which has these issue points may be worth a great deal more than any other issue which does not have these points.

A point need not necessarily consist of an error, however. It could, for example, be in the binding. The first issue of Ralph Waldo Emerson's *Essays*, published in Boston in 1841, did not carry the designation "First Series" on the backstrip. Apparently the publisher was none too hopeful that Emerson's work would be sufficiently popular to merit his publishing more to constitute a series. However, after the Second Series did actually appear, the remaining copies of the First Series were bound—with "First Series" on the spine.

A great deal of the bibliographical information concerning a book may be concerned with the minutiae of points. Another example of points is found in *The Adventures of Tom Sawyer*, by Mark Twain, published in 1876: in the first state of the first edition, the half-title is printed on a separate leaf, followed by two blank pages, but in later printings the half-title appears on the reverse (verso) of the frontispiece. This first issue was printed on calendered paper, and it measured only one inch across the top of the covers, whereas later issues, printed on appreciably heavier paper, were thicker. The earliest printed copies have perfect type in the last line of the first page of the text and in the lines appearing last on page 202. All the foregoing items of information constitute issue points.

Without spending years of study oneself, the only way to become familiar with all the points for any first editions is to acquire the bibliography or bibliographies for the author. Checking the *Encyclopaedia Britannica* or other standard encyclopedia often provides the name of the standard bibliographical works for a well-known author.

Point In printing, a unit of measurement. In the Didot (French) system, the 72nd part of an inch.

Polite literature A somewhat derogatory term sometimes applied to belles lettres, essays, or poetry dealing with the niceties of social communication.

Pollard and Redgrave A. W. Pollard and G. W. Redgrave, editors: *Short Title Catalogue of Books Printed in England, Scotland, and Ireland, and of English Books Printed Abroad, 1475–1640.* Now out of print. (See also **Wing.**)

Polybiblist A person who owns many books.

Poor A book in poor condition may be one pretty battered. Poor, in the dealer's lexicon, means less than fair. About the only standard left for a book in poor condition is that it should still have all the important pages. A book in poor condition may still, however, qualify as a reading copy.

Pornography A kind of obscene writing, possibly subject to legal discipline. One of the best sources for information on this subject as it may affect the old-book dealer is the 1973–74 (Silver Jubilee) *AB Bookman's Yearbook*, Part I of which is largely devoted to a comprehensive discussion of definitions of pornography, current attitudes, and recent court decisions on issues involving obscenity. Available from *AB* (*Bookman's Weekly*) (q.v.) at $5.

Portfolio A fancy kind of wrap-around case designed to

protect a book, a collection of maps, or of prints, pamphlets, etc. It may possibly have a tuck-in flap or be shaped as an envelope which snaps shut.

Portrait A picture of a person, often used as a frontispiece in a book. Sometimes called portrait plate. Abbreviated port.

Précis French for summary.

Preface An introductory section to a book, in which the author presents himself to the reader, possibly explaining the purpose of his book and suggesting how the reader may get the most from it. The author may also explain how he came to write the book. The preface, since it is part of the front matter of a book, is also the customary place for an author to thank any persons who helped him in the book's preparation. The foreword or the introduction, on the other hand, may be a statement by someone other than the author. However, all these terms may be used interchangeably.

Preisgekrönt German for award-winning.

Prelims Prelims, or preliminary matter, also called front matter, may consist of all or some of the following parts of a book which appear first: bastard title, frontispiece, title page, copyright notice, dedication, preface, foreword, table of contents, list of illustrations, introduction, and half-title. Many books, of course, lack some of these as published. When present, all, however, except the frontispiece and the copyright notice, occupy the right-hand side of the page (recto). Sometimes these pages are numbered separately from the rest of the book, with Roman numerals. Occasionally it will be possible to decide whether all the preliminary matter for an old book is still present by counting back from the first Roman numeral: if iv appears first, there should be three earlier pages, etc.

Presentation copy The copy of a book given by the author, or sometimes publisher, to someone else, usually a relative, friend, or person who helped him with the book. It is often a first edition. Since the author customarily scribbles a message in this book, it then becomes also an inscribed copy. John Drinkwater, the English poet and dramatist, once had the rare good luck, when browsing in an old-book store in New York, to come across the copy of *Moby–Dick* which Melville had inscribed to Nathaniel Hawthorne, on the very page on which he had dedicated the book to him.

Preserving old bindings A highly recommended source for information on preserving old bindings is *Pamphlet No. One* of a series on conserving library materials, Publication 16 of the Library Technology Program of the American Library Association: *Cleaning and Preserving Bindings and Related Materials*. Second edition, revised, by Carolyn Horton, illustrated by Aldren A. Watson, Chicago, 1969. Available at $4.50 from the A.L.A., 50 East Huron Street, Chicago, Ill. 60611.

Lacking the technical guidance offered by this publication, it might be useful to remember that any substance used to preserve an old leather binding should meet these four basic requirements: (1) not be sticky, (2) not harden with age, (3) not evaporate, and (4) not stain. If nothing else is available, Vaseline may be used as a preservative for leather, although over a long period it will tend to evaporate. Another simple and time-tested preservative for old bindings is a solution of paraffin wax in castor oil: a small amount of castor oil is placed in an earthenware jar and about half of its weight in paraffin (a wax) is shredded into it; the mixture is warmed slightly so that the wax melts into the oil. A little goes a long way, and it is inexpensive.

The problem of preserving old books extends, however, far beyond the simple measures it is possible to take to preserve a leather binding. The subject can be complicated indeed, and amateurs are advised to either hand their problem books over to the expert or study the advice of the professionals with some care before proceeding on their own. Again, we highly recommend Carolyn Horton's book.

Press book A book-trade term for a book which is the

product of one of the private presses. A press book is often issued in limited edition, sometimes limited to as few as twelve copies. Since most press books are produced outside the normal routines of book production and without the usual pressures for a large sale and commercial success, they are often outstanding examples of fine printing, frequently set by hand with special type, often on handmade paper, with illustrations to order and sometimes even colored by hand. Some press books are bound by hand. Such books customarily carry a colophon at the back of the book, in the style of the first printed books, and they carry a statement of the number of copies issued and the individual number assigned to this particular copy. Press books are often signed by the artist, and sometimes by the author and/or designer. Collecting press books is a hobby for those who enjoy beautiful books and are willing to pay for them. Any press book offered as an example of the art of printing is expected to be in close-to-mint condition. For an authoritative and comprehensive work on the private press, see *The Private Press* by Roderick Cave, published by Watson-Guptill in 1971 at $35.

Presswork   Printed matter in general.

Price code   The supposedly secret code developed by each old-book dealer as his own private method of indicating, for each book he has for sale, the ratio of the price he hopes to get for the book to the price he himself had to pay for it. A fairly obvious code, for example, might be a-b-c for 2-3-4 times the price. A dealer might pencil $1.50/b to indicate that his asking price ($1.50) is three times the amount he paid for the book (50¢). Most price codes are a great deal more elaborate. One clue: many book dealers like to peg their code to their own name or that of their shop.

Prices, average   In spite of the publicity which is sometimes given to the prices paid on some occasions for rare volumes, few books in the old-book trade go for much more than $10. Sol. M. Malkin, editor of *AB*, fairly recently said he thought that most out-of-print fiction was still selling at dealers for between 50¢ and a dollar, most non-fiction at less than $3. Even doubling his figures does not present a picture of a hobby for rich men only. For every $28,000 paid for a copy of Thomas Aquinas thought to have been printed by Gutenberg before 1460 (sold at auction by Swann Galleries in December 1974), there must be hundreds of thousands of book transactions involving less than $5.

Pricing books There can never be a "right" price for a book. Even experts will appraise the same book differently, depending in part upon their judgment of the market.

To make a guess at the going price for any particular book, the experts go to *American Book Prices Current*, *Book Auction Records*, or *Book Auction Prices* which reports more modest prices, or to some other similar compendium which keeps up to date. Sources of information which are not current, such as Wright Howes' *U.S.Iana*, must be used with caution and as a general guideline only.

Primer A first book, for children; a book of simple instructions.

Printer's mark A symbol used by printers, particularly in the early days of printing, to identify their work.

Printing First printing, second printing, third, etc. The first printing is the first delivery off the press; this first printing is usually the only one which book collectors want. A second or third printing might be accepted by a collector only until he can replace it with the desired first. Modern books sometimes carry the words "first printing" on the copyright page of the first edition.

Printing processes There are six basic printing processes: planography, relief printing, intaglio, stencil, photography, and xerography.

Privatdruck German for not issued for sale.

Private press Definitions vary, but the one generally accepted is that of a small amateur press free from pressures for commercial success. Occasionally the term is used more inclusively to mean any commercial press (or amateur) which both limits its work in the interests of technical excellence and adheres to high standards. Will Ransom, author of *Private Presses*, said "a private press may be defined as the typographic expression of a personal ideal, conceived in freedom and maintained in independence." Proprietors of private presses are usually equally concerned with fine typography and with literary content, and much of their production has consisted of new editions of the classics, or books considered classics at the time, or original works, in handsome new format, employing a special font of type, frequently set by hand and printed by hand on handmade paper, even bound by hand, invariably in limited edition. Handcrafting is the specialty of the private press, and on occasion it has included weaving the cloth for the binding, inserting initials by hand, hand-coloring the illustrations. By experimenting with layout, type faces, and kinds of binding, and by making a practical demonstration of the beauty of sometimes startlingly innovative ideas and techniques, the private presses have often set new standards of excellence for the printing industry and publishing business as a whole. Some amateurs may play at printing with only indifferent results, of course, but there is a strong tradition of painstaking craftsmanship which commands great respect from connoisseurs of good bookmaking and typography, and which makes collecting press books an expensive hobby, though perhaps one of the most thoroughly soul-satisfying areas of collecting. Although the private press might be said to have had its beginnings in the clandestine press producing political documents, the modern private press dates from the work of William Morris at the Kelmscott Press from 1891. Among the most notable of the English private presses have been the Ashendene Press, Vale Press, the Golden Cockerel, Doves, and Daniel, to name just a few; in America, the most notable of the early presses was the Village Press operated by Frederic W. Goudy with his wife Bertha. The interesting individual qualities of these presses can be glimpsed by scanning a short list of their names: the Press of the Woolly Whale, the Golden Hind, Bird and Bull, Perishable, Snail's Pace Press.

A valuable work on the private press, with a checklist, is *Private Presses and Their Books*, by Will Ransom, published in 1929. A recent work is *The Private Press*, by Roderick Cave, published by Watson-Guptill in 1971 at $35. *A Select Bibliography* by G. S. Tomkinson (1928) is now available in reprint at $20 from Alan Wofsy Fine Arts, 150 Green Street, San Francisco, Cal. 94111.

Probe-Abdruck   German for the proof of an engraving. *Probedruck* by itself means trial proof.

Process engraving   The art of producing printed surfaces by means of photography and the chemical treatment of the plate.

Procès verbal   French for proceedings, or minutes.

Proctor order   A system of bibliographical arrangement for cataloguing books by country, town, press, and date; named after Robert Proctor (1868–1903).

Proem   An introductory discourse; a preface.

Prologue   An introductory statement, sometimes explaining the main body of the work which is to follow.

Proof   A sample impression of the work of a printer, made so that it can be inspected for errors. Proof sometimes comes into the old-book market, but not often. In printers' jargon, a "proof is pulled off the press."

Proofreader   A person charged with the responsibility for seeing that a printed text corresponds exactly to an original manuscript or text. Making corrections in the text is not the job of the proofreader.

Proprietary type   A type face designed especially for the use of one particular press, usually a private press, which then becomes the sole proprietor.

Protective box   A box of cardboard made to encase a book. Many book-club books are issued in this type of box. Usually the box is open along one long end to display the book's spine. Unless the box which is still with a book is in almost-mint condition, a dealer may not bother mentioning it in his description of a book.

Professional bookbinders are often glad to construct special protective boxes for valuable old books.

Protective tissue   A thin piece of paper inserted into the binding of a book, between the pages, to prevent an illustration from offsetting onto the opposite page. Unfortunately, sometimes acid content in the tissue itself will cause browning on the opposite page. Tissues which are lettered with the legend for the illustration may add elegance to a book.

Protokoll   German for minutes of a meeting; or proceedings.

Pseudonym   A name other than one's own, used to conceal one's identity.

Pseudonyma   The body of work by an author who has used a name other than his own. Some authors have produced both pseudonyma and works under their own name. (See also **Anonyma**.)

Pseudonyms   A standard work on pseudonyms by William Cushing, titled *Initials and Pseudonyms: a Dictionary of Literary Disguises*. Published in reprint in 1969 and available from Mark Press at $44.50 for the two-volume set. Another standard work is the *Handbook of Pseudonyms and Personal Nicknames* by Harold S. Sharp, published by Scarecrow Press at $27.50. The granddaddy work is by Samuel Halkett and John Laing, titled *Dictionary of Anonymous and Pseudonymous English Literature*. The first edition, in four volumes, came out in 1882–88, and there is still a seven-volume edition in print, greatly enlarged, from Haskell at about $100.

Publié   French for published; appearing often on a title page where "edited" would be the English equivalent.

Q

Quarto A book size, from 11 to 13 inches tall in American book measurement, or from $8\frac{1}{2}$ x $6\frac{1}{4}$ to 15 x 11 inches according to British terminology. Abbreviated to 4to or 4°. Also, a book larger than octavo (8vo) and smaller than folio. Historically, any size of paper (page) attained by folding a whole sheet twice, so as to form four leaves, or eight pages.

Quire To the book collector, this means a gathering (section) of the leaves of a book. But to the manufacturer of paper, it may be one-twentieth of a ream of paper. The term "in quires" means that a book is as yet unbound.

Quote A statement of the price at which the owner of a book is willing to sell it. The owner "quotes" his price. The specialized use of the word is seen in this advertisement in *AB* (*Bookman's Weekly*): "Please quote me. I buy something about Texas every day."

Over the years a simple and uniform method for quoting has been agreed upon by bookmen. Each quote is listed on a separate card, so that if it is not acted upon immediately it can be held for future action. Index cards are preferred, although a postcard will do. The following information should be supplied on one side of the card in the following order: name and address of the seller of the book; title, author, publisher, and edition (most important); briefly, the condition of the book; price; and, possibly, the length of time you will hold the book if necessary.

Books should always be quoted prepaid. This could make

a big difference in the case of, say, a ten- or twelve-volume set.

Weekly, long lists of the books for which quotes are being sought are printed in both *AB* and in the *Out-of-Print-Bookfinder*.

Quoting is often worthwhile even if the book is not sold, since sometimes it sets up a correspondence and an exchange of information about general needs.

The quickest way to alienate a potential buyer for your book is to provide all the information except the price you want for the book and then coyly conclude "make offer?" The quote card will be filed in the wastebasket.

R

Radierung German for etching.

Rag Fragments of cloth from which a high-quality paper is made; or, the paper itself.

Raised bands Horizontal bands across the back (spine) of a book. Such bands were once the result of the method of binding used; today they are sometimes added simply for decorative effect.

Randall David A. Randall and John T. Winterich, authors of the classic *Primer of Book Collecting*. A third edition is available from Crown at $5.95.

Randleiste German for an ornamental border.

Rarity A book which an active dealer in old books might expect to see only once in his lifetime. A merely scarce book, on the other hand, might turn up every ten years or so.

Rattle A means of judging the amount of sizing used in paper: the more the rattle when the paper is pulled and shuffled about, the more the sizing.

Reading copy A book which still has all its pages carrying text, but is generally in only fair or even poor condition.

Rebacked Repaired by being furnished with a new backstrip or spine. A good job of rebacking may be extremely difficult to detect, but any binding more than two hundred years old which appears to be in extraordinarily good shape may be suspect. In books bound in leather, there will be a faint telltale line between the sides and the back of the book, so faint as to be almost invisible.

Rebinding Any old book should be rebound only after

careful thought and when there would appear to be no other way of preserving it. One advocate of mending rather than rebinding is Douglas Cockerell (*Bookbinding, and the Care of Books*): "If the old boards have quite perished, new boards of the same nature and thickness should be got out and the old cover pasted over them. Such places as the old leather will not cover must first be covered with new of the same color. Generally speaking, it is desirable that the characteristics of an old book should be preserved, and that the new work should be as little in evidence as possible. It is far more pleasant to see an old book in a patched contemporary binding, than smug and tidy in the most immaculate modern cover."

However, once the hinges of an old book have become badly cracked and the pages are coming loose, the book must be rebound; in almost all cases this will require the services of an expert in book repair. Most book dealers deal with some professional bookbinder and can recommend his services. When any book is rebound, it is important that the new binding be appropriate to the content of the book and the period when it was first published. If a book is worth rebinding, it is often worth the extra expense of putting into leather.

For further information about bookbinding in general and about the various individual processes involved, a good source is *Basic Bookbinding*, by A. W. Lewis, first published in England and now available in America through Dover at $1.75.

Any book which is in need of rebinding should be carefully wrapped in an acetate or other type of acid-free covering. Putting an elastic around the book to hold the covers on will only mark the covers and deface the book.

Rebus   A basically enigmatic representation of a name by means of figures, drawings, a special arrangement of letters, etc.

Recased   Rebound within the old covers.

Récit French for story.

Recto The right-hand page of a book when it is lying face up in the reading position. The recto is given the uneven page numbers.

Recueil French for collection. *Recueil de modes* is a collection of fashion plates.

Redigé French for compiled or edited, as might be true of a conference report prepared for publication.

Redigiert German for compiled or edited.

References, bibliographical For information on the variety of bibliographies available on a wide scale, consult Theodore Besterman, *World Bibliography of Bibliographies*, at your library. Or check out the subject or author in the *Encyclopaedia Britannica* or other standard large reference work of reputation, for the list of references often provided at the conclusion of the article. A good introductory work, which you may also find in the library, is *An Introduction to Bibliography*, by R. B. McKerrow. This is good for browsing and general information as well as for the specifics.

Register German for an index, or list.

Register "In register" means that printed material has been placed correctly on a page and, specifically, that the margins on a series of pages are properly aligned. In color work, off-register printing results in blurry outlines and muddy colors.

Register of National Bibliography A standard British subject catalogue, compiled by W. R. Courtney; sometimes, therefore, known as a Courtney.

Reimpression French for reprint.

Reiseführer German for a traveller's guidebook.

Relié French for rebound. *Reliure de luxe* is a luxury binding.

Relief printing Printing from a raised surface, as is done from type and from engraved wooden blocks.

Remainder A remainder is a book left over from publishers' stock and therefore offered for sale at reduced price. Many old-book stores also handle remainders, whether or not they call them that. Particularly good buys may sometimes be found among these remainders, particularly in art books.

Rémaniée   French for revised, as in revised edition.

Remargined   Said of a page when its outer edge has been repaired, usually with a close-to-invisible mending paper or tape. Such a page may appear darker around the edges, but a skillful repair job may be difficult to detect without holding the page up to a strong light.

Repairing tears   In repairing any torn page, by all means avoid applying cheap popular "sticky tape." It will eventually dry out, but—worse—when it does, it peels off, leaving an ugly brown stain. Try, instead, a glassine paper backed with a water-soluble adhesive, such as Dennison's Mending Tape. This may yellow with age, but it will not stain the page itself. There is a better way of mending, of course, but it involves the careful use of special librarians' paste and a strong-fibered fine paper such as used to be imported from Japan and is now hard to find.

Réparé   French for mended. In German it is *repariert*. The French word for restored, however, is *restauré*.

Replica   A reprint which is a direct copy of the original book, either from the original plates or through the offset process. Some replicas, on the appropriate paper, can fool the eye (and hand). Any replica should carry the statement that it is not the original. Reprint is the more common term.

Reprint   A re-issue of a book, either in the original form or with changes and additions. Any reprint should indicate, somewhere between its covers, that it is not the original reprint. Unfortunately, in some reprints this information is hard to find.

Reprints may be valuable in their own right. A good copy of the first edition of *Moby-Dick* may be worth thousands of dollars, but the Lakeside Press edition of 1930, illustrated by

Rockwell Kent—a reprint—or the two-volume Limited Editions Club version may be valuable, too.

Reserve The confidential minimum price agreed upon between the consignor of books and an auction house, below which any specific lot (individual book or bundle of books) will not be sold.

Reset Put into new type. A book may be reset for a new deluxe edition, for example.

Or, in another sense, a leaf or a plate which has become loose or detached in a book may be reset—restored firmly to its original place.

Revidiert German for revised.

Review copy A copy of a book furnished to a reviewer for his comment, customarily before the announced date of publication. Books stamped "review copy" frequently come into the old-book market in fine condition, having very often been read, or glanced through, only once.

Revue French for periodical.

Rezensionsexemplar German for a review copy.

Rights Those rights specified in a publisher's contract. Or, the copyright rights in different parts of the world, such as the American rights, Colonial (British) rights, or the Continental rights. Or, copyright rights in general: literary, dramatic, performing, radio, serial, or translation.

Road book A book listing itineraries or stops, for the traveller.

Roan A soft leather of sheepskin, used sometimes for bookbinding. In the late eighteenth century roan was used in half-binding, to cover the spine only; this enabled the frugal publisher to call his book "leather bound." However, since it is usually pared very thin, it is not particularly durable, and old books backed with roan have a peculiarly brittle look. Roan comes in red and sometimes blue, as well as black, and sometimes other colors.

Rogers Bruce Rogers (1870–1957), an American, who has been called the first modern type designer. Some people consider his 1935 Oxford Lectern Bible the most important printed book of the twentieth century. Between 1896 and 1912 Bruce Rogers designed sixty books for the Riverside Press, each with an original and different combination of text, format, type, paper, and binding. Among his most notable achievements were the 1915 design for Maurice de Guerin's *The Centaur*, which employed type he had especially designed and cut, and the 1917 Grolier Club reprint of Dürer's *On the Just Shaping of Letters*. In 1920 he joined William Edwin Rudge's press at Mount Vernon, where in the next eight years he produced another one hundred books. In his last years he also designed a number of books for the Limited Editions Club.

Rogné   French for trimmed or cut, as the edges of a book are cut.

Roman   A style of type based on that used in ancient Roman inscriptions and manuscripts. Modern Roman is a style of type which is scarcely modern any longer, having been originated about two hundred years ago. Examples in current use are Bodoni and Scotch Roman.

Roman   In German, fiction; story is *Erzählung*.

Roman numerals   In the days when Latin was a much more familiar language than it is today, many books were published with the date of publication in Roman numerals. Many publishers still continue to use Roman numerals in a manner which seems affected to many readers—especially those legions who have difficulty reading the Roman numerals. Occasionally book dealers try to make life a bit easier by pencilling in the date under the numerals; it is not unusual, however, to find MDCCXL interpreted as 1760 instead of 1740, or MCMIX as 1899 rather than 1909, to take just two fairly easy numbers. The best thing to do is to learn the following chart, remember that the basic rule is to read from left to right . . . and don't succumb to panic.

1	I
5	V
10	X

50	L
100	C
500	D
1000	M

The Romans, in some ways an orderly people, wrote first the century, then the decade, and finally the year. Any symbol appearing to the right adds to the value of the number, whereas a symbol to the left of the next greater number subtracts from it. Thus V is 5, VI is 6, whereas IV is 4. Sample dates are: for 1500, MD; for 1600, MDC; for 1620, MDCXX; 1626, MDCXXVI; 1629, MDCXXIX. The later centuries are:

1700	MDCC
1800	MDCCC
1900	MDCCCC *or* MCM

Rosenbach A. S. W. Rosenbach (1876–1952), an American book dealer who had the good fortune to represent wealthy clients, and a writer on the subject of old and rare books. He has been aptly called the very Napoleon of booksellers. Through his capable hands passed several Shakespeare folios, several copies of the Gutenberg Bible, a Chaucer manuscript in the original binding, and Benjamin Franklin's personal account book. He proved himself an expert bibliographer with his *Early American Children's Books* which has become a standard reference work and is now available from Dover in an unabridged reprint at $5. Rosenbach is also author of *An American Jewish Bibliography*, published in 1926, now available from Kraus Reprint at $14.

Rounding Shaping the spine of a book during the process of its manufacture. A well-rounded book has a hollow back. When the book is opened out as flat as possible, light can be seen through the tunnel of its spine.

Rousseurs French for rust stains; foxing.

Roxburghe A style of binding in plain leather, with a gilt top edge and the other edges untrimmed, and with the title on the back (spine) enwreathed in a border. So named for the

Duke of Roxburghe, an early nineteenth-century collector who devised this style of binding for his own collection of books.

Royal folio (Ry Fol)   A British book size, 20 x 12½ inches.

Royal octavo (Ry 8vo)   A British book size, 10 x 6½ inches.

Royal quarto (Ry 4to)   A British book size, 12½ x 10 inches.

Roycroft   The Roycroft Shop began business as a private press in 1896 under the direction of Elbert Hubbard, at East Aurora, New York. Although this press quickly went commercial, its first 43 publications, issued through 1900, are generally conceded to be within the definition of private press books. Hubbard is credited with having introduced the private press concept to an extensive new and admiring public.

Rubbed   A book's covers are called rubbed when they have been damaged by friction of some sort. Rubbing can often be simply the result of ordinary heavy shelf wear. The term rubbing does not really tell you the extent of the damage. Rubbing should, however, as a descriptive term, be well this side of chipped, gouged, torn, etc.

Rubricated   Reddened. Initial letters are sometimes rubricated in a book otherwise without decoration. Rubricated prayer books are those with the headings printed in red.

Rücken erneuert   German for rebacked.

Rückenschild   German for label.

Rückseite   German for verso.

Running title   A title which is repeated at the top of successive pages of a book, usually on the same top printing line as the folio (page number).

Russia   A fine, smooth leather, usually dark red in color. It originated in Russia, and is made by impregnating calfskin in oils distilled from birchbark.

S

Sabin Joseph Sabin (1821–1881), author of *A Dictionary of Books Relating to America from Its Discovery to the Present Time.* One of the greatest authorities on Americana, Sabin was himself an Englishman who came to the United States in 1848. He began his monumental work in the sixties and by the time of his death in 1881 had managed to work down the alphabet as far as "PA-." Wilberforce Eames, with Harry M. Lydenberg, completed the task which Sabin had begun. As a source of bibliographic information concerning any author, Sabin remains incomparable. Yet, for the average book collector of fairly specialized interests, Sabin contains vastly more information than is required. Perhaps fortunately, since the edition of Sabin in fifteen volumes, published by Barnes and Noble, costs about $450, and the two-volume reprint from Scarecrow is still a hefty $95.

Sachregister German for subject index.

Sadleir Michael Sadleir, author of *Excursions in Victorian Bibliography* first published in London in 1922 and considered a fine authority on such Victorian authors as Trollope, Disraeli, Reade, and others.

Sain French for in good condition; healthy.

Sali French for dirtied or soiled.

Sammelwerk German for the collected work; *Sammlung* is collection; and *sämtliche Werke*, complete works. *Sammlung von Modekupfern* is collection of fashion plates.

Sans serif A style of type which lacks serifs—projections at the top and/or bottom of the character.

Scarce A book which is considered scarce is one which it might take you two or three years of fairly steady hunting to find. A rare book, however, might not be located by a dealer in ten or twenty years.

Scarcity need not simply evolve; often it is created by the publisher, who may issue a book in an edition of only several hundred, or even less than one hundred copies. A great deal of the output of the specialty and private presses is scarce from the moment it is released on the market. A book need not be considered valuable, of course, simply because it is scarce.

Schlussvignette German for tailpiece or endpiece.

Schmal German for narrow, or tall (format in a book).

Schmutztitel German for half-title.

Schoolbooks According to the Antiquarian Booksellers Association, very few old textbooks, no matter how quaint, have value in the old-book market. It might be assumed that the McGuffey Readers would be an exception to this rule, but since over one hundred million copies of this popular schoolbook series were sold, there are still quite a few around, and there is some market only for the earliest, those *Eclectic Readers* of William Holmes McGuffey published between 1836 and 1857. One of the few geographies worth much is the 1784 *Morse's Geography Made Easy,* published at New Haven. Latin grammars, most spelling books, arithmetic books, etc., are worth almost nothing, with certain exceptions. The most notable exceptions are the schoolbooks of some lad who later became President of the United States—but his signature must be there to prove it was his book.

Schuber German for slipcase.

Schutzumschlag German for dust jacket, or wrapper.

Scout An individual who searches for books for a dealer or on behalf of a collector. A scout usually works on a commission basis. He is also known in some localities as a picker. On assignment, he may attend book auctions to bid for certain books. Scouting has a history which goes well back to before the invention of the printing press in Europe. In his *Philobiblon*, Richard de Bury, in 1345, discoursed on "the manifold opportunity we have had for gathering a multitude of books," explaining that he had managed to become a patron of a number of religious mendicants "wherefore we deserved to have them as our peculiar favourers and promoters, both in word and work. Traversing sea and land, casting their view over the circuit of the world, and searching the universities and schools of various provinces, they studied to do service for our wishes, for their hope of reward was most certain. What leveret could miss the sight of so many keen-eyed hunters? What fry could escape now their hooks and now their nets and snares? From the body of the Sacred Divine Law up to the quarto of yesterday's sophists, nothing escaped these searchers."

Today's book scouts must be equally keen-eyed, and also extremely knowledgeable about all manner of books.

Script A style of type face simulating handwriting and rarely encountered in books.

Scuffed The covers of an old book may become scuffed in just the same way that shoes become scuffed and worn. Either leather or cloth books may be termed scuffed. "Rubbed" is used in the sense of light scuffing.

Sealskin An extremely strong and durable leather for bookbinding, soft, and of an even grain, which can be used only on expensive books because of its cost.

Search service An agency which attempts to locate books at request. Search services are operated by individuals, sometimes out of their own homes, by old-book stores, and sometimes by new-book stores as a service for customers trying to find books recently out of print. Most search services do not make a charge for the search itself, but add a modest fee to the price of any book they locate. Most collectors prefer to find one good search service and stick with it. Sometimes it may be years before the service can find a truly scarce book, but for a regular client it will keep trying.

Secondary binding　Not a second printing, but a later binding of the earlier printed sheets. Sometimes a publisher may bind only as many copies as he thinks he will need at once; later, if there proves to be sufficient demand, he will bind more of the printed quires, frequently, as it chances, in a different color of binding, kind of cloth, or even with a different stamping.

Section　A gathering of the printed sheets for a book.

Sehr selten　German for exceedingly rare.

Seite　German for page.

Selbstbiographie　German for autobiography.

Selbstverleger　German for author-publisher of his own works.

Self-cover　A cover of the same weight of paper (stock) as the pages of the book.

Selten　German for rare or scarce.

Semestriel　French for semi-annual.

Separatabdruck　German for reprint or offprint.

Sepia　The rich brown color of ink sometimes used in printing illustrations. This ink is supposed to come from the inky secretions of a cuttle fish.

Serié complète　French for a completed series.

Serientitel　German for the general title for a whole series.

Set off　In press work, the process of the ink of one printed sheet coming off on the next sheet as it is delivered off the press. The result is called offset. Offset, however, may also refer to the transfer of ink from one page to another in an old book.

Sewing　The earliest means of binding a book together, by cords or bands, five for most books and seven for a folio. Holes had to be punched in the covers through which the cords might be laced so that the book would lie perfectly flat when opened. Today, each signature is first sewn separately and then the signatures are all gathered together.

Sextodecimo The page size of a book made by folding a sheet of paper into sixteen leaves, thus creating thirty-two numbered pages. But by custom the term has come to mean a book which is from six to seven inches tall. Pronounced sexteenmo, abbreviated 16mo or 16°.

Shagreen A kind of untanned leather with a roughened surface, usually prepared from the skin of a horse or ass, or possibly from shark or seal; often dyed green.

Shaken A book may be termed shaken when it is loose within its covers. A shaken book moves fairly freely loose of its binding when it is moved to and fro within the hands.

Shaw-Shoemaker *A Checklist of American Imprints*, originated by R. R. Shaw and continued by R. H. Shoemaker; 29 volumes, for the years 1801–29, plus addenda, corrections and author-index, along with title-index, making a total of 32 volumes. Shaw and Shoemaker continued the work begun by Charles Evans and brought his bibliography up through the first quarter of the nineteenth century, citing tens of thousands of books, pamphlets, and related kinds of material. Now out of print, this set may bring about $300 at auction today. Reprints of the separate years are available from Scarecrow Press at $14 or less per volume. Most collectors need to refer to the *Checklist* infrequently; dealers sometimes make a point of the fact that a work is sufficiently rare so that it is not found in Shaw-Shoemaker.

Sheepskin A traditional kind of leather binding often used for law books, even though it has a number of drawbacks in use, including cracking and drying. A sheepskin binding will eventually split at the book's joints. Sheepskin is occasionally prepared to look like goatskin; in fact, there are two kinds of "morocco" which are actually sheep: Niger, which is a coarse-grained leather, and Venetian, which is highly polished.

Short title An abbreviated form of the title of a book, used frequently to denote the book in a checklist comprising many titles. Also, any contracted form of a book's title. *Not,* however, a term with the same meaning as any of the following: bastard title, fly title, half-title. See also **Pollard and Redgrave, Wing** and *Gallery of Ghosts,* for examples of the short title catalogue. *The Short Title Catalogue of Books* is a specific catalogue, covering the years 1475–1640 and 1640–1700.

Side note   A short paragraph inserted into a paragraph from either the right or left side, where the text has been indented for the purpose. Not the same as marginalia (q.v.).

Sides   The front and back covers of a book.

Signature   The folding of a single sheet of paper to make up the pages of a book: signatures must then be gathered in the proper sequence to constitute the book as a whole. Originally, the term signature meant a letter, figure, or a combination of these two which the printer would place at the bottom of the first page of the signature to indicate the order in which all the signatures were to be bound together. From being the designation of the folded sheets' order in a series, the word has eventually come to mean the sheets themselves. If you will examine the folds of paper against the spine of a book, you can see the signatures—the consecutive foldings of paper which make up the pages.

Signed   The term signed appearing in a book dealer's catalogue means that this book has been signed by its author. Any other signature would have to be more fully explained.

Singleton   A single leaf in a book not conjugate (joined) to any other.

Sitzungsbericht   German for proceedings.

Sixties book   In the old-book trade, "sixties" usually refers to the 1860's, except in the case of material clearly of very recent date. Thus, a sixties book is one over one hundred years old; and specifically the term refers to a kind of elaborate souvenir book or annual, a parlor-table book similar to the coffee-table book of a later day.

Size   For the most part, beginning collectors need know no more about the niceties of size than to be able to recognize the four major categories: folio, quarto, octavo, and duodecimo. These categories are abbreviated in dealers' catalogues to F, 4to, 8vo, and 12mo.

The folio is considerably larger than a sheet of typewriter paper—thirteen inches or more tall. Quarto is eleven or twelve inches, a size often used, for example, for books on art. Octavo, approximately eight-and-a-half to nine inches tall, is the most common size for modern hard-cover books. Many paperbacks are issued in sextodecimo size, between six and seven inches to duodecimo, only slightly larger.

The names of the sizes are derived, historically, from the number of times a full sheet of paper was folded to create the leaf of a book: thus, once for folio, twice for quarto, three times for octavo, etc., creating two, four, and eight leaves respectively (four, eight, and sixteen pages). Although at first the sizes of the sheets of paper so folded were not standardized, by custom these terms eventually came to mean a certain approximate page size. Actually, a single term for size, in the strictest sense, means nothing unless the size of the original sheet is known. For example, an 8vo of a particular size of sheet (folded three times) might be more properly described, in modern terms, as 4to.

A modern trend now gaining some headway is to give page sizes in inches or centimeters rather than the old-fashioned and out-of-date categories.

The British system for indicating size is not only different from the American, but also much more precise.

Size categories, American The most generally accepted definitions for size appear to be the following:

Miniature	less than 3 inches tall
Sixtyfourmo (64mo)	about 3 inches tall
Fortyeightmo (48mo)	less than 4 inches tall
Trigesimosecundo (32mo)	4 to 5 inches
Vigesimoquarto (24mo)	5 to 6 inches
Sextodecimo (16mo)	6 to 7 inches
Duodecimo (12mo)	around 7 inches or slightly taller

Small Octavo (Sm. 8vo)	$7\frac{1}{2}$ to 8 inches
Octavo (8vo)	8 to 9 inches
Small Quarto (Sm. 4to)	about 10 inches
Quarto (4to)	between 11 and 13 inches
Folio (F)	13 inches or larger
Elephant Folio	23 inches or more
Atlas Folio	25 inches
Double Elephant Folio	larger than 25 inches

For some time the trend has been away from precise measurements; approximate measurements are satisfactory for the most part, and if exact measurements seem to be required, they are provided in inches or centimeters. Rare and unusual books, of course, require exact measuring.

Size categories, British British book sizes are more precise than the American. Within octavo alone there are seven different categories, measured by both width and height. Beginning with the size comparable to the American sextodecimo, they are:

Octavo

Foolscap (F 8vo)	$6\frac{1}{2}$ x $4\frac{1}{2}$
Crown (Cr 8vo)	$7\frac{1}{2}$ x 5
Large Crown (L Cr 8vo)	8 x $5\frac{1}{2}$
Demy (Dy 8vo)	$8\frac{3}{4}$ x $5\frac{5}{8}$
Medium (M 8vo)	$9\frac{1}{2}$ x 6
Royal (Ry 8vo)	10 x $6\frac{1}{2}$
Imperial (Imp 8vo)	11 x $7\frac{1}{2}$

Quarto

Foolscap (F 4to)	$8\frac{1}{2}$ x $6\frac{3}{4}$
Crown (Cr 4to)	10 x $7\frac{1}{2}$
Demy (Dy 4to)	$11\frac{1}{2}$ x $8\frac{3}{4}$
Medium (Med 4to)	12 x $9\frac{1}{2}$
Royal (Ry 4to)	$12\frac{1}{2}$ x 10
Imperial (Imp 4to)	15 x 11

Folio

Foolscap (Fo Fol)	$13\frac{1}{2}$ x 10

Crown (Cr Fol)	15 x 10
Royal (Ry Fol)	20 x $12\frac{1}{2}$
Imperial (Imp Fol)	22 x $15\frac{1}{2}$

Slip case   A box open at one end and usually covered with paper, leather, or cloth, possibly linen, into which a book may be neatly slipped, leaving the backstrip exposed. Many fine examples of the printer's art are issued in slip cases to protect the book—and to emphasize the fine quality of the book. A slip case is sometimes called a protective box, although slip case is a more precise term.

Slip sheet   A blank piece of paper inserted by the publisher between printed pages, often against a full-page illustration, for the purpose of preventing offset (set-off).

Small quarto (Sm. 4to)   An American book size, about 10 inches tall. Or, specifically, an American book size based strictly on the number of times a sheet was folded to create pages (twice). In eighteenth-century books, the pages may be numbered in a series of four leaves, and yet such books, to the modern eye, may have the appearance of octavos or even duodecimos.

Solander   The solander case, made to protect a book, was the invention of D. C. Solander, who died in 1782. The case has a fall-down lid which is usually secured with a spring latch. Not only does it effectively keep out dust, but it is particularly valued because it makes it possible to open the book and examine it without actually removing it from its case.

Sold as is   The expression probably preferred in the old-book trade is sold "with all faults" (w.a.f.).

Sommaire   French for list of contents.

Sonderausgabe   German for reserved copies; of a limited edition.

Songster   Not a female singer (songstress), but any kind of early book of songs.

Sophisticated copy   A made-up copy, in which the missing leaves of a book have been replaced by taking leaves from another, close-to-identical copy of the same book.

Souffert   French for injured or damaged.

Sous-titre   French for sub-title.

Souvenir book   A book intended as a keepsake, a token of remembrance. Popular in the mid-nineteenth century, such books were usually compilations of poetry and prose in the popular style of the day, usually profusely illustrated and sometimes elaborately decorated as well, and customarily ornately bound. Souvenir books were frequently issued in time for the Christmas season; an especially popular book might be subsequently issued as an annual.

Spanish calf   A calf binding which has been decorated with splashes of either red or green dye.

Specialist collection   A collection which has been built around one subject or one type of book. The subject may be dolls, archery, bonsai, plants, antique cameras, old automobiles, enamels, firefighting equipment, Indian captivities, oil drilling . . . or dentistry. The type of book may be all those illustrated by an artist such as Arthur Rackham or Rockwell Kent or Phiz, or even an artist who is still at work but whose earliest publications are already hard to find. Then there are the collections of the works of one author, which usually lead the collector quickly to concentrate on first editions and then, possibly, first issues, so that an author-collection has pretty much come to mean a collection of first editions. Some specialist collections are limited to books of certain size, or to odd shapes, or leather bindings, or some other facet of the book's physical appearance. The term cabinet collection is sometimes applied to a very highly specialized collection which by its nature will admit few books, although cabinet collecting is also used to mean collecting miniature books.

There is no doubt a specialist dealer somewhere to help out a collector no matter what he decides shall be his specialty. Collectors interested in finding out the names of dealers who are specialists in their area have three excellent sources of information to which they may turn. The first is the *A B Bookman's Yearbook*. The latest edition of this annual may be obtained for $7.50 (or $5 for the list of specialist dealers alone), by writing to *A B* (*Bookman's Weekly*). The second source is a book in hard-cover by B. Donald Grose, *The Antiquarian Booktrade: an International Directory of Subject Specialists*, published in 1972 by the Scarecrow Press of Metuchen, N.J. 08840, at $5. And the third is *American Book Specialists*, available from Continental, 1261 Broadway, New York, N.Y. 10001 at $12.

Speculation in books Most dealers will tell you frankly that betting on the horses is safer and a more reliable way to make money. It is true that there are fads and fashions in the old-book business as in any other area of human activity, so that buying old books for potential resale can be a risky business. Yet this is, of course, precisely what the dealers are doing to earn their living. Few become rich—but some do. The sad fact appears to be that on the whole the books already known to be rare, in high demand, and therefore expensive today are those which are going to most rapidly escalate in value and bring a great deal more money tomorrow. The conclusion must be drawn that speculation in books is not a game for the moderate buyer. Most of us may console ourselves with the fact that buying books for investment is considered by most bibliophiles as bad form, and therefore spend our money where our instinct and whim lead us—and probably as good a method as any of spending money today to ensure the happiness of our heirs.

Spine Sometimes called the backbone of a book. That part which performs the function of connecting front and back covers and gives some rigidity to a book. In catalogue descriptions of old books, the spine is more frequently called the back, to include both the spine itself and the backstrip which covers it. The back of a book is apt to show wear first, being subject to fraying, chipping, and discoloration; the back of a book, which is its exposed portion as it rests on the shelf, frequently becomes time-darkened while the sides of the book remain bright, and the lettering on the back often flakes off before the lettering on the front cover begins to disappear. None of these conditions necessarily mean that the book has been abused.

Spiral Press This American press, which is noted for its fine work, issued its first book in 1926, under the direction of Joseph Blumenthal.

Spitzenverzierung German for lacy tooling or other type of ornamentation in a leather binding.

Split The joints of a book may show wear by first starting to crack, then cracking, splitting, and will, finally, be sprung. A split means that the cover and the back are starting to part company. By the time that a joint is split, the book probably should be rebound, since the pages are usually already starting to come loose or will shortly.

Sporting books There is a steady trade in the old-book market in books on all manner of sports, including tennis, fox hunting, football, boxing, basketball, wrestling, ice hockey, even the relatively non-strenuous billiards. Possibly chess should also be included in this category. The hard-cover books in demand include sports guide annuals and annual record books. Many of the hard-cover books, however, are more esteemed for their illustrations (plates) than text, and among this type of book the publications of the Derrydale Press are consistently popular. Sports ephemera are also eagerly collected, and these include football programs and the programs for other sports, score cards, trading cards which describe a player or team, even manufacturers' catalogues for equipment, bats, balls, and uniforms.

Spots on pages and covers Rain is the most common cause of spotting in a book. No book should ever be left where it might possibly be damaged by rain, even for a few minutes.

Spots on pages: removal For the removal of spots caused by dust or simple grime, an artgum eraser applied very lightly may be effective, but it should always be tried first in the most inconspicuous spot. Many people swear by a good wallpaper cleaner. There are a number of such cleaners available commercially. A cleaner of this type will not also pick up pencil or ink notations, which may or may not be a good thing depending on who made the notations—the author, some prominent person, or anonymous scribbler. Sometimes, if the stain is not deep, the soft part of a loaf of white bread will work fairly well in removing a slight smudge. Great care must be exercised, whatever agent is used, to refrain from digging so deep as to harm the texture of the paper.

Sprinkled   Splashed with dots. The edges of the leaves of a book, for example, may be sprinkled. Dark red is a favorite color for such decoration. This decorative style was popular in books printed before the mid-nineteenth century, but sprinkled edges are, by now, mostly confined to reference books. A natural calf binding may also be sprinkled.

Sprung   Gatherings which have become displaced, *proud*, as it is termed, or separated from the binding, are called sprung. It is difficult, if not impossible, for a person unskilled in book repair to either glue or sew a sprung binding back together again. The job should be given to an expert.

Square book   A book which is more than the customary one-to-three proportion between its width and height. Such a book definitely impresses the eye as more square than oblong, although it is rarely perfectly square. The square book is frequently found in the octavo size, where it may vary from 7 x 8 inches to 8 x 9 inches.

Squares   A technical term used in bookbinding: the amount of the boards which project beyond the body of a book. Should these squares project too far, the book's appearance will be poor, rather droopy. Also, the book will quickly show wear.

Square serif   A modern style of type face made popular in the 1930's—geometric, even chunky in design—with stubby serifs, projections top and bottom from the main part of the character (letter). Examples: Clarendon, Stymie.

Stahlstich   German for a steel engraving; print, or engraving.

Stained   The most common cause of staining is water. Books should never be stored in a damp place or where there is an inadequate circulation of dry air. Dampstaining is often first seen at the top or bottom margin of a book, where it may sometimes be forgiven provided that it does not interfere with the text, the plates, or the title page. Any dampstaining, however, may lower the value of a book.

Foxing is not the same as staining, since foxing occurs naturally in old papers. It is therefore much more readily forgiven than staining which may be the result of some liquid having been spilled on a couple of pages.

Stamping   The process of making an impression by pressing type upon leather, paper, or cloth. Blind stamping creates only an indentation, but stamping may employ ink or create an impression in gold or silver by pressing through foil.

A library stamp, which is often blind, is considered a defacement of a book, especially if the stamp appears anywhere on the title page.

Start   Pages are said to start or to be starting when they begin to spring away from the spine of a book. The binding has become weakened. Starting pages may be the first sign, as a matter of fact, that a binding is weak. A start in the leaves—pages projecting beyond the others—is sometimes caused in a book newly bound or rebound, if the book is carelessly or violently opened from the middle rather than carefully inward from the sides.

Starting joint   In a book with a starting joint, the closure of the pages with the binding at the joint has been substantially weakened. Eventually the pages in this book will come loose.

State   In a book, a variant form of the typesetting or

make-up of an edition. The difference between one state and another is caused by making alterations in the sheets for an edition—*before* any copies of the edition are circulated, according to some authorities. The difference between one state and a following state is often described in old-book catalogues, however, as a difference in the binding—sometimes as minute a difference as $\frac{1}{16}$ of an inch in the placement of an insignia.

Artists' proofs may also appear in different states.

Stealing   (See **Books, stolen;** or **Theft.**)

Stempel   German for owner's stamp.

Stich   German for print or engraving.

Stitched as issued   The term applies when a gathering of leaves has been sewed together but the book is neither bound nor as yet wrapped in any type of cover.

Stock   In printing, the paper used for any printing job.

Stockflecken   German for foxing.

Stoff   German for cloth.

Streeter   T. W. Streeter, a famous collector and bibliographer. A reference to "Streeter," however, usually means either his five-volume *Bibliography of Texas, 1795–1845* or the catalogue for the sale of the Streeter Collection, which was conducted by Parke-Bernet over several years, from 1966 to 1969. The eight-volume catalogue for this sale has now itself become a collectors' item, bringing as much as $300 at auction.

Suite   French for a set of plates (illustrations).

Super-calendered   Paper which is super-calendered has been treated to give it a medium gloss, not the glassy finish which the name might suggest. Paper with this type of finish is considered especially suitable for fine art work.

Supplement   An addition to a book, possibly appearing in a separate volume.

Supralibros   German for a book stamp.

Synoptique, tableau   French for synopsis.

T

Table alphabétique des Matières French for an alphabetical index by subject.

Tache French for stained. *Tache d'humidité* means a dampstain; and *tache de rouille* means foxed.

Tafel German for plate.

Tagebuch German for diary, or memoirs.

Tail With reference to the makeup of a book, the tail is the bottom of the spine; but in printing it is the descender on a character of type which goes below the line on which the body of the character rests, as does the tail in the letter Q.

Tailpiece An ornament placed at the end of a chapter or section of a book, usually filling up a space which would otherwise have been vacant. Headpiece is the similar device used at the beginning of a chapter or section.

Tall copy A book printed on paper of the customary size but scarcely cut down at all at the bindery; a book printed on extra-size paper and therefore with unusually wide margins; a book printed from the first setting of type, but this time on larger paper.

Tall-paper copy Specifically, a book which is a bit larger than octavo (8vo) but not quite so large as quarto (4to). Examples of books which are in this in-between size may be found among the books issued in limited edition by many of the private presses. See also **Large copy.**

Tamerlane In the old-book trade, a term used sometimes as a synonym for Shangri-La—searching for his own brand of Tamerlane! The reference is to the first book written by

Edgar Allan Poe: *Tamerlane and Other Poems*, published in 1827. Exceedingly rare, yet it may still possibly turn up in some neglected corner of an out-of-the-way New England attic (as it did once before). Any new copy might be worth $123,000, the sum it brought at a Parke-Bernet auction in New York City in December, 1974. There are said to be some expertly done facsimile copies around, extremely difficult for any but an expert to tell from the original.

Taschenatlas   German for a pocket atlas.

Teil   German for volume; or one part of a longer work.

Témoins   French for untrimmed edges.

Tête de série   French for the first in a series.

Tête doré   French for top edge gilt.

Tetrachromie   French for a four-color print.

Text   The main content of a book, usually beginning with Chapter One. The text does not include the preface, if there is one, or the foreword, introduction, table of contents, or the index.

Text block   The leaves of a book, exclusive of the book's binding or covering.

Textile binding   An ornate style of binding which employs a luxury fabric such as satin, velvet, or needlework. Such binding was popular in the early days of book publishing when each book might be highly valued; in England it was used until the eighteenth century. Limited edition books or private press books, or books which are bound by hand, are almost the only books with such binding nowadays.

Theaterstück   German for play.

Theft   Dealers in old books, like other retail merchants these days, sometimes have occasion to complain of the disappearance of some of their stock through shoplifting. Many book dealers have become convinced that book-stealing is the work of professional thieves for the most part, possibly the work of drug addicts who steal rare books as a means of supporting their habit. Be that as it may, there are numerous instances of well-spoken, well-mannered gentlemen extremely knowledgeable about books who seem to have lifted the most expensive books by pretending to pay for them by check. Professionals are interested in stealing only those volumes for which there is a known market. Many dealers in old and rare books believe that professionals, like everyone else, shop from the dealer's catalogue and know exactly what they are looking for when they enter his shop. For this reason, many dealers do not keep shop hours and prefer to work on a check-with-mail-order basis. Those dealers who do run shops open to the public often do not display their most expensive books but will show them to customers they know upon request. This is, of course, one explanation why so many old-book shops appear to have so little of real value out on their shelves.

Thick paper   A paper which is usually not only thick but also luxurious—and expensive. Thick-paper copies (sometimes the same as large-paper) are often a special printing to serve a particular purpose. A few copies of a first edition may be issued on this special paper, for example.

Thomas, Isaiah   An early American printer and publisher (1749–1831) associated with the early Colonial cause for independence, publisher of the *Massachusetts Spy* (a newspaper) and also of the first American illustrated folio Bible, in 1791, the first Greek grammar in this country, and the first American dictionary. He is also the author of *The History of Printing in America*, published in 1810 and still a highly respected source of information.

Three-decker   A novel published in three separate volumes, in cloth binding. This type of publication was extremely popular in Victorian England during the last half of the nineteenth century.

Three-fourths   A three-fourths leather binding is one which has the backstrip and the corners of the binding in leather, with the leather extending about a third or halfway across the boards; it is, therefore, a book predominantly but not entirely bound in leather. A book may also be bound three-fourths in cloth or imitation leather of some sort.

Ties Narrow strips of linen, leather, cloth, or similar material attached to the edges of a book's cover so that the book may be securely tied together. Such ties are seen, for example, on artists' portfolios. Their purpose is often to hold a large and unwieldy volume together or to keep vellum from buckling. They also probably help keep the dirt out.

Tight Dealers' catalogues employ the word tight to indicate that a book's inner joints (hinges) are holding firm. Clean-and-tight is another expression used, meaning that the general appearance of the interior of the book is very good—even though the binding might be worn or shabby.

Tipped in Attached lightly to a page of the book, or to the book's binding. Errata slips, for example, are often tipped in by the binder at the last possible moment as the book is being bound. However, the binder can, if desired, also tip in extra pages; in addition to the pages which are a part of the folded signatures, additional pages such as those carrying illustrations may be inserted by means of wrapping a short stub of the extra leaf around an adjoining signature. Novice bookmen sometimes think this stub means a page has been snipped out.

Tipping-in can also mean pasting something lightly into a book. An illustration which has been produced by a process different from that used for the rest of the book may be tipped in on the proper page. (See also **Laid in.**)

Tirage French for a run, or successive series of issues. *Tirage limité* means a limited run, or edition; whereas *tirage nouveau* means a reprint. *Tiré* by itself simply means printed.

Tissue A thin piece of paper sometimes laid against a plate (illustration) to protect it and to protect the page opposite from being marred by any offsetting.

Title page The title page is "the face of the book. It speaks the author's personality. If pleasant spoken, well favored to the sight, instinct with intelligence, direct of purpose, it invites desire for fuller knowledge and better acquaintance, just as a smile and friendly glance welcome to conversations." (Preface of Volume I, Evans' *American Bibliography*.)

More prosaically, it is the recto of an early leaf of a book, providing the particulars concerning the book—customarily including the book's title, the name of the author, of the editor if appropriate, the contributor of any preface, and sometimes a quotation or a motto for the book; also, the name of the publisher or the printer, or both names, and the place and date of publication.

In old books, the title page is considered an essential part of the book as published and without it a book is defective. However, it should at once be added that not all books are necessarily published with a title page. In the earliest days of publishing, both vellum and paper were so costly that it probably would not have occurred to a printer to "waste" a leaf providing information at the front of a book when he could more economically squeeze it in at the back, in less than a full page. The first title page did not appear until some fifteen years after the Gutenberg Bible. There are a few early examples of Americana without a full complement of information on the title page; Thomas Jefferson's *Notes on the State of Virginia*, published in Paris in 1787, appeared without the author's name or publisher's imprint on the title. Occasionally, even today, the information generally conveyed on a title page is switched to a book's cover, or there may be only a caption title heading the text rather than a full title page. (See also **Colophon.**)

Titre French for title. *Titre de collection* means the general, over-all title, as for a series. *Faux titre* means half-title.

Toile French for cloth, as in the covering of a book.

Tomaison French for volume number.

Tomkinson G. S. Tomkinson, author of *A Select Bibliography of the Principal Modern Presses, Public and Private, in*

Great Britain and Ireland (London, 1928). This useful reference book is now available in reprint at $20 from, among others, Alan Wofsy Fine Arts, 150 Green Street, San Francisco, Cal. 94111.

Tooling A decorative tracing on a leather binding. Blind tooling is an indentation without the use of ink or gold or silver foil or other color.

Topography A British term for the kind of books known in the United States as local, town, or county histories.

Toy book Attractive books, with the text in large print and with brightly colored illustrations, intended for small children, possibly before they have learned to read. There was a great vogue for toy books during the nineteenth century, and many of these are now especially valued for their bright and charming lithographs.

Trade book A work, either fiction or non-fiction, which is offered by the publisher to the general public and sold commercially, as opposed to a book of limited edition or for a special limited public. Almost all the stock of new-book stores is made up of the trade editions of books. In the most strict sense, a trade book or a trade edition would exclude textbooks, law books, medical tomes, book-club publications, many books of a religious nature, and all other publications for a special reading public which receives its books through a special distribution agency.

Trade catalogue An advertising bulletin issued by a merchant or other businessman. Two of the first known American examples of a trade catalogue are both from the versatile Ben Franklin: his 1744 catalogue of books inviting orders by mail, and his brochure of the same year in which he advertised his new kind of "fireplace." Another early catalogue was that of William Prince of Flushing, Long Island, who in 1771 advertised the various varieties of fruit trees which he had for sale. During the period immediately following the American Revolution, the idea of trade catalogues seems to have caught hold, with many being issued to advertise such diverse products as silver-plate, surveying instruments, stationery, and drugs. Thus trade catalogues, which some people think began with Sears, Roebuck, actually date back to the eighteenth century.

Today, collectors are taking an increasing interest in this kind of material; a great deal of it is apparently still hidden away in out-of-the-way places. In his *Guide to American Trade Catalogs, 1744–1900*, issued by Bowker in 1960, Lawrence B. Romaine listed the kinds of trade catalogues under no fewer than sixty-two headings. His own interest in catalogues, he stated, sprang from the hope that he might "pinpoint those goods, products, and manufacturers time has proven the leaders in the development of the United States economically, politically, and socially." Valuable as it may be to expose more of this material, the fact remains that this field of collecting still remains relatively untouched, and most prices are still moderate.

Traducteur   French for translator.

Traité   French for treatise.

Tranche   French for edge (of a book).

Transformation book   A book for children designed with movable figures, usually operated by means of tabs or a wheel.

Transitional   Specifically, a kind of type face more delicate and graceful than some, Oldstyle Roman for example. Examples of transitional faces include Century and Baskerville.

Tree calf   A bright brown or buff calf used for bookbinding, with a distinctive bark-like design characteristically bisected longitudinally.

Trial binding   The first binding of a book, which is then submitted to the book's editors for their approval. There are, probably, few times when the trial binding is not accepted and would not, therefore, be identical with the binding of the first issue.

Trichromie   French for three-color printing.

Trick book   A type of children's book fancifully designed to perform as a toy. Occasionally one turns up for sale in fairly good condition, preserved no doubt by some admiring adult. An example of a trick book is the *Book of Revolving Scenes* (c. 1890), which contains five large circular color plates with a string to pull which moves various new views into sight. The modern pop-up book constitutes another example.

Trigesimosecundo   The size of a book between 4 and 5 inches tall, just one step larger than the miniature category. Abbreviated to 32mo or 32°.

Trimestriel   French for quarterly.

Trimmed   In the process of binding a book, the trimming is the process by which the edges of the book are shorn, at least roughly. Trimming and cutting are about the same, but cutting usually means that the edges are sheared to a smooth edge. A book must be cut rather than trimmed, for example, if it is to take a fore-edge painting.

Truffé   French for grangerized.

Turkey   A kind of morocco, in which the leather is tawed (steeped) in oil, with the hairy side not removed until after the tawing. Turkey morocco is considered almost as fine a leather as Persian.

Turn   Or turn-over: the transfer from the end of one line of verse to the beginning of the next line. Such a turn sometimes proves useful in identifying the issue of a first edition, thus constituting an issue point.

Type   An individual piece of type is a small, rectangular block of metal or wood having on its end a raised letter, figure, or some other character used in printing. Such pieces collectively are known as type. For styles of type, see Jenson, Caslon, Baskerville, Bodoni. (See also **Xylography.**)

Type faces   The face of the type is the printing surface and thus the term type face has come into use to designate a particular style of alphabet devised for printing. The first type face, which was initially used when printing was invented around 1450, was closely modelled on letters written by hand. Since that time many changes have gradually taken place, many in the direction of greater simplicity of type and thus greater legibility. Of the thousands of type faces which have been invented over the years, only a few have survived to be accepted for general use. Some small private presses have their own type, a factor which helps to contribute to the individuality of their work. It is customary to specify the kind of type face used only in books of limited edition. (See also **Font.**)

Typescript The typed manuscript of a book, often containing corrections in the author's own hand, inserted as the book was being prepared for the printer. A corrected typescript sometimes comes into the old-book market, where it may command a higher price at times than the first edition, first issue, of the printed book. However, a great deal will depend upon the collectibility of the author.

Typography The overall manner in which type is used in a book; or the science of printing; or the art of arranging type. Layout, on the other hand, means the way in which both type and decoration, or illustration, are arranged on the page. George Macy of the Limited Editions Club had his own definition of typography: "The art . . . of arranging letters upon a sheet of paper, and of so decorating the sheet of paper, that the reader of the letters more fully comprehends the words which the letters compose."

Typophile Chap Books A series of publications (numbered with Roman numerals) on various typographic achievements, and illustrating different styles of typography and type, issued in limited edition beginning in 1940, by a variety of presses. The presses include Marchbanks, Spiral, Anthoensen, George Grady, Watch Hill, Plimpton, and others. Some of these small books of few pages are now worth more than $20 in the old-book market, where interest in books on typography is always high.

U

Uebersetzen German for translating. *Uebersetzung* means a translation.

Uebersichtstabelle German for synopsis.

Umgearbeitet German for revised; or, newly edited, with additions. *Umgearbeitete Ausgabe* means revised edition.

Umschlag mitgebunden German for with the wrappers bound in. *Neuer umschlag,* in German, means *not* in the original wrappers.

Unbound Simply never bound at all, at any time. Not, therefore, to be confused with "disbound," which means that the volume, which was once bound, has now become separated from its binding.

Uncorrected page proof The initial printing of a book before it goes to the editor and the author for final corrections. Sometimes this page proof is offered for sale in the old-book market, though not often. The leaves, often stitched but without printed wrappers, may be enclosed in a wrapper stamped "Uncorrected proof."

Uncut A book which is uncut has not been trimmed down in any binding process. Uncut is therefore not the same as "unopened." The latter means that no one has as yet sliced open the pages so that the book might be read. The two terms are, unfortunately, often confused. An uncut book may have the pages left untrimmed for decorative effect. (See also **Unopened.**)

Uneven page A page which bears the odd-numbered

folio, thus a page on the right-hand side of the book in reading position; the recto.

Unfrisch German for faded or soiled.

United States Booksellers Antiquarian Booksellers' Association of America, Inc., with headquarters at 630 Fifth Avenue, New York, N.Y. 10020. (See also **British booksellers**.)

Unopened An unopened book is one which has not as yet had any closed leaves slit open with a sharp instrument such as a paper knife or letter opener, so that the pages might be read. An uncut book, on the other hand, is one which has not been trimmed at the bindery.

Books which are unopened should always be left that way, according to the tradition of the old-book trade. An unopened book may be more valuable; certainly its pages have a greater chance of remaining clean so long as they are not read. Collectors purchasing any book for investment should certainly not open it; book-lovers, however, may find it almost impossible to resist opening a book in order to enjoy it, especially since it is often the limited edition, private press book which is unopened, and such books may be triumphs of layout and design.

Unpressed A book is unpressed when it has not been subjected to the final process at the bindery. It is, therefore, fatter than one which has been properly pressed. Leaving a book unpressed is done for artistic reasons or, possibly, to make the book appear "different" and thus merit a higher price.

Unrecorded This term is applied to any book which has not been listed as yet in any of the standard bibliographies where it might be expected to be found.

Unsprung An unsprung book is one which is still securely fastened within its binding. Unsprung and tight are two terms used much in the same sense.

Unterdrückt German for censored.

Unterschrift German for signature or autograph.

Untertitel German for sub-title.

Unverdorben German for in good condition.

Unveröffentlicht German for unpublished.

Unvollständig German for incomplete.

Updike Daniel Berkeley Updike (1860–1941), primarily associated with the Merrymount Press, which he founded in 1893. This press is noted both for its scholarship and for its typographic excellence. Probably Updike's best-known achievement is *The Book of Common Prayer* (1930). He is also the author of an authoritative two-volume work, *Printing Types: Their History, Forms, and Use* (1922), still a standard work. A second edition appeared in 1937.

Upright pages Those in which the width of the printed matter is less than the depth. Most pages, this one included, are upright.

Urtext German for the original text.

Usagé French for worn.

Used A used book is one which simply has had a previous owner. The term need not imply that the book is out-of-print. A used book is not, therefore, always a good buy, if a better copy can still be obtained at about the same price from a new-book store.

Used Book Price Guide, The A directory to the prices asked by dealers in the United States and Canada in recent years for rare, scarce, used, and out-of-print books. Unlike most other price guides, this one lists books offered for sale for as low as $3. Compiled and edited by Mildred S. Mandeville, a five-year, two-volume edition is available from Price Guide Publishers, 525A Kenmore Street, Kenmore, Wash. 98028, in hard cover at $45, in paper at $37.

U.S.Iana (See **Howes.**)

V

Value According to the Antiquarian Booksellers Association, "A book may be rare but not necessarily valuable. There are thousands of *rare* books, of which there are less than ten copies in existence, that are of no value to dealer or collector." If we have the only copy in the world, but no one is interested in acquiring it, our book cannot be said to have value. "A book's value is governed by three factors operating together: intrinsic importance, collectors' interest, and scarcity. Generally speaking, the books which are sought after are first editions of great books in literature, art, and science, which includes discovery in all fields. These are source books revealing the development of man, and are of intrinsic importance, their value being influenced by scarcity and the demand for them at any particular time." (From the Association's Publication No. 5.)

Value, little With some exceptions, the following types of material are in very little demand and therefore have little value in today's market: single copies of newspapers—unless they not only record some great event in history but are scarce, having been printed in Colonial America; old schoolbooks and textbooks of all sorts (exception: some early books of instruction in mathematics or astronomy, or the earliest of the *McGuffey Readers*); school atlases (unless it should happen to be the first American atlas or some other first); old family Bibles, no matter how old or treasured (unless associated with some truly famous family or person; or the first Bible printed in America or other first); old encyclopedias printed before 1911, including the *Britannica* (except for one which contains thousands of pictures from everyday life or science and mechanics and is still bright and clean); the late editions of any popular work, or reprints of any sort (unless the illustrations are of special interest, or the book is signed).

Value, rising Among those types of books which appear to be assured of rising value are the following: works of fiction in fine condition by those authors who are already popular with collectors; first editions and especially the first issues of works rated as classics; the earlier works of well-known authors, written well before they achieved their fame; books signed by the author (if he is collected) and books inscribed by famous people (even if the book itself is not notable); books setting forth new scientific principles or facts; books on subjects currently of high interest, such as the American western migration, the beginnings of various American industries, aeronautical history, early photography, furniture, china, etc. This is by no means an exhaustive list. It could be extended by including the many new types of items being collected today under the general expanded heading of book-collecting: postcards, photo albums, trading cards, the Sunday comics, movie mags, etc.

Vanity press A publishing firm in which the author pays all or part of the cost of publication of his work.

Variants Published works in which various copies of one edition have different readings as the result of corrections having been made in the original work.

Variorum *Cum notis variorum* (Latin): from the hands of various editors.

Vélin French for vellum or imitation vellum.

Vellum A fine kind of parchment prepared from the skin of the calf, lamb, or kid, by stretching the skin and scraping it after it has been treated with lime. The term may also be applied sometimes to any superior parchment or even to its imitation. Vellum may be used for either pages or the binding of a book. It is considered particularly appropriate for the covers of a precious book.

Vellum finish In papermaking, a vellum finish is one which is waxy like real vellum; it is therefore frequently used in arty books. However, in printers' jargon, a vellum finish is also one which is toothy: permits fast ink penetration.

Velvet calf Calf with the grain side buffed off, a type of leather occasionally used for bindings.

Vendre aux enchères French for to sell at auction.

Verblasst German for faded or discolored.

Verfasser German for author.

Vergriffen German for out-of-print.

Verlängert German for a tall format.

Verleger German for publisher.

Vernis-mou French for etching *(eau-forte)*.

Veröffentlichung German for publication.

Verso In a book which is laid open in the reading position, the verso is the page at the left, and the recto is the right-hand page. The verso bears the even numbers in a book's pagination. The verso of the title page customarily conveys the copyright information.

Very good A term of fairly exact meaning in the old-book trade, used to describe an old book which is better than good but less than fine. In such a book there is no major sign of wear, no rips or tears, no water-staining. The interior pages must be bright and clean. The binding is still tight. If there is a book jacket present, it may be permissibly worn but not tattered. Occasionally, if a book is in very good condition overall, a dealer may describe it as such but then note any conditions which might not fit.

Verziert German for ornamented, or decorated. *Verzierter Rücken* means a decorated back (spine).

Viable Occasionally a dealer's catalogue will state "still a viable copy." Since the literal meaning of viable is able to live, possibly what is meant is that this copy stacks up fairly well against any competing copy the dealer has seen—or simply that it is still in passable condition.

Vierfarbendruck German for a four-color print.

Vierteljährlich German for quarterly.

Vigesimoquarto The size of a book which is from 5 to 6 inches tall. This is one size smaller than sextodecimo and one larger than trigesimosecundo. Abbreviated to 24mo or 24°.

Vignette In printing, a technical term meaning a half-tone in which the engraving blends off into the color of the surrounding paper. In books, however, an embellishment or decoration, usually a small design, sometimes round or oval, with or without an enclosing border. Vignettes are used, for example, as head- and tail-pieces.

Volksausgabe German for a popular edition.

Vollständige serie German for a complete set. Note that *unvollständig* means defective or incomplete.

Volvelle A design motif which may be used on book bindings, consisting of a series of graduated or figured circles, patterned after an old device which had served historically to ascertain the rising and setting of the sun and moon, the state of the tides, etc. Also, a movable figure operated by a disk or pull-tab.

Vorbericht German for a notice or announcement to the reader.

Vorderschnitt German for fore-edge.

Vorsatzblatt German for preliminary leaf (or simply *Vorsatz*).

Vorwort German for foreword.

W

Wagner-Camp Henry R. Wagner's *The Plains and the Rockies, a Bibliography of Original Narratives of Travel and Adventure, 1800–1865*, in the third edition, published in 1953, revised by Charles L. Camp. This is a standard reference work on books describing trips over the Rocky Mountains (not, however, currently in print).

Want card The card or paper on which dealers record the titles of books for which they are searching for their customers. Many dealers are glad to set up permanent want cards for steady customers and frequently continue looking over ten or twenty years for that particularly rare and elusive book.

Washing A specific process by which experts in book repair or in restoring plates can clean and de-fox the pages of a book. Amateurs are warned against trying it with a book of any value.

Wasserfleck German for a waterstain.

Wasserzeichen German for the watermark in paper.

Water: enemy of books Fire, surprising as it may seem, unless it totally consumes a book, frequently does it less damage than water. A fire may only smudge the book's binding, whereas even a slight dampness may penetrate a book with devastating effect. Ugly wavy stains may appear on the pages, and the pages themselves may crinkle. Most water damage to a book can be repaired only by an expert. If a book is not worth the expense of professional repair, it is often better simply to throw it out and forget about it.

The techniques used by libraries to repair books damaged by flood are described in a booklet titled *Procedures for Salvage of Water-Damaged Library Materials*, by Peter Waters. Waters helped save many of the books damaged at the Biblioteca Nazionale in Florence in the flood of 1966. Single copies of his booklet are available free from the Preservation Office of the Library of Congress, Washington, D.C. 20540. The booklet includes information on the techniques of cleaning, freezing, and freeze-drying as well as on sources for services, supplies and equipment, and places to go for further assistance.

Watermark In papermaking, the watermark is the light mark or design made in the stock (paper) during its manufacture, through the imprint of some projection in the wire frame over which the paper is made. Individual manufacturers may employ special insignia to leave a distinctive watermark. Sometimes, therefore, it is possible to identify a particular edition of a book by holding a page to the light and examining the watermark. Some of the private presses have developed different watermarks for different books. Kelmscott had, for example, a watermark, at various times, of a primrose between the initials "W. M." (William Morris), a perch with a spray in its mouth, and the initials, and an apple with the usual "W. M."

Wearing A general term used to describe the condition of a book which is less than very good. Wearing may denote some scuffing, or even spotting. Because the term is so vague, it should never be employed to describe a book of any real value.

Welche *A Bibliography of American Children's Books Printed Prior to 1821,* by d'Alte Welche. This bibliography describes about eight thousand items, with comprehensive descriptions of about fifteen hundred titles. It is available at $45 from the University Press of Virginia, Box 3608, University Station, Charlottesville, Va. 22903.

White calf   A type of calf binding which has traditionally been associated with law books.

White-line   White-line engraving is engraving on wood, as differentiated from engraving on metal. The part incised appears white in the print.

Widmung   German for dedication.

Wie neu   German for as new, or mint condition.

Wing   Donald A. Wing, Editor: *A Short-Title Catalogue of Books Printed in England, Scotland, Ireland, Wales & British America & of English Books Printed in Other Countries—1641–1700* (1945–51). Volume One of the revised second edition is available at $60 from the Modern Language Association of America, 62 Fifth Avenue, New York, N.Y. 10011. As of this writing the next two volumes, as yet unpriced, are scheduled for publication in the near future.

Winterich   John T. Winterich, author, with David A. Randall, of a classic on book collecting: *A Primer of Book Collecting*. The third edition was published by Crown in 1966. Still in print, this is a fine book to own—available at $5.95.

Wire marks   In the manufacture of paper by hand, the light lines which are created in the paper where it thins over the wires at the bottom of the mold. The chain marks, on the other hand, are the lines which run at right angles across the paper.

Wochentlich   German for weekly.

Woodburytype   The invention of Sir Walter Woodbury (1834–1885), whereby an image is transferred through photography from a hardened gelatine plate onto a metal printing surface. Woodburytypes, extremely lifelike, were popular for book illustration in the second half of the nineteenth century.

Woodcut   An illustration for a book which is produced by the process of engraving on the grain end of a block of wood.

The design which is to take the ink is left raised by cutting away the rest of the surface of the block. Woodcuts were used as a method of illustration for the earliest printed books.

Working copy   A book in poor condition. It may be still hanging together, but that is about all that can be said. A reading copy is pretty much the same thing.

Wormholes   It would probably be quite possible to spend a lifetime collecting modern first editions and never see a wormhole. Modern methods of book manufacture, as well as improved methods for storing books, have by and large rid us of the bookworm, that traditional symbol of the book-lover. Books from the eighteenth century and earlier, however, often demonstrate the extent of the damage which could be done by these larvae burrowing straight through the pages. For this reason, the presence of wormholes is sometimes cited as proof of a book's antiquity.

Wove   Wove paper, in contrast to laid paper, is made in a mold of closely woven wire, is generally machine-made, and therefore shows no chain marks.

W.P.A.   The Works Progress Administration, established by President Roosevelt in 1935 to help meet the pressing problems of unemployment, hired writers among others. The W.P.A. guidebooks to the various states are now collected. Individual guidebooks, if the map is still present, may be worth $10 or more in good condition. A bibliographic checklist of over 1500 W.P.A. publications, both major and minor, is available at $3.95 from publisher Evanell Powell, Box 381, Palm Beach, Fla. 33480. The W.P.A. ceased to exist in 1943.

Wrappers   The covers of a book, made from a heavy stiff paper rather than from boards. Such wrappers are often employed to cover small books or pamphlets. A dust jacket is not a wrapper, since it is not a permanent part of the book.

Wright   Lyle H. Wright: *American Fiction, 1774–1900: a*

Contribution toward a Bibliography. Wright was modest in calling his work merely a contribution. This valuable bibliography is available in a three-volume set at $30 from the publisher, Huntington Library. It is also available in paperback for the years 1851–75 and for 1876–1900.

X

Xerography   A form of inkless printing not to be confused with xylography.

Xylography   The process of producing an image or a print from the impress of a block of wood. The wood employed is usually fruitwood; the end-grain is carved into lines in fine relief which, when inked, will produce a picture. The more common term for xylography is wood-engraving.

Y

Yapp Yapp was a bookseller in London who, around 1860, had the first circuit binding made up for a book. This is a binding of limp leather with edges, or flaps, overlapping the body of the book. A book which is bound in this manner is said to be yapped. Divinity circuit is another name of this type of binding, since it is often used for Bibles.

Yellow-back A publication issued in a bright dust jacket —of any color. It is designed for mass appeal and may be considered vulgar. A yellow-back is a publication of "low appeal."

Z

Zeitgenössisch German for contemporary.
Zeitschrift German for periodical. *Zeitung* means newspaper, or journal.
Zensur German for censorship.
Zusammen German for together, in all. *Zusammenfassung* means summary.
Zusätzlich German for additional. *Zugefügt* means added.

About the Author

MARGARET EKERN HALLER is presently a cataloguer for the Swann Galleries of New York, one of the outstanding auction houses devoted exclusively to scarce and rare books. She is a native of Boston, and attended Smith College, from which she graduated as a Phi Beta Kappa in 1938. After marrying and working for a number of years, she retired to devote herself to raising a family, which eventually numbered six children. She returned to work in 1961, first in public relations and then as editor of a college alumni magazine. She has tried her hand at editing and writing, and has worked experimentally in a bookstore. In addition to her present association with a book auction house, she has her own "rather low-key" old-book business and a slowly growing personal collection which is diversified among handsome bindings, children's books, and a select number of publishers.